A Student's Guide to Education Studies

Written specifically for students on Education Studies courses, yet also relevant for students on teacher training courses, *A Student's Guide to Education Studies* covers a diverse range of topics and issues. With a revised structure, new chapters and fully updated content, this 2nd edition continues to introduce alternative visions of education theory and practice.

The chapters are divided between three sections: Education Policy and Politics; Global and Environmental Education; and Learning, Knowledge and the Curriculum. Coverage includes:

- Every Child Matters
- Gender and educational achievement
- Religious and cultural plurality in education
- Education for democracy and citizenship
- The global dimension in education
- Education for sustainability
- The ecology of learning
- Young children learning
- The effective teacher
- Educational research.

Each chapter contains introductions, summary points, questions for discussion and annotated suggestions for further reading.

With a distinctive international and global focus, *A Student's Guide to Education Studies* (orginally published as *Education Studies: A Student's Guide*) continues to be a valuable resource for all students of Education Studies as well as students on initial teacher training courses.

Stephen Ward is Dean of the School of Education at Bath Spa University, UK.

A Student's Guide to Education Studies

2nd edition

Edited by
Stephen Ward

Routledge
Taylor & Francis Group

LONDON AND NEW YORK

Second edition published 2008
by Routledge
2 Park Square, Milton Park, Abingdon, Oxon OX14 4RN

Simultaneously published in the USA and Canada
by Routledge
270 Madison Ave, New York, NY 10016

First published 2004 by RoutledgeFalmer as *Education Studies: A Student's Guide*

Routledge is an imprint of the Taylor & Francis Group, an informa business

Typeset in Bembo by
HWA Text and Data Management, London
Printed and bound in Great Britain by
TJ International, Ltd Padstow, Cornwall

British Library Cataloguing in Publication Data
A catalogue record for this book is available from the British Library

Library of Congress Cataloging in Publication Data
A student's guide to education studies / edited by Stephen Ward. – 2nd ed.
    p. cm.
  Includes bibliographical references and index.
  Rev. ed. of: Education studies. 2004.
  1. Education. 2. Teaching. 3. Learning. I. Ward, Stephen, 1947– II. Education studies.
  LB1025.3.E334 2008
370.71´1--dc22   2008005548

ISBN10: 0–415–46537–0 (pbk)

ISBN13: 978–0–415–46537–3 (pbk)

Contents

Illustrations

Contributors

All the authors are members, or former members, of staff of Bath Spa University and have taught on the Education Studies (ES) programme there.

Viki Bennett is Principal Lecturer in Early Years Education and Programme Leader of the Education Studies Foundation Degrees. A former teacher, she became Early Years Adviser for Bristol City Council and has published training guidance for practitioners. Her research interests are transition and creativity in the early years.

June Bianchi is an artist, National Teaching Fellow and Senior Lecturer in Art Education. She manages and teaches courses in the arts across the spectrum of undergraduate, post-graduate and Masters programmes, as well as acting as Leader of the Centre for Research in Arts Education. June's research focuses on issues of identity within the arts and arts education, and she works in a collaborative way, exploring constructions of the self across an intercultural context, through exhibitions, video films and publications.

David Coulby is Professor of Education and Head of International Activities at Bath Spa University. His latest book is (with Evie Zambeta) *The World Yearbook of Education 2005: Education, Globalisation and Nationalism*. He is a member of the Editorial Board of Intercultural Education.

Denise Cush is Professor of Religion and Education and Head of the Department of Study of Religions. Her best-known book is *Buddhism*, a textbook for A level. Recent publications include several articles on teenage witchcraft, co-editing an Encyclopedia of Hinduism, and articles on the place of religious education in state schools internationally. She co-wrote a commissioned report (2007) on the state of religious education in schools in England for the Department for Children, Schools and Families (DCSF) and the Religious Education Council (REC) of England and Wales.

Dan Davies is Professor of Science and Technology Education and Head of Applied Research and Consultancy in the School of Education. His current research projects concern science assessment at GCSE level, evaluating active learning in primary science and developing dialogic teaching in primary science teacher education. He has published books on primary design and technology education, early years science teaching and science 5–11.

Graham Downes has a special interest in technology and learning. He spent five years with the Central Bristol Education Action Zone with a brief to develop creative teaching and learning approaches using technology. He teaches on a range of Education Studies modules with a particular focus in technology, creativity and research.

Christine Eden is Assistant Dean of the School of Education with an interest in using her background in sociology to explore education systems and access to educational opportunities. In recent years she has undertaken evaluation research into the interface between education and the needs of the labour market. Her research interest is in educational inequalities with a particular focus on gender.

Howard Gibson leads the Full-Time Masters in Education. He lectures and writes on issues concerned with literacy, links between language and power, Citizenship Education and the assumptions underpinning current models of Economics Education in England.

Don Harrison is a part-time lecturer in citizenship and human rights education. He has previously worked for Oxfam and Save the Children producing materials and supporting teachers for global learning and children's rights.

Susan Haywood's research interests are in the use of information and communication technology (ICT) in education, particularly new literacies and electronic texts. She teaches ICT-based modules within Education Studies and has co-authored a book on the ICT Strategy at Key Stage Three. She is Assistant Dean and Head of Partnership in the School of Education.

David Hicks is Visiting Professor in the School of Education and internationally known for his work on the need for a global and futures perspective in education. His most recent books are *Lessons for the Future* and, with Cathie Holden, *Teaching the Global Dimension*.

Alan Howe is co-subject leader for Education Studies. He has published in the areas of science and technology education, early years education and Education Studies. His research interest is in creativity in education.

Mim Hutchings' two main specialist teaching areas are social and educational inclusion, and language and literacy within Education and Childhood Studies and Masters programmes. Current research focuses on the learning experiences of undergraduate students in Education Studies. Her previous lives have included teaching in schools (nursery through to secondary) and universities, working as an Advisor for Special Educational Needs, and within Ethnic Minority Support Services.

Elaine Lam is Lecturer in International Education. She has written on aspects of culture in secondary Mathematics and is completing her PhD on education borrowing in the Caribbean.

Tilly Mortimore joined Bath Spa from Southampton University in 2007 as senior lecturer in Education Studies and Inclusion and is also developing Masters programmes in SpLD/dyslexia and inclusion. She currently researches dyslexia, inclusion and vulnerable learners. Previously she taught and lectured in a range of international educational and training cntexts. Her recent publicatoins include a second edition of *Dyslexia and Learning Style* and with Jane Dupree *Supporting Learners withSpLd/dyslexia in the Secondary Classroom*.

Nicki O'Brien is Senior Lecturer in Early Years Education. She coordinates professional studies in the Early Years and Primary Postgraduate Certificate in Education (PGCE). She leads on the Reggio Emilia Approach to Early Years Education module and her research is linked to this. A former early years practitioner Nicki is passionate in promoting the rights of children.

Catherine Simon is Senior Lecturer in Education and Childhood Studies. She has experience of teaching in both secondary and primary settings and for a number of years taught in Forces schools in Germany. She teaches a broad range of Education modules, with a particular interest in Education policy, which was the focus for her MA. She is currently researching the Every Child Matters agenda and has contributed to both undergraduate and post-graduate training in this field.

Stephen Ward is Professor of Education and Dean of the School of Education. He was formerly the subject leader for Education Studies. A founder member of the British Education Studies Association, he was Chair in 2006–7. He has published books on the primary curriculum, primary music teaching and Education Studies. His research interests are education policy and university knowledge.

Heather Williamson entered teacher training after a period as Head of Department in a secondary school. She was Assistant Dean of the Faculty of Education and Human Sciences at Bath Spa University College. She has taught philosophy to students studying for degrees in Education, Study of Religions and the Social Sciences. Her research interests are in applied philosophy. She has written papers on moral and political philosophy.

Acknowledgements

The ideas in these chapters were developed with Education Studies students at Bath Spa University. We learned from their enthusiastic and critical responses and they were the inspiration for this book.

Figure 7.1 on p. 71 and Table 7.3 on p. 72 are from *In the Global Classroom2* by Graham Pike and David Selby, copyright © 2000 by Pippin Publishing Corporation. Reprinted with the permission of the copyright holder. All rights reserved.

Figure 7.2 and Tables 7.4–7.6 on pp 73–6 are reproduced from the *Curriculum for Global Citizenship, 1997* with the permission of Oxfam GB, Oxfam House, John Smith Drive, Cowley, Oxford OX4 2RY, UK www.oxfam,org.uk/education. Oxfam GB does not necessarily endorse any text or activities that accompany the materials.

Abbreviations

The following abbreviations are used in the text:

AIDS	acquired immune deficiency syndrome
BEd	Bachelor of Education
BESA	British Education Studies Association
CAP	Common Agricultural Policy
CIDA	Canadian International Development Agency
CSO	civil society organisations
CSR	Comprehensive Spending Review
DCMS	Department for Culture, Media and Sport
DCSF	Department for Children, Schools and Families
DE	development education
DEA	Development Education Association
DEC	Development Education Centre
DES	Department of Education and Science
DfEE	Department for Education and Employment
DfES	Department for Education and Skills
DfID	Department for International Development
EAZ	education action zone
ECHR	European Convention of Human Rights
ECM	Every Child Matters
EE	environmental education
EFA	education for all
EfS	education for sustainability
ELLI	Evaluating Lifelong Learning Inventory
EYPS	Early Years Professional Status
FSM	free school meals
GCSE	General Certificate of Secondary Education
GM	genetically modified

HESA	Higher Education Statistics Agency
HIV	human immunodeficiency virus
HMI	Her Majesty's Inspectorate
HMSO	Her Majesty's Stationery Office
ICT	information and communication technology
ILEA	Inner London Education Authority
IMF	International Monetary Fund
IPCC	Intergovernmental Panel on Climate Change
KS	Key Stage
LA	local authority
LDC	less developed country
LEA	Local Education Authority
LMS	local management of schools
MDG	Millennium Development Goals
MP	member of parliament
NATO	North Atlantic Treaty Organisation
NESTA	National Endowment for Science, Technology and the Arts
NFER	National Foundation for Educational Research
NGO	non-government organisations
OECD	Organisation for Economic Co-operation and Development
Ofsted	Office for Standards in Education
PFI	Private Finance Initiative
PGCE	Postgraduate Certificate in Education
PSHE	Personal, Social and Health Education
QAA	Quality Assurance Agency
QCA	Qualifications and Curriculum Authority
REC	Religious Education Council of England and Wales
SACRE	Standing Advisory Council on Religious Education
SAT	Standard Assessment Test
SCAA	Schools Curriculum and Assessment Authority
SMSC	Spiritual, Moral, Social and Cultural
TDA	Training and Development Agency for Schools
TIDE	teachers in development education
TNC	transnational corporation
TRIPS	The Research Informed Practice Site
TTA	Teacher Training Agency
TVEI	Technical Vocational Education Initiative
UDHR	Universal Declaration of Human Rights
UN	United Nations
UNEP	United Nations Environmental Programme
UNESCO	United Nations Educational, Scientific and Cultural Organization
UPIAS	Union of Physically Impaired People Against Segregation
USAID	United States Agency for International Development
VA	voluntary aided
VC	voluntary controlled
WTO	World Trade Organisation
YDoL	Young Designers on Location

Introduction: The Study of Education

Stephen Ward

INTRODUCTION

Education Studies is one of the fastest growing new university subjects. It is concerned with understanding how people develop and learn throughout their lives, the nature of knowledge and critical engagement with ways of knowing. It offers intellectually rigorous analysis of educational processes and their cultural, social, political and historical contexts. We live in a time of a massive and rapid change in the world and education is about how we both make change and manage change. So Education Studies includes perspectives on international education, economic relationships, globalisation, ecological issues and human rights. It also deals with beliefs, values and principles in education and the way that they change over time.

In the four years since this book was first published, education has moved on and this second edition discusses the most recent events, findings and ideas. This introduction explains how the subject has developed and gives a taste of some of its topics through a summary of the chapters.

THE ORIGINS OF EDUCATION STUDIES

During the last ten years, Education has become a fully fledged university subject in its own right. Before that it was a part of teacher training: the theory to inform the practice of teachers. As an academic subject it began during the 1960s and 1970s when teaching became an all-graduate profession and Bachelor of Education (BEd) degrees were introduced. The universities awarding BEd degrees were suspicious that teacher training was simply 'tips for teachers' and so degree courses were to be made more theoretical and 'academic'. Psychology, sociology, philosophy and the history of education were introduced as the theory for professional practice. Crook (2002) gives an interesting account of how educational theory came into being.

It has to be said that education theory in this form had an unhappy start: students often found their studies of psychology, sociology and philosophy *too* theoretical and unrelated to their practice in school.

Similarly, practising teachers distrusted their training, saying, 'you only learn to teach when you get into school'. Simon (1994) explains that these problems occurred because the academic theory in BEd degrees failed to relate theory to students' and teachers' practice. The result was the progressive discrediting of theory in teacher training. This led to government intervention in teacher training and the formation in 1966 of the Teacher Training Agency (TTA), now the Training and Development Agency (TDA). The TTA was, as a government agency, to take the control of teacher training away from universities and to make it practical and less theoretical. Universities were made to comply with a set of requirements and national 'standards' (TTA, 1998, TDA, 2007) and courses were to be rigorously inspected by the Office for Standards in Education (Ofsted).

The 'de-theorizing' of teacher training left many university staff dissatisfied with the courses they were teaching and there were moves to create non-teacher training Education Studies free from the control of the government agency and from Ofsted inspection. At the same time there was increasing interest from students in studying education as an academic subject in the university, but not as teacher training.

Education Studies has become a subject of interest to a whole range of students with different career intentions. Some intend to be teachers, going on to take a PGCE course. It gives them a critical analysis of the policy and practice going on in schools, which they are not likely to get from a teacher training course. Other graduates work in the new posts in schools and children's centres as teaching assistants, family link workers or advisers. Some work in education and training in art galleries and libraries and commercial industry. Finally, Education Studies can simply be a subject of study for those who are interested in education as a feature of human activity and experience.

THE NEW EDUCATION STUDIES

The Universities of York and Lancaster had Education Studies courses from the 1960s. However, for most universities it has been in recent years that the academic community has created the 'new Education Studies'. The present author (Ward, 2006) researched the way the subject has been formed by interviewing course leaders in universities and found a wide range of content and origins. Some had based the subject on what had been in the BEd teacher training degrees, with practical work in the school curriculum linked to the TTA standards. But usually course leaders had been determined to make the subject distinctly different from teacher training and tried to find new areas of study that defined Education Studies as a subject in its own right.

As noted above, the first attempts at theory in the old teacher training courses had been to import the 'foundation' disciplines of psychology, sociology, philosophy and history and to apply these to education. So Education Studies might simply be modules called 'psychology' or 'sociology of education'. But the course leaders said that, while the disciplines are included in their course to provide academic rigour, they wanted to see the new subject having its own distinctive identity, rather than being a collection of the old disciplines. They also wanted to open up the political analysis of education as well as ecological and global perspectives, which were not possible within the constraints of TDA-regulated courses. They all said that Education Studies should provide a critical analysis of policy and practice in education.

Most of the new courses have been drawn up by a group of academics in a university deciding what they consider to be important content for the subject. It is interesting that there was relatively little interaction between the academics in different institutions and most courses have been derived from the particular knowledge and interests of the staff involved. In recent years an organisation has been formed to create an academic network for tutors and students in Education Studies: the British Education Studies Association (BESA) http://www. besa. ac. uk. There is a journal and an annual conference that share academic practice and research in Education Studies.

The Quality Assurance Agency (QAA) regulates university degree courses to ensure that their content is appropriate and rigorously assessed. The QAA Benchmark for Education Studies (2007) states that education courses should provide:

> ... an intellectually rigorous study of educational processes, and the cultural, political and historical contexts within which they are embedded ... provide students with opportunities to engage in critical reflection and debate.

> Students should have the opportunity to engage with a number of different perspectives and to evaluate aims and values, means and ends, and the validity of the education issues in question. (para. 5. 1)

Also necessary is an understanding and knowledge of research and research methods and the different disciplines such as psychology and sociology:

> ... students will need to draw upon contemporary research and other relevant educational literature. Students will also require an awareness of relevant concepts and theories from across a range of appropriate disciplines. (para. 5. 2)

Education Studies is not just about education in the UK, but in other cultures and contexts, as well as the underlying political and theoretical perspectives. The Benchmark requires:

> the effects of cultural, societal, political, historical and economic contexts on learning, including education policies, moral, religious and philosophical underpinnings, and issues of social justice; formal and informal contexts for learning. Educational contexts will include some understanding of their own education system and other education systems, and the values underpinning their organisation. (para. 5. 5)

CRITICAL ANALYSIS IN EDUCATION STUDIES

We all know about education because we have had some kind of education or schooling and experienced discussions about education in the media and among family and friends. Discussion of education can be uninformed 'chat' about pet theories and opinions. Education Studies challenges everyday thinking and assumptions about education. It deconstructs taken-for-granted ideas and asks us to analyse what is really known and what is just belief or assumption. The theme that runs through this book is the 'critical analysis' of policy and practice in education.

This does not mean 'critical' in the sense of being negative; it is easy to grumble about the government, schools, teachers, parents and pupil behaviour. Critical analysis in a university means asking questions, such as: Why have we got the schools and the curriculum we have? What is education for? Is it about training children to become skilled workers in industry, or helping them to become autonomous citizens who can effect change in society and the world? A critical analysis of education is to have ideas about what alternatives there are for education in the future: to know what education *is*, but also what education *could be*, and *might be*. To answer the questions we need to look at the conflicting theories about the subject. This means making an analysis of where ideas and thinking have come from and how they have been shaped by different philosophical and political viewpoints.

And this is where the disciplines come in. Asking the questions is a philosophical activity. A critical analysis of learning, teaching and schooling needs the theoretical perspectives and hard research evidence from psychology and sociology. Education systems need political theory and global economics. Education is worldwide and a critical understanding is to compare and contrast education in different countries and cultures. This requires an understanding of the world in which we live and global issues such as poverty, human rights and environmental sustainability. So Education Studies includes historical, economic and ecological perspectives. These are the broad theoretical perspectives used by authors in this book.

STRUCTURE OF THE BOOK

The curriculum in a school or university course is a tiny selection of the vast range of topics that exist on the supermarket shelves of human knowledge. This book is written by tutors on the Education Studies programme at Bath Spa University and reflects the selection that they made in creating the subject. The topics have been chosen to give the reader a sample of the current thinking. Chapters are designed to introduce the reader to the breadth of knowledge and understanding that Education Studies offers. They are starting points and further readings give directions for study. In order to help with critical analysis, each chapter presents a set of questions that can be asked about the topic.

There are three parts: *1 Policies and politics, 2 Global and environmental education, 3 Learning, knowledge and, the curriculum*. Each chapter draws on the different disciplines, knowledge and skills in Education Studies.

1 Policy and politics

Part 1 is about education in society, the policy, practice and political thinking behind education. Education used to be a social service determined by teachers in schools. Chapter 1 shows the ways in which governments have taken more and more control over schools and the curriculum to skill young people for Britain to compete in the global economy. It has 'marketised' education by making schools compete with each other to sell education as a 'commodity'. The chapter takes a historical approach to explaining education policy and some of the economic theories that have influenced politicians.

Recently education has become part of the government's overall social policy for health and welfare with the Every Child Matters agenda. Chapter 2 analyses the policy and the political theories about childhood and society on which it is based. Chapter 3 extends the discussion of social policy and explains the inequalities in the education system in gender, class and ethnicity. It draws upon the extensive data that is available on government websites and shows how to use data in making an analysis. There are recent moves to make education and society inclusive and Chapter 4 explores the way this has come about and the thinking behind it. It discusses the ethical case for inclusivity.

Cultural and religious diversity is a major issue for society and politicians. Chapter 5 examines how education responds to diversity, examining the role that religion has played in the development of the education system; it considers the controversial role of faith schools and the current political support for them. The National Curriculum of the 1988 Education Act left pupils learning nothing about politics and society. The Citizenship curriculum introduced in 2000 is discussed in Chapter 6 and questions are raised about the political assumptions that lie behind it and the role of education for democracy. It takes further the political and economic ideas in Chapter 1.

2 Global and environmental education

Education is a global phenomenon, but can vary in different contexts. It is easy to imagine that the education we know, or were brought up in, is the only one possible. A problem discussed in Part 1 is that strong government policy tends to lead to a single vision of what education is about. Part 2 is intended to make us aware of what happens in the rest of the world and to be able to hold alternative visions of education. It emphasizes the crucial role of education in creating a sustainable future for the planet through environmental education and helping children to understand their democratic role as citizens of the future.

Chapter 7 introduces the idea of global education and the ways in which schools can bring global and international perspectives into the curriculum, helping children to understand the world in which they live. The other aspect of global education is the divergence between education in different countries and cultures. Europe, while a geographically small area of the world, has a long cultural history of conflicts and differences between its member states. Chapter 8 examines the contrasts between the educational systems of the European countries and the attempts to forge convergence in the European Union.

International differences in education mean that some children – particularly girls – are simply not educated. Chapter 9 looks at education in the so-called 'developing countries', drawing attention to the effects of global poverty. There are attempts to redress this with the United Nations 'Education for All' by 2015 campaign, but education in some African countries still follows the old colonial pattern of nineteenth century British or French curriculum and teaching methods. All children have the right to education and Chapter 10 takes the idea further to explain why human rights are so varied across the world. It explains the philosophical underpinning of human rights legislation and questions whether children should have the right to determine their education and their futures. It suggests that children in the west may now be overprotected in a 'risk-avoidance' culture.

Education must be about the future. Chapters 11 and 12 together explore the implications of education for a sustainable future for the planet. They examine the ways in which schools can educate children to be aware of their role in the future as citizens and what they can do to affect change, not just be passive recipients of change.

3 Learning, knowledge and the curriculum

There are lots of books about teaching the curriculum. Education Studies deals not with 'how to teach', but with 'epistemology': what knowledge *is*, debates about what counts as knowledge and how the curriculum is determined. There is a long history of debate about how people learn. The third part of the book explores the nature of knowledge and learning.

Chapter 13 explains knowledge and the curriculum. It argues that knowledge is not simply inert 'stuff' that we load into children's heads, but is highly controversial and contested. Using science as an example, it looks at the debates about the curriculum and what should be taught in schools. These political arguments surfaced at the time of the development of the National Curriculum and it is shown that we should not take what is in the school curriculum for granted.

Just as knowledge itself is contested, so is the way it is learned and taught. The next two chapters explore the latest thinking about the nature of learning. The study of learning has been an essentially psychological discipline. Chapter 14 goes beyond the psychological to show the importance of cultural contexts in learning and how the individual can take control of her learning in different situations. The chapter also gives us ways to reflect on and analyse our own learning. Chapter 15 looks at the distinctive qualities of learning in young children and some of the theories that help us to understand the nature of early learning and the importance of play.

The next chapters offer new ideas about knowledge and learning. Chapter 16 looks at children's learning through computer games. This is a controversial topic and some would want to see such activities barred from schools. However, it is shown that games are a new medium for learning and can lead to thinking of a high quality. Chapter 17 argues that knowledge in the school curriculum has been too 'cognitive' with an overemphasis on language and mathematics. It shows how the Every Child Matters agenda can be met through 'cultural connections' in an art-based curriculum and how there can be culturally different ways of thinking about intelligence and learning.

All the authors in the book refer to research findings. The final chapter discusses the role of educational research. It argues that an understanding of the nature of research, and the ability to carry out research, is an essential part of an Education Studies curriculum. There are examples of the ways in which Education Studies students can carry out collaborative research projects with schools in order to understand children's learning and to improve their educational experiences.

SUMMARY POINTS

- Education Studies is a new university subject in its own right, which has grown from its origins in teacher training.
- Research shows that courses have developed differently in various universities.
- The QAA Benchmark for Education Studies provides a guide to the content of the subject and emphasises critical analysis and alternative visions or education.
- The foundation disciplines of psychology, sociology, philosophy and history play an important role in the academic rigour of the subject.
- There are new global, international, economic and ecological perspectives that inform the 'new Education Studies'.

QUESTIONS FOR DISCUSSION

1   Why did you choose Education Studies?
2   What are your career plans?
3   Does Education Studies have to include the foundation disciplines of psychology, sociology, philosophy and history?
4   What do you think about the new perspectives: global, international, ecological and economic?

REFERENCES

Crook, D. (2002) Education studies and teacher education, *British Journal of Education Studies*, 50, 1, March 2002, 55–75.

QAA (2007) *Subject Benchmark Statement: Education Studies*. Online. Available http://www. qaa. ac. uk/ academicinfrastructure/benchmark/honours/Education07. asp (accessed 23 November 2007).

Simon, B. (1994) 'The study of education', in *The State and Educational Change: Essays in the History of Education and Pedagogy*, London: Lawrence and Wishart.

TDA (2007) *QTS Standards and ITT Requirements*, London: TDA.

TTA (1998) *Teaching: High Status, High Standards. Standards for the Award of Qualified Teacher Status*, London: DfEE.

Ward, S. (2006) Undergraduate Education Studies as an Emerging Subject in Higher Education: The Construction and Definition of University Knowledge, Unpublished PhD Thesis, Bath: Bath Spa University.

Part I

Policies and Politics

1   Education Policy and Politics

Stephen Ward

INTRODUCTION

This chapter explains the political and economic influences on education in England. There have been similar developments in Scotland, Wales and Northern Ireland, and across many industrial nations. However, it is England where state control of education has swung between apparent indifference to micromanagement in a story that is still unfolding. The chapter introduces:

- trends in government policy in England since 1870;
- some political theories and their effects on education policy;
- the links between education and the economy;
- the development of market forces in education.

THE BEGINNINGS OF EDUCATION POLICY

We tend to take government education policy for granted, but the degree of control varies in different countries and it has varied in England over time. In the 1830s and 1840s there was schooling for factory and workhouse children and some schooling provided by church foundations (see Chapter 6). But education was mainly for the rich who could send their children to independent schools and it was not until 1870 that the Forster Education Act introduced compulsory state schooling for all.

It is important to understand why, later than other countries in Europe, the government in Britain finally got round to providing state education. In the nineteenth century the Industrial Revolution and its colonial powers made the British economy the envy of the world. A secret of its success was what economists call 'liberal economics': low taxation, no state interference in production with employers free to charge as much for their products and pay as little as they need to their workers. Providers compete with each other and the economy grows. However, the effect of liberal economics is to create a wide differential between rich and poor. By 1870, after years of unfettered free markets, British society was close to breakdown and it was time for the government to intervene. A series of reforms to protect the welfare of the poor included the 1870 Education Act, providing elementary education for all (Gray, 1998).

When a government provides education, it wants to make the service 'accountable' to ensure that the taxpayer is getting 'value for money'. The first attempt at education policy was simple: children were taught a basic curriculum of reading, writing and arithmetic and given moral and religious instruction, as set out in the Ministry of Education's *Handbook for Teachers*. To ensure that children were taught the curriculum Her Majesty's Inspectorate (HMI) tested them in order to determine the level of teachers' pay: the so-called 'payment by results scheme'.

THE 'POLITICAL CONSENSUS' ON EDUCATION

The 1902 Education Act saw the abolition of payment-by-results, effectively handing control of schooling and the curriculum to the teaching profession. It was an implicit statement of faith in teachers and, for the greater part of the century, left England with no national curriculum and no structure for monitoring education. Midway through the century the 1944 Butler Education Act introduced compulsory secondary education, but again did not stipulate the curriculum, except for religious education. In setting up compulsory secondary education, a tripartite system of selective and non-selective schools was constructed: grammar schools for the 'academically able', technical schools for the 'technologically able' and secondary modern schools for those destined for a non-academic and non-technical future. The system was based upon the psychological theory that intelligence testing at age 10 could sort the child population into these categories. As White (2006) points out, the idea assumes predestined futures for people that came culturally from the non-conformist religious ethic that underlies British society: just as some are destined by God for salvation, so some are destined for professional careers and economic success.

The two main political rivals in the UK are the Conservative and Labour parties. The *right-wing* Conservative Party has been committed to 'freedom' in the liberal economic tradition, whereas the *left-wing* Labour Party has been inclined to state intervention in publicly funded services – schools, hospitals, social workers – to protect the welfare of all. Traditionally, the Labour Party would have higher taxation to fund welfare services, whereas the Conservative Party would charge lower taxes to leave people with more personal wealth to spend on services as they wish. Conservatives have criticised Labour for intervening in people's lives.

During the twentieth century free-market liberalism receded and the economic theories of J. M. Keynes became dominant. Keynes argued that the economy would be successful in a more equal society in which the population was supported by state-provided social services, health and education. From the end of World War II this became the direction of social policy in Britain, with the creation of a national health service, social services and free education for all. Political interest in education lay mainly in debates about types of schools, social class and access to schooling. Conservatives argued for selective grammar schools to preserve high standards for an elite, usually middle class, group. Labour wanted to see equal access for all, regardless of social class, and from 1965 tried to introduce secondary comprehensive schools open to all pupils regardless of income or ability. However, schools were controlled by local authorities (LAs) and some Conservative authorities retained selective grammar schools. Independent fee-paying schools, of course, also continued.

During this long debate about access and social class, central government took little or no interest in the curriculum, in teaching or in the running of schools. The administration and monitoring of education was left to the LAs and a small number of inspectors in HMI. It is as though the political parties were so concerned with social class and equality that they disregarded other aspects of education. The tacit agreement not to interfere with schools Lawton (1992) calls a 'political consensus' on education. Economics, again, are important in understanding this 'hands-off' approach. During the twentieth century the British economy continued to be strong, and so, for politicians, there was no need to worry about the education system: it could be left to the local authorities and teachers.

EDUCATION AND THE GLOBAL ECONOMY

The oil crisis of the 1970s brought the indifference about education to an end. Conflict in the Middle East and the loss of Britain's colonial control led to increasing oil prices, which hit production in all the European economies. At the same time, there were concerns about rising crime, lower moral standards and the breakdown of traditional moral codes. Politicians looked around for the culprits and sent the first shots across the bows of the education professionals. In 1973 Anthony Crosland, Labour Secretary of State for Education, famously complained that the school curriculum was 'a secret garden in which only teachers and children are allowed to walk'. Jim Callaghan (1976), Labour Prime Minister, criticised primary teachers and accused schools of failing to equip young people for industry. 'Moral panic' set in, with schools portrayed as failing their children and falling standards as the cause of the nation's economic and social ills.

By the 1980s the effects of the global economy were being realised with the 'Asian tiger' economies of Japan, South Korea and Taiwan producing better industrial goods more cheaply and sucking away customers from Britain. Their education systems appeared to benefit from teaching basic skills through traditional methods. Multinationals, such as the Ford Motor Company, invested in Britain by establishing manufacturing plants and providing jobs. But they threatened to go elsewhere if the workforce was not suitably skilled. Making the curriculum suited to industrial production was seen as one of the means of enabling Britain to compete. The government began to treat education as the principal means of training industry for competition in the world, and it had to become more vocationally oriented.

THE NEW RIGHT: NEOLIBERAL ECONOMICS AND THE MARKETISATION OF EDUCATION

The 1979 general election saw the Conservative government elected under Margaret Thatcher. She criticised Keynesian economics and social policy for creating a 'nanny state' in which people ceased to be independent, functioning human beings. Her plan was to reduce taxation, 'roll back the state' and to allow people to have greater personal control over their lives. This was the birth of so-called 'New Right' politics, derived from nineteenth-century liberalism and so known as 'neo(new)liberalism'. Its ideas are based on the social philosopher Friedrich von Hayek (1899–1992) who argued in his book *The Road to Serfdom* that the welfare state disables people's creative energy and that individual freedom, while it appears to be self-serving and greedy, actually brings public good. For education, neoliberal economics means introducing the competition that made private businesses successful. Neoliberals want a 'free market' in education: education becomes a commodity that is bought and sold; schools are the providers and parents and children the consumers, or 'customers'.

It took Thatcher into her third election win, and ten years after Callaghan's warning speech, for neoliberal politics to arrive with the Education 'Reform' Act of 1988. The act is well known for introducing a national curriculum and standardised testing, but it also introduced 'local management of schools' (LMS). This took financial control away from the local authorities by delegating the spending budget directly to schools. Schools were to use the money as they wished: to appoint teaching staff or non-teaching assistants, purchase more computers or repair the roof. Such decisions were now to be taken by the head teacher and the governing body of the school, not by local authority officials. While the National Curriculum had an immediate impact on schools, LMS was a bigger change, making schools into business corporations that had to compete for pupils. The role of school governors was strengthened to get rid of 'provider capture': education is determined by the 'customers', not the providers, the education professionals.

But for parents to be able to choose in the market, the goods need to be on display: the performance of schools and teachers was to be out in the open. The reason for setting up the machinery of a national curriculum, testing, league tables and Ofsted inspection was to bring education into the market. The ambitions of the New Right Conservative Hillgate Group (1987) were realised in taking the control of education away from the 'self-interested' professionals. Schools are not adjacent to each other like shops in the high street and a family may need to be equipped to transport children to the school of their choice. But the principle was that education must be accountable to its 'customers'. The move from education as a public service provided by professionals to education as a commodity that can be purchased is referred to as 'Thatcherism'. It is part of a broader political movement taking place in many parts of the world (see Chapter 6).

LMS seems contradictory. On the one hand, the government had taken central control of the curriculum and national testing, but had de-centralised spending and management. In fact, the devolution of funding was designed to reduce the power of the local authorities that had run education. It was the Conservative government's political intention to limit the power of left-wing Labour-controlled local authorities, particularly the Inner London Education Authority (ILEA). Some had exercised strong equal opportunities policies with action against racism and sexism, which the Conservative government saw as dangerous 'social engineering' and against the liberal tradition (see Chapter 3). So while the 1988 Act appears to devolve power from government to schools, it actually increased the power of central government by disempowering the local authorities. The noose tightened around the education service with legislation in 1992 to introduce the Office for Standards in Education (Ofsted) with powers to inspect every school in the state system every four years. The Ofsted Framework for Inspection gives the most detailed list of every possible dimension of a school's work and it can be seen as part of a general trend in society towards increased accountability and surveillance.

It is difficult to convey the magnitude and complexity of the systems that were put in place for education by the legislation of the late 1980s and early 1990s. They generated prodigious amounts of consultative documents and a variety of government agencies. They also led to furious debate among professionals and politicians, particularly in setting up the content the National Curriculum. (See Coulby and Ward, 1996; Chitty, 2002; and Chapter 13 for further discussion of the National Curriculum.) The logic underlying the 1988 Education Act was to make education accountable to the rest of society and to put it into the marketplace with freedom of choice for consumers. What was going on was never entirely evident to teachers at the time. They thought they were dealing with a national curriculum and testing. They were really facing a social and economic revolution in education.

IMPROVING SCHOOLS AND CONTROLLING TEACHERS

A historical assumption about education in England has been that schools cannot compensate for society: some children are bound to achieve less because of cultural background, poverty or 'low intelligence'. The Conservative government in the 1990s seized on the research by Mortimore et al. (1988) who showed that children in some London schools learned more than in others. The differences were due to the quality of teaching and management, not just to the pupils' backgrounds. As part of the marketing of schools, the notions of 'the Effective School' and 'School Improvement' were introduced. The role of the head teacher was recast as a manager who can produce the goods and attract customers. The well-managed school concentrates on pupils' learning and achievement in the national tests.

In the National Curriculum there was an explicit statement that the legislation was to cover only content, not the way in which the curriculum was taught. However, government intervention in education had begun and by December 1991 the Secretary of State, Kenneth Clark, announced an inquiry into primary teaching and requested a report to be made available by January 1992. Those appointed to the task, Alexander, Rose and Woodhead (1992) worked over the Christmas period and their efforts became known as the *Three Wise Men* report. Their summary of the findings of 1980s research on primary teaching indicated weaknesses in individualised teaching and group work in primary schools. They recommended an increase in the level of whole-class teaching, more subject-specialist teaching and grouping by ability.

Ofsted inspection enabled the government to control the practice of teachers. If a school was not operating in the prescribed way, then it could fail its inspection and be threatened with closure. The appointment in 1994 of Chief Inspector of Schools, Chris Woodhead, as the 'scourge of poor teachers' ensured that the tightest control was exercised and a bitter campaign against the profession was underway. The so-called 'naming and shaming' of schools began to create a climate of fear that had been unknown to teachers before. This criticism of teachers by politicians, government officers and the media has been described as 'a discourse of derision'.

The 1988 Act brought enormous changes to education in England. While the National Curriculum was the most public element, the introduction of LMS, competition between schools and national testing to create the marketisation of education was the major reason for the Act and these could be seen as a contradictory: if the idea is for 'customers' to choose their school, they ought to be able to choose their curriculum. So why have a uniform curriculum for all? Chitty (2004) notes from his interview with one of Thatcher's advisers, Stuart Sexton, that he saw the National Curriculum as 'a quite separate and unnecessary piece of legislation serving mainly to divert attention from the free market objectives...' (p. 53). So why was Thatcher, a neoliberal politician who talked of 'rolling back government' introducing this welter of legislation designed to control and regulate education? Gray (1998) explains that free-market economics cannot actually happen without government intervention:

> ... encumbered markets are the norm in every society, whereas free markets are a product of artifice, design and political coercion. *Laissez-faire* must be centrally planned: regulated markets just happen. The free market is not, as New Right thinkers have imagined or claimed, a gift of social evolution. It is an end-product of social engineering and unyielding political will. (p. 17)

So there was no contradiction in the paraphernalia of education legislation in 1988 and the early 1990s. The free market needed customers to be able to choose between schools by comparing their performance on the same curriculum, by the results of standardised tests and by the evidence from Ofsted inspections. They were the government controls needed to create a free market. The National Curriculum was not principally to entitle all children to a good education; it was to ensure that parents could compare school with school. The idea of neoliberals that free markets do everything and no government is needed is just too simple.

NEW LABOUR AND THE 'MODERNISERS'

The Conservatives had enjoyed four terms of office until 1997 when Tony Blair swept Labour to power in a landslide election victory. Teachers looked forward to a return to the consensual days when they would be able to control education and the criticism of schools would end. They were soon disappointed. For this was 'New Labour' and Blair soon showed that his three priorities – 'Education, Education and Education' – meant more of the same politics of education as under the Conservatives. Blair claimed that he had not been elected to return to 'old Labour' methods of high taxation and leaving education to the professionals. 'Modernisation' meant continuing the marketisation of education and keeping the pressure on schools to deliver education fit for a modern industrial society. This does not mean that the politics of New Labour were identical with the Conservative New Right. New Labour did not see market forces as a philosophical doctrine as the neoliberal Conservatives did. Instead, Blair claimed that market forces were simply a pragmatic and effective way of operating to get the best from the system. The political philosophy was different, but the effect was much the same.

New Labour's 'modernisation' went even further. Old Labour's commitment to equality of opportunity through comprehensive education faded with the refusal to abolish independent and grammar schools. Alistair Campbell, Tony Blair's Head of Communications, casually mentioned that the government wanted to get rid of 'bog-standard' comprehensive schools and the 2002 Education Act encouraged diversity, with specialist schools allowed to select their pupils. All this, Blair claimed, makes sense 'because it works': increasing quality and standards to create an education system that provides the educated workforce for industry in globally competitive markets. Even if this allows inequalities, it is worth it.

The doubts about contradictions in 'the Conservative mind' (Lawton, 1992), where neoliberals believe in the free market with as little government as possible, did not exist for New Labour. Blair's modernising approach meant 'intervention' and the political will to take on big issues such as child poverty, inequality and underachievement through a mixture of legislation, funding and persuasion. But central control did not mean the abolition of the market. In fact, New Labour proved to be an even more enthusiastic proponent of market forces and privatisation than the Conservatives. Assessment and school league tables were strengthened with the setting of targets at all levels: national government targets for literacy and numeracy, as well as targets for local education authorities (LEAs), for schools and for individual pupils. Performance-related pay for teachers was introduced, failing local education authorities were taken over by private companies and school building was financed by profit-making organisations in the Private Finance Initiative (PFI). The privatisation of school meals, cleaning and other services begun by the Conservatives continued. All were designed to bring capital and private enterprise into the system.

Labour took up the Conservative government's desire to prescribe teaching methods and introduced the National Literacy and Numeracy Strategies. These required primary teachers to take a one-hour daily lesson in each subject, with a high proportion of interactive class teaching: the 'three-part' lesson. Such prescription of methods was previously unknown, and it is interesting that the profession should have allowed it to occur. It is unlike the prescription made to any other professional body and a result of the lack of response of the educational profession to its own research findings, which largely failed to make significant impact on teachers' practice (see Gipps, 1992). It was an extraordinary invasion into profession practice and indicates the extent to which the government was prepared to 'micromanage' education. The strategies were replaced by the Primary National Strategy (DCSF, 2007), which is less prescriptive. But the same appetite for direction was shown in the government demand for the use of synthetic phonics as recommended by the Rose Report (2006).

EDUCATION FOR THE ECONOMY AND THE STANDARDS AGENDA

Old Labour policy had been to reduce inequalities both in society and in education by providing high levels of resources to schools. Labour governments in the past, though, had not succeeded in actually producing the finances. Blair's policy was to ensure that the economy was successful by maintaining a neoliberal economy. New Labour intended not to return to the old arguments about equality and abandoned its commitment to the egalitarian comprehensive school movement. The priorities for education were to be 'standards' of achievement, not the 'structures' of schools. New Labour's enthusiasm for privatisation and the market is shown by the policy of introducing privatisation into education by establishing Academies: state-funded schools owned by private individuals or organisations. Academies set their own curriculum and are free from other constraints of state schools. Like privatising the railways, the assumption is that a school run by a private enterprise will be more efficient and more effective than one run by a state body. The same idea is inherent in School Trusts. Any school, or group of schools, is able to apply for 'Trust Status' (DfES, 2006). The school is not, like an Academy, owned by another company, but by the Trust, which has control of all its property and assets. Members of the trust can be individuals, businesses or a university and take part in the governance of the school. A trust school is able to devise its own curriculum and set its own admissions requirements.

Trust schools and Academies bring private interests into schooling and reduce the role of the state. The theory of markets and privatisation extends to diversification: the market prefers diverse offerings to give choice. The 2005 Education Act encouraged the expansion of faith schools as a means of diversification (see Chapter 5). The theory is that faith schools have a record of high achievement, so more faith schools will contribute to the raising of standards. However, research by Gibbons and Silva (2006) shows that the higher achievement of faith schools is probably due to the higher socio-economic intake of their pupils, rather than anything to do with religion.

New Labour's policies might be seen simply as an extension of the neoliberal policies of the Conservative governments in that they were designed to enhance the economy through market forces and reduce the Old Labour agenda of social equality. In ten years Blair had shifted Labour policy onto the centre ground and away from the old Labour tax and spend, socialist image. New Labour governments were successful with one of the most efficient economies in Europe. The ten years saw increases in teachers' salaries, numbers of teaching assistants, better provision for early years, improved resources, raising the school leaving age to 18 and a commitment to rebuild all secondary schools by 2015. 2007 brought a new Labour Prime Minister, Gordon Brown, who argued for an end to the conflict between education as a market and as a social service:

> We need both strong public services and we need a dynamic market economy to have a fair and prosperous society. Arguments about the size of the state and the funding of public services mark important dividing lines in politics, investment in public services in my view is absolutely critical. But we don't believe in a zero sum game in which there is only one winner between state and market forces in advanced economies. Each, markets and government, have their place.
>
> (Brown, 2007)

CONCLUSION

Government policies have been to employ market forces to introduce efficiency in education and to equip the labour market for a global economy. The assumption is that a vocationally educated workforce will improve the economy and the economy will provide a good education system in a virtuous circle. However, Wolf (2002) shows that there is no evidence of a link between education and a successful economy: vocational education and investment in higher education does not improve the economy in itself. The stress on numeracy and literacy has had the effect of narrowing the curriculum in primary schools, supposedly to suit vocational needs. But the government's priority for literacy and numeracy to meet the challenges of the global economy is questioned by Coulby (2000) who suggests that a twenty-first century economy needs a curriculum that emphasises *breadth* of skills and knowledge.

It had always been New Labour policy to reduce child poverty and to improve the working prospects of the whole population. Another aim was to promote social cohesion through 'joined-up' government with coordinated health, welfare and education policies. The SureStart Scheme and Early Years Professional Status (EYPS) in nurseries were introduced to coordinate the physical, intellectual and social development of young children. It is becoming evident that education policy can no longer be simply about raising standards to equip children for industry. The Interim Report of the Enquiry into Primary Education (Alexander, 2007) indicates the limited impact on children's learning of government policy on teaching strategies and the broad concerns about the society in which children are growing up. Some of these are the anxieties that children feel about assessment in schools, a direct result of government policy. Education should now be seen as part of a wider picture of the regeneration of society and the removal of extremes of inequality and class. 'Every Child Matters' is the Labour government's attempt to do this and is discussed in the following chapter.

SUMMARY POINTS

- After three quarters of a century of political consensus and little state control of education, legislation brought stronger controls than any other country in the world.
- Market forces were introduced to make education more efficient. Legislation was needed to enable customer choice.
- New Labour increased the controls of education beyond the curriculum, testing and inspection to include the control of teaching methods.
- New Labour education policies have continued the neoliberal marketisation process and extended it to the privatisation of education services and privately owned Academies.
- Recently the government has tried to use educational reform as a part of overall social policy with the Every Child Matters agenda.

QUESTIONS FOR DISCUSSION

1   How far should governments be involved in education?
2   Is the principal role of education to help people to get jobs and to serve the economy?
3   Should education be a public service, or be left to market forces?
4   Can education compensate for social disadvantage?

FURTHER READING

Barber, M. (2001) High expectations and standards for all, no matter what: Creating a world class education system in England, in M. Fielding, *Taking Education Really Seriously: Four Years Hard Labour*, London: RoutledgeFalmer. Argues for the 'modernizing agenda' of New Labour policy. See Fielding's introduction for a critique of New Labour's 'standards agenda'.

Bottery, M. (2000) *Education Policy and Ethics,* London: Continuum. Bottery gives a thought-provoking critique of managerialism in schools (Chapter 3), the school improvement movement (Chapter 5) and the effects of Ofsted in the 'surveillance' culture (Chapter 7).

Chitty, C. (2004) *Education Policy in Britain*, Basingstoke: Palgrave Macmillan. A thorough and detailed account of education policy.

Whitty, G. (2002) *Making Sense of Education Policy*, London: Paul Chapman Publishing. Outlines the tensions between pupils as consumers and as citizens (Chapter 5) and explains New Labour policy (Chapter 8).

Wolf, A. (2002) *Does Education Matter?* London: Penguin. Challenges the idea that vocational education improves the economy.

REFERENCES

Alexander, R. (2007) *Primary Review: Children, Their World, Their Education*, Cambridge: Esmee Fairburn Foundation, University of Cambridge. Online. Available http://www.primaryreview.org.uk/ (accessed 9 November 2007).

Alexander, R., Rose, J. and Woodhead, C. (1992) *Curriculum Organisation and Classroom Practice in Primary Schools: A Discussion Paper*, London: DES.

Brown, G. (2007) Speech on education policy at the University of Greenwich, 31 October, 2007. Online. Available http://www.number10.gov.uk/output/Page13675.asp (accessed 15 November 2007).

Callaghan, J. (1976) Towards a national debate, speech at a foundation stone-laying ceremony at Ruskin College, Oxford, 18 October 1976.

Chitty, C. (2002) *Understanding Schools and Schooling*, London: RoutledgeFalmer.

Chitty, C. (2004) *Education Policy in Britain,* Basingstoke: Palgrave Macmillan.

Coulby, D. (2000) *Beyond the National Curriculum: Curricular Centralism and Diversity in Europe and the USA*, London: RoutledgeFalmer.

Coulby, D. and Ward, S. (1996) *Primary Core National Curriculum: From Policy to Practice* (2nd edn), London: Cassell.

DCSF (2007) *The Primary National Strategy*. Online. Available http://www.standards.dfes.gov.uk/primary/ (accessed 30 November 2007).

DfES (2006) *Trust Schools*. Online. Available http://findoutmore.dfes.gov.uk/2006/09/trust_schools.html (accessed 16 November 2007).

Gibbons, S. and Silva, O. (2006) *Faith Primary Schools: Better Schools or Better Pupils?* London: London School of Economics.

Gipps, C. (1992) *What we Know about Effective Teaching*, London: Institute of Education.

Gray, J. (1998) *False Dawn: The Delusions of Global Capitalism*, London: Granta.

Hillgate Group (1987) *The Reform of British Education*, London: Claridge Press.

Lawton, D. (1992) *Education and Politics in the 1990s: Conflict or Consensus*, Lewes: Falmer Press.

Mortimore, P., Sammons, P., Stoll, L., Lewis, D. and Ecob, R. (1988) *School Matters*, London: Open Books.

Rose, J. (2006) *Independent Review of the Teaching of Early Reading*, London: DfES.

White, J. (2006) *Intelligence, Destiny and Education: The Ideological Roots of Intelligence Testing*, Oxon: Routledge.

Wolf, A. (2002) *Does Education matter?* London: Penguin.

2 Every Child Matters: Social Cohesion, Schooling and Success

Catherine Simon

INTRODUCTION

The purpose of this chapter is to explore the policy document *Every Child Matters: Change for Children in Schools* (DfES, 2004a) and its contribution to New Labour social policy. After examining the social, political and historical context, questions are raised about the validity of constructing social policy around issues of child welfare. There is a discussion of New Labour's understandings of society, in particular, the role and power of the state, the nature of childhood and responsible parenting. Finally the role of education in partnership with other key agencies as a means of achieving social cohesion and stability is questioned.

BACKGROUND

According to government documentation the catalyst for Every Child Matters and its legislative spine The Children Act (HMSO, 2004) was the Victoria Climbié case and the findings of the ensuing inquiry. Significant here was an emphasis on a new social agenda founded on public participation and investment. Old protectionist models of child welfare provision in place since 1945 were no longer considered effective and needed to be replaced. Central to this new social order is the child:

- as part of a 'family' in its wider, more liberal constructs;
- as a 'citizen in waiting'; and
- as an expression of cultural values and aspirations as defined by government and mediated through schools.

The policy changes encapsulated in *Every Child Matters: Change for Children* (DfES, 2004b) were engendered by the notion of children at risk from their parents/guardians or communities. As such they represent the government's attempt to codify perceived risks in society and to formulate its responses. The result is a complex array of initiatives and strategies that seek to tackle the long-term effects of deprivation by making children the strategic focus of wider social policy reform, the effects of which are to be felt first within education.

Every Child Matters is about shifting the principles and assumptions upon which education is founded. It spells out the government's policy and purpose for the most vulnerable and at risk in society by altering the focus of intervention from protection to prevention. It is also a restructuring and redefining of the education sector itself to encapsulate all aspects of children's lives that can be incorporated under the umbrella of 'well-being': fiscal, social (including family and community), emotional, spiritual, educational and health. This in turn is part of a wider political process involving a redefining of the role of the state and modernising governance in response to global pressures including the effects of marketisation.

POLITICAL CONTEXT

In 2003 the government published the Green Paper *Every Child Matters* alongside the response to the Laming Inquiry (HMSO, 2003) into the death of Victoria Climbié. The consultation period that followed resulted in the publishing of *Every Child Matters: Next Steps* (DfES 2004c) and The Children Act (HMSO, 2004). In November 2004 *Every Child Matters: Change for Children* was published, extending the remit of the original policy into the current 'change agenda' relating to children, young people and families. It was to: 'explain how the new Children Act 2004 forms the basis of a long-term programme of change' (DfES, 2004a: 1). Supporting documents were provided describing the implications of the policy for different services including schools, health, social care and the criminal justice system.

Change for Children in Schools (DfES, 2004a) focuses on two distinct approaches to achieving the overall aim of raising standards and improving the opportunities and outcomes for children: alterations to institutional processes and accountability. It aims to achieve this through the five outcomes:

1   being healthy;
2   staying safe;
3   enjoying and achieving;
4   making a positive contribution;
5   achieving economic well-being.

As such it stands in the tradition of neoliberalism and the 'Third Way' based on market principles, borrowing much of the language and practices of the business world. Terms such as 'partnership', 'providers', 'services', 'evaluation', 'core offer' are prominent. Justification of the initiatives in the document is couched in the language of competition. It is 'highly successful' schools that already display many of the features set out by the government. The new school Profile is a means by which schools are to 'set out for parents the full range of services they offer' (DfES, 2004a:2). Schools are part of a competitive market with parents (and children) as both consumers and stakeholders. The Profile is just one way in which schools are encouraged to advertise their wares. This, together with league tables and stringent new inspection arrangements, including assessing a school's contribution to pupil well-being, gives an illusion of transparency by setting out schools' perceived successes and failures upon which they will be judged.

The Victoria Climbié case provides the background. However, it would be naive to believe that a major government policy initiative such as this is created in such an extemporised manner without reference to previously considered aims and objectives. New Labour's election victory in 1997 elicited promises to halve child poverty by 2010 and to eradicate it by 2020. The emphasis on child poverty, social exclusion and inequality is pivotal to 'Third Way' social policy of the Blair governments since 1997. According to Rustin (2004) the case itself and the Laming Report that followed provided a populist rationale for the social policy that had already been determined.

Since 1997 the government has introduced a staggering array of measures and initiatives targeted at children and those responsible for them. They were aimed at reducing the negative impacts (perceived or actual) of the wider forces implicit in modern society that reduce the life chances and opportunities of the most vulnerable children, families and young people. They gave precedence to the role of schools in this new social democracy of the 'Third Way'. 'Raising standards' and 'opportunity for all' became the new discourse for education reform. The first line of attack was to raise literacy and numeracy standards enabling access for all to a redefined 'broad and balanced curriculum', which in turn would produce an educated British workforce that could compete confidently on the world stage. Family learning and basic skills were also prioritised, enabling families to support children's learning more effectively, whilst at the same time improving their own life chances and opportunities. Looked-after children also featured in these earlier reforms, with public service agreements aimed at improving the continuity of care and educational attainment of those in local authority care. The Care Standards Act of 2000 began the implementation of a Children's National Service Framework to set national standards for those involved in childcare. Other reforms have included the establishment of Youth Offending teams, the Connexions service for the careers of young people and fiscal reforms, including the tax credit system in 2003, and a National Childcare Strategy (DfEE, 1998).

Historically education has been one of several conduits for social reform, but it is the pace of change since 1997 that is significant and forms a fundamental part of the discourse of 'Third Way' politics. The plethora of reform emerging since 1997 appears to serve three purposes:

1   to open up education to market forces and private investment;
2   to limit 'provider capture' – the control and influence of professionals over education – and to give more power to government and other stakeholders;
3   to develop the creation of New Public Management, which promotes public participation and a subsequent shift in relationship between government and the governed. (Dale and Robertson, forthcoming)

Indeed it can be argued that it was the notion of 'provider capture' itself that provided the stimulus for the creation of the New Public Management. Furthermore, in terms of Every Child Matters, the expectation is that all agencies to do with child welfare – education, health, youth offending, social services – work together. This multi-agency 'resectoralisation', or the breaking down of traditional sectors, enables the deconstruction of existing 'provider' strongholds such as the various sector unions, once again facilitating the strengthening of government control.

However, rather than promoting a strong centralised state, which was a feature of neoliberal politics in the 1980s, the role of the state under New Labour has been that of the 'enabling state' whereby citizens at a local level take an active part in running their own lives. Giddens (cited in Olssen et al., 2004) argues that in order to be effective the enabling state must be underpinned by a level of social cohesion and sustained by a flourishing civil society. It calls not only for a new relationship between the individual and the community, but also a new relationship between those individuals, the community and the state itself.

It is upon this new relationship that current education and child welfare policy is constructed. Every Child Matters is premised on the belief that education is the prime means by which children can be raised out of poverty. The focus is not so much on the advantages accrued by the individual child but rather the family unit as a whole, supported as it is by a benefits system and a belief in 'family learning' through the extended schools agenda. Schools are to make up the perceived deficiencies in the home or community. The role of the 'enabling state' is to facilitate communities in the construction, and/or accessing, of local initiatives that will target those families who have traditionally failed to equip their children to benefit fully from the school system on offer (see Chapter 3).

'Third Way' politics is characterised by tensions generated between two seemingly opposing principles: centralisation to establish state control over key agencies such as education; and marketisation, which empowers the individual with choice, acting on the basis of self-interest, rather than as a citizen with social responsibility (Moore, 2004). Under this model local communities can be viewed as both the originators of the perceived evils in society and the very means by which the problems can be addressed. It is, therefore, not surprising that in the past decade the political focus has turned its attention to notions of social cohesion, public participation, community and citizenship under the auspices of child welfare.

CHILDHOOD IN THE TWENTY-FIRST CENTURY

Such discourses form the background to understanding expectations for children in the first decade of the twenty-first century. It is important to assess what constitutes the norm for children today and what are perceived as threats to their quality of life and opportunities. The Thomas and Hocking (2003) report for Demos examines how children's quality of life is changing and might be improved for all children over the next generation. They argue that focusing on children's quality of life has the potential to reconnect society with those shared values that are being lost to individualism.

Across the UK and Organisation for Economic Co-operation and Development (OECD) countries, changes for children have been positive, especially where they have been supported by economic growth, wider choice and access to broader experiences. However, for those families with the least economic, social and political power the trend has been one of wider disaffection and exclusion from the mainstream. Thomas and Hocking define the new childhood as one where:

- Child welfare is increasingly understood as a parent's direct responsibility – an effect of the new individualism.
- The experience of caring for children across society is diminishing – children are a lifestyle choice for many.
- Parents are becoming more risk averse – a child playing freely in open spaces is less acceptable.
- The privatisation of childhood means more contractual relations with the wider caring community such as paid-for childcare; home–school contracts.
- Private consumption has grown in scope and influence, reflected in the growth in sales of 'private' toys used in the home – PlayStations, PCs and televisions – rather than 'communal' street and park toys such as roller-skates and bicycles.

Three new social trends are identified:

1   risk aversion – the tension between the adult's 'guardian' mentality and the desire to give children freedom to learn from experience runs through every aspect of children's lives;
2   colonisation – intensive adult-based supervision of children in itself may reduce a child's quality of life and increase pressure and fear;
3   commercialisation – the rise in children's spending power makes them targets of commercial pressure.

These trends are set against a backdrop of major changes in society: social diversity, family, economy, the environment, health and crime have all impacted on the lives of children over the past thirty years. Although many of the factors that threatened children's lives have been radically reduced or removed in the last generation, poor children, as a group, are most likely to suffer other forms of deprivation and risk. Yet for all children the changes in British social structures have meant that they are limited to roles and spaces for which they are ill-equipped to adjust. Furthermore, those social changes mean that adults no longer always hold a positive, shared vision for children. This results in fragmentation, which serves to threaten the quality of life and opportunity for children.

PERCEIVED THREATS TO GOVERNMENT IN THE CURRENT ERA: THE WEAKENING OF THE STATE

The rise of neoliberalism and globalisation during the last quarter of the twentieth century, whilst bringing economic advantage to some, has served to alter the contours of state power (see Chapter 1). Neoliberalism reduces opportunities for political control over economic affairs: the market becomes the mechanism through which wealth is redistributed. Brown and Lauder (1996) view the role of the state as having the power and responsibility of ensuring prosperity, security and opportunity. Yet marketisation militates against this, promoting self-interest and undermining social cohesion. State borders are no longer supremely significant; transnational corporations have greater control over the distribution of wealth, cultural capital and the breakdown of national trade barriers.

One consequence of the weakened state is that the development of welfare state principles, the social wage and the powers of trade unions are seen to act counter to the market, with the result that wealth is polarised: unemployment for certain groups increases and welfare benefits decline. Social cohesion is thereby threatened. The rise in poverty for some has had a profound effect on children. Open markets and the ease of travel and communication systems are among the many complex factors relating to globalisation and migration of workers. Western societies are no longer (if indeed they ever were) homogenous, but are made up of a diverse ethnic mix, which calls into question traditional understandings of citizenship and national loyalties. There is evident unease amongst national governments about recent social change, and the rise in ethnic and religious fundamentalism serves to threaten state control and social cohesiveness. Citizens are citizens on many levels: local, national, ethnic, religious and global, encouraging loyalties not only within, but beyond, state borders. That national or state loyalty will come first is no longer a given, as the 7/7 bombings in London illustrate.

A further threat to the power and role of the state is current apathy towards political engagement and democratic processes. The percentage of people voting in elections is declining in Western democracies with the most significant drop amongst those under thirty-four years of age (Social Trends, 2002). Governments represent a decreasing percentage of the population. This contributes to political indifference and lack of trust in political leaders and processes, thereby weakening the power of the government mandate (see Chapter 6).

In addition, according to Brown et al. (1997) the breakdown of economic nationalism since 1970 has been coupled with shifts in social institutional structures. The family is far less stable and work is no longer secure; the hold of these institutions on the processes of socialisation and control has itself weakened. This serves as a further threat to social cohesion and stability. That certain families 'fail' their children and keep them trapped in a world of economic and educational disadvantage is, under the current 'Third Way' model, not so much a result of the failures of government policy but the renewed focus for state intervention.

EVERY CHILD MATTERS: THE NEW SOCIAL AGENDA

The answer to these perceived threats to government and society has been to redefine the power and role of the state by re-conceptualising the notion of governance in the public sector. The underlying assumption is that New Public Management is dependent upon an active citizenry and will be the means by which social cohesion is promoted through participation. *Every Child Matters* (DfES, 2003) conforms to New Labour's interventionist view of government in the public service sector and is in line with other 'Third Way' policy initiatives since 1997. Principal among these has been Sure Start, rolled out initially in each of the 20 per cent most deprived neighbourhoods (DfES, 2003: 7). These were linked to the education action zones (EAZs) in the first phase of Sure Start. Sure Start can be viewed as a pilot for the wider Every Child Matters initiative through the modelling of approaches to public participation and multi-agency working that will serve to address the systemic failures of the past and the government's desire for more effective governance in the public sector.

Sure Start emerged from one of the Comprehensive Spending Review (CSR) reports *Modernising Public Services for Britain* (HM Treasury, 1998). At its heart is the notion of public participation and multi-agency working, providing 'wrap-around care' across health, education and social services as well as voluntary and private sector services. Sure Start centres are run by local communities for local communities based on the assumption that local involvement will produce a service better tailored to the needs of its consumers.

The same notions of public participation and multi-agency working are fundamental to Every Child Matters and the mechanisms by which *Change for Children* is implemented. Most notable have been the structural changes across government and local authority departments to accommodate new and collaborative ways of working involving public, private and voluntary sectors. Responsibility for identifying and commissioning children's services at local authority level has fallen to the newly created Children's Trusts. Under this model local authorities have become facilitators, rather than providers, of services. Thirty-five 'pathfinder' Children's Trusts were established between 2004 and 2006 and their final evaluation was published in early 2007 (NFER, 2007). Whereas much of the evaluation centres on systematic restructuring and working practices (especially models of leadership and management) significant amongst the findings is the discussion concerning levels of involvement in, and understandings of, the services provided amongst its users: children, young people, parents and carers. Only in some of the pathfinders were users included in the planning, design and evaluation of services. The recommendation of the report was that more could be done. This is especially significant in the light of the assumption that local involvement will lead to more effective services tailored to local need.

Sure Start centres model the notion of multi-agency working in that they bring together health, social services and education to improve opportunities and life chances for young children and their families. However, the call for an integrated and coordinated approach to service provision is far from new and has been evident in government policy as far back as the Plowden Report (1967). That this was a recommendation in the Laming Report (HMSO, 2003) is symptomatic of a lack of such coordinated multi-agency working. Restructuring of service provision is still viewed by government as the way forward in developing holistic child welfare and protection, especially for the most vulnerable and hard to reach: 'Local leadership, dynamism and ownership are vital if change is to succeed' (DfES 2004b:6). Furthermore the model has been welcomed by users, frustrated by the lack of coordination and communication between the multiple services on which they depend (NESS, 2007).

Every Child Matters: Change for Children is built on the assumption of local participation through multi-agency working across both private and public sectors in order to achieve its five outcomes for children listed above. At each level, parents, families and carers are viewed by government as having a crucial role in promoting, achieving and sustaining these outcomes for children. This constitutes a 'new relationship' with parents. In order to promote it from the outset, parents together with children were involved in the initial consultation process from which the outcomes emerged – a direct attempt by government to appear to be conceding ownership of the aims of the policy to the communities for which they were designed. Parents are encouraged to 'actively support children's learning and development' (DfES, 2004a: 2) In order that they may do this effectively 'parental support opportunities' and 'family learning' form an essential element of the extended schools agenda embedded within *Every Child Matters* and outlined in *Change for Children in Schools* (DfES, 2004a: 3).

There are, however, confused messages to parents. Indeed it could be argued that the policy in general, and the five outcomes in particular, have been generated by the assumption that children are at risk from their parents in a variety of ways. Pugh (2006) points out in relation to Sure Start that, whilst there is recognition of the key role played by parents in the upbringing of their children and an expectation that they are to be actively involved, parents will be penalised if they fail. In the same way, parental responsibility is promoted through the expectation that they will buy into and support the five outcomes of *Every Child Matters*, with warnings of punishment for those who fail to comply and fines for those whose children persist in absconding from school. There is an assumption that parents are both the key cause of failure for children and the primary solution to the problem. One means of ensuring that 'every child (fulfils) their potential, regardless of their background or circumstances' is 'engaging and helping parents in actively supporting their children's learning and development' (DfES, 2004a: 2). These conflicting messages are further evident: parents are under pressure to return to work with more accessible childcare available to them; yet at the same time they have to be better parents.

An evaluation of Sure Start offers a clear indication of the real levels of parental and community involvement that might be expected in Every Child Matters. Gustafsson and Driver (2005: 533) argue that what is understood by 'public participation' and the extent to which it takes place depends on a number of assumptions: who constitutes 'the public' and how representative are they? Participation may be understood in a number of ways: hierarchical, consumerist or democratic. Furthermore, the nature of state power and the degree to which people participate, if at all, is also central. Using Arnstein's (1969) hierarchical 'ladder of participation', which judges participation in terms of power relationships, Gustafsson and Driver (2005) view the level of parental participation in Sure Start as that of compliance and consultation, far behind the higher orders of 'citizen control' or 'power sharing. 'Compliance' here is described as a situation where public involvement is severely limited. Tasks are assigned and incentives given, but the agenda and management of the strategy are decided by outsiders. Consultation is similarly indicative of low levels of participation. Local opinion may be canvassed but it is outsiders who analyse the information and decide on the course of action. In reality parents are powerless in the governance of Sure Start programmes and they are subjugated to the aims of outsiders.

Whether those who fail to participate are doing so by choice or because of exclusion is open to debate. Compliance or non-compliance has to do with a number of factors, not least the sense of 'community' that has yet to be defined. Community, like citizenship, can be experienced on many levels. Which 'community' and whose 'values' are being promoted will have implications for non-participatory groups who can simultaneously be viewed as 'hard to reach' or 'socially excluded' depending on perspective.

Community involvement and parental participation are promoted throughout Every Child Matters, particularly through the extended schools agenda where schools can buy in or signpost a variety of services such as family learning, parenting classes, youth clubs and extra-curricular activities. However, evaluations of extended/full service schools both in the US and UK suggest that typically schools have not succeeded in offering the 'full service' extended school model where education, health and welfare needs are met on site (Wilkin *et al.*, 2003; Cummings *et al.*, 2004). The experience for the majority of schools has been to operate in a cluster and/or to signpost services already on offer within the community. How far this will actively increase community involvement, if at all, remains to be seen, especially for those so-called 'hard to reach,' and when such extended services are expected to be self-financing.

CONCLUSION

Every Child Matters represents the government's response to urban disadvantage in promoting social cohesion, modernisation of public service provision and raising educational standards. The document sets out the values that the government wish to promote and in so doing to define, by inference, those for whom the initiative is targeted. New Public Management means that responsibility and accountability are transferred from the state to the market, individuals and families. It is where families and communities 'fail' their children that they become the focus for state intervention.

By centring social welfare policy on the child, the government has set out its vision for redefining the very nature of the education sector. There is a fundamental shift in the remit and responsibilities of education, which extend far beyond the traditional responsibility for teaching and learning. A clear indication of this is the formation of the Department for Children, Schools and Families (DCSF) in 2007. In order to break the cycle of deprivation, education is to link in partnership with other agencies to provide dedicated support to the most vulnerable and their families. To this end, schools have become strategic in their connectedness with parents, families and communities. Working practices that were once implicit have now become explicit. In this way education in general, and schools in particular, have become the universal service for delivering this new social agenda.

SUMMARY POINTS

- Every Child Matters (ECM) is a social policy that stands in the tradition of neoliberalism and 'Third Way' politics.
- ECM represents the government's response to contemporary social, cultural, political and global changes.
- ECM has emerged from a process of redefining the role of the state.
- EMC challenges traditional understandings of the role and nature of the education sector.

QUESTIONS FOR DISCUSSION

1 ECM is about new ways of thinking rather than new forms of professional practice. How far would you agree with this statement?
2 What do you envisage being the barriers to multi-agency working and how might these be addressed?
3 In what ways do you think the ECM agenda will affect the lives of all children?
4 Has ECM created new groups of disaffected children, young people and adults?

FURTHER READING

Brown, P., Halsey, A.H., Lauder, H. and Stuart Wells, A. (1997) The transformation of education and society: an introduction, in A.H. Halsey, H. Lauder, P. Brown and A. Stuart Wells (eds) *Education, Culture, Economy and*

Society, Oxford: Oxford University Press. An excellent overview of the political, social and cultural change in post-war Britain.

Cheminais, R. (2006) *Extended Schools and Children's Centres: A Practical Guide*, London: David Fulton Publishers. A practical guide to extended school policy and services including case study examples.

Hughes, P. (2006) Education and integrating children's services, in J. Sharp, S. Ward and L. Hankin (eds) *Education Studies: An Issues Based Approach*, Essex: Learning Matters. An exploration of inter-agency working and its impact on the children's workforce in schools.

Williams, F. (2004) What matters is who works: why every child matters to New Labour. Commentary on the DfES Green Paper Every Child Matters, *Critical Social Policy*, 24, 3, 406–27. A critical account of ECM and New Labour politics.

REFERENCES

Arnstein, S. (1969) in Gustafsson U. and Driver S. (2005) Parents, power and public participation: Sure Start, an experiment in New Labour governance, *Social Policy and Administration* 39(5): 528–43.

Brown, P. and Lauder, H. (1996) Education, globalisation and economic development, in A. H. Halsey, H. Lauder, P. Brown and A. Stuart Wells (eds) *Education, Culture, Economy and Society*, Oxford: Oxford University Press.

Brown, P., Halsey, A.H., Lauder, H. and Stuart Wells, A. (1997) The transformation of education and society: an introduction, in A.H. Halsey, H. Lauder, P. Brown and A. Stuart Wells (eds) *Education, Culture, Economy and Society*, Oxford: Oxford University Press.

Cummings, C., Dyson A. and Todd, L. (2004) *Evaluation of the Extended School Pathfinder Projects*, NFER Report 530, Nottingham: DfES Publications.

Dale, R. and Robertson, S. (forthcoming) Reflections and directions, in K. Martens, A. Rusconi and K. Leutz (eds), *New Arenas of Global Governance and International Organisations*, London: Palgrave.

DfEE (1998) *National Childcare Strategy*, Sudbury: DfEE Publications.

DfES (2003) *Green Paper: Every Child Matters*, Norwich: The Stationery Office.

DfES (2004a) *Every Child Matters: Change for Children in Schools*, Nottingham: DFES Publications. Online. Available http://www.everychildmatters.gov.uk (accessed 7 October 2007).

DfES (2004b) *Every Child Matters: Change for Children*, Nottingham: DfES

DfES (2004c) *Every Child Matters: Next Steps*, Nottingham: DfES

Gustafsson, U. and Driver, S. (2005) Parents, power and public participation: Sure Start an experiment in New Labour governance, *Social Policy and Administration*, 39(5): 528–43.

HMSO (2003) *The Victoria Climbié Inquiry: Report of an Inquiry by Lord Laming*. Online. Available http://www.victoria-climbie-inquiry.org.uk/finreport/finreport.htm (accessed 6 April 2008).

HMSO (2004) The Children Act, Norwich: The Stationery Office.

HM Treasury (1998) *Comprehensive Spending Review: Modernizing Public Services for Britain*, Norwich: The Stationery Office.

Moore, R. (2004) *Education and Society: Issues and Explanations in the Sociology of Education*, Cambridge: Polity Press.

NESS (National Evaluation of Sure Start) (2007) *National Summary: Understanding Variations in Effectiveness among Sure Start Local Programmes: Lessons for Sure Start Children's Centres*. Online. Available http://www.ness.bbk.ac.uk/impact.asp (accessed 6 April 2008).

NFER (2007) *National Evaluation of Children's Trusts Pathfinders – Final Report*. Online. Available http://www.everychildmatters.gov.uk/aims/childrenstrusts/ (accessed 6 April 2008).

Olssen, M., Codd, J. and O'Neill, A. (2004) *Education Policy: Globalisation, Citizenship and Democracy*, London: Sage Publications.

Plowden Report (1967) *Children and their Primary Schools*. Online. Available http://www.dg.dial.pipex.com/documents/plowden.shtml (accessed 6 April 2008).

Pugh, G. (2006) *Every Child Matters: Change for Children Challenges and Opportunities*. Online. Available http://www.tactyc.org.uk/pdfs/2006Joint_pugh.pdf under the title of *Professionalism in the Early Years: A Policy Update* (accessed 6 April 2008).

Rustin, M. (2004) Learning from the Victoria Climbié Inquiry, *Journal of Social Work Practice*, 18(1): 9–18.

Social Trends 32 (2002) TSO. Online. Available http://www.statistics.gov.uk/downloads/theme_social/Social_Trends32/Social_Trends32.pdf (accessed 6 April 2008).

Thomas, G. and Hocking, G. (2003) *Other People's Children: Why Their Quality of Life is Our Concern*, London: Demos.

Wilkin, A., Kinder, K., White, R., Atkinson, M. and Doherty, P. (2003) *Towards the Development of Extended Schools: NFER Report 408*, Nottingham: DfES Publications.

3 Gender and Educational Achievement

Christine Eden

INTRODUCTION

Media interest in education tends to focus on the information that it is believed interests parents: how different schools have performed in various tests and examinations and their place in published league tables. During the last twenty years, equality of opportunity discussion has focused on whether schools are able to affect test results, irrespective of the social background of children. This has led to debate about what is perceived to be boys' underachievement. The emphasis on boys has obscured other significant inequalities in achievement. So while the main focus of this chapter is on gender, data will be used to show that not only is much of the current understanding of the gender gap too simple, but it has failed to give due prominence to ethnicity and social class.

The data in research and government statistics show the patterns of educational achievement that require explaining. Explanations involve schooling, but also the growth of self-awareness and identity. These impact on both gendered and ethnic expectations of pupils' roles as adult men and women, which are developed within a system fragmented by class. This complex social construction of identity helps explain why inequalities are so problematic and why research does not give definitive answers.

The chapter:

- introduces the changing debate about gender and educational achievement, including the relationship between gender, social class and ethnicity;
- shows recent trends, using the wide range of data available on gender, social class and ethnicity in relation to educational achievement;
- considers the explanations for the relationship between gender and educational achievement, particularly gender formation;
- highlights the continuing dissonance between girls' achievements at school and their place in the labour market.

THE CHANGING DEBATE

Gender has always received attention in discussions of pupil attainment. But the particular focus is located in wider debates about the position of men and women in society at different historical moments. In the nineteenth century the Schools Enquiry Commission of 1868 compared girls' and boys' school performance and suggested that differences could be attributed to characteristic mental differences between the sexes, although the Commission did not argue for a differentiated curriculum. Reports during the twentieth century did, however, argue for such differentiation. In the mid-twentieth century two government reports, Crowther in 1959 and Newsom in 1963, argued that the prime destination of girls was as wives and mothers and so their curriculum should reflect the nature of their ambitions and their future domestic role. Concerns centred on working-class male pupils and explanations for low achievement ranged from the characteristics of the home background to mechanisms within the school that stratified pupils on the basis of social class.

The 1960s and 1970s saw significant changes with the introduction of comprehensive schooling and the Sex Discrimination Act of 1975 and it became possible to question female underachievement and curriculum differentiation. The feminist movement tried to build on such a view by promoting subject choices for girls and initiating a number of projects aimed at breaking down traditional assumptions and promoting greater access across the curriculum. Projects such as Girls into Science and Technology, Women into Science and Engineering and the government initiative, Technical Vocational Education Initiative (TVEI), all challenged stereotypical choices within the curriculum and tried to enhance girls' achievement. Feminist writers made gender inequality visible and articulated the reasons for change, arguing that girls and women were disadvantaged in education and the labour market. They rejected ideas of differences in the biological capacities of males and females, offered social explanations for gender inequality in education achievement and proposed strategies for change.

The 1988 Education Act had considerable impact on gender equality in that it established a common curriculum to General Certificate of Secondary Education (GCSE) level for boys and girls. Subject stereotyped choices could still be made at A level, but the National Curriculum itself made at least the theoretical assumption that the sciences, technology and mathematics are as much for girls as they are for boys. This helps to explain why girls' attainment is now higher than that of boys. It has become increasingly visible since the early 1990s, initially revealed through the results of GCSE examinations. The gap between female and male attainment has continued to widen in favour of females and even the traditional advantage of males over females in science areas has to a large extent disappeared. So after a relatively short focus on girls' achievements, discussion of gender inequality now focuses on boys' underachievement, but without considering men and women in the economic and power structures of society.

Inequalities associated with ethnicity and social class have been surprisingly invisible until recently compared to the focus that has been given to the gender gap. This may lie in the belief that strategies to tackle boys' underachievement can be found in the school system itself. Issues of social class and ethnicity appear more difficult to deal with through policy initiatives, rooted as they are in power relations in society, whereas the gender gap in education is not often discussed as part of wider issues of gender inequality in society.

GENDER DIFFERENCES IN EDUCATIONAL ACHIEVEMENT

Both boys' and girls' educational performance have significantly improved during the last twenty years. But the rate of increase for females is greater and more rapid and the differences vary across pupils' school careers. The difference actually widens across key stage 2 (KS2) to KS4. In the last few years the gap in performance, which had existed in favour of boys at A level, has also been eliminated (Arnot *et al.*, 1998).

The results for Standard Assessment Tests (SATs) and GCSEs in 2005, 2006 and provisional results for 2007 confirm girls achieving at a higher level than boys in most, but not all, subjects: the most significant gap is in literacy, which is an international phenomenon.

Drawing on selected DCSF data for 2007 (provisional) we see at KS1:

- girls continue to out perform boys at Level 2b and above in all subjects with the largest gap of 16 per cent in writing in 2007;
- but at Level 3 and above between 2005 and 2007, boys out perform girls by 4 per cent in mathematics and by 2 per cent in science. (DCSF, 2007a)

The picture becomes more complicated when ethnicity is introduced with greater differences in achievement across ethnic groups. Teacher assessment in Reading in 2006 showed:

- Level 3 was achieved by 22 per cent of white boys compared to 28 per cent of Chinese;
- this dropped to 10 per cent for Pakistani, 11 per cent for Bangladeshi and 12 per cent for Black Caribbean groups. (DCSF, 2007b)

The data for girls achieving Level 3 show that across all the ethnic groups girls are achieving at a higher level than boys with a 9–10 per cent difference but, as with boys, the biggest gaps are between different ethnic groups.

- Level 3 was achieved by 32 per cent of white girls, 37 per cent of white and Asian, 38 per cent of Chinese;
- this dropped to 15 per cent for Pakistani and Bangladeshi girls;
- 21 per cent of Black Caribbean girls achieved this level, which is significantly higher than the 12 per cent for boys from that group. (DCSF, 2007b)

Eligibility for free school meals (FSM) is used as a crude indicator of deprivation, and reveals even greater differences. In the 2006 teacher assessment at Level 3 the gap between those eligible for FSM and those not (the FSM gap) exists across all ethnic groups and is larger than the gender gap and larger than differences between ethnic groups:

- 8 per cent of FSM boys achieve Level 3 compared to 24 per cent of non-FSM boys;
- 13 per cent of girls achieve Level 3 compared to 34 per cent of the non-FSM girls. (DCSF, 2007b)

The FSM gap varies in its impact for different ethnic groups: it is very high for white boys but much less strong for Bangladeshi boys (DCSF, 2007b).

Key Stage 2 data for 2005–7 continues these trends:

- girls continue to outperform boys in all aspects of English at all levels;
- there are significant differences in performance at writing with 17 per cent more girls achieving Level 4 compared to boys in 2005, 16 per cent in 2006 and 15 per cent in 2007 showing a small downward trend across those three years;
- boys' performance at Level 3 and 4 mathematics is slightly better than girls'.;
- in 2007 at Level 5 or above, boys have extended their lead over girls in mathematics to 5 per cent and marginally outperform girls in science by 1 per cent. (DCSF, 2007c)

A different measure of the impact of socio-economic differences can be seen in the relationship of attainment to types of school where again the socio-economic gap is wider than the gender gap. Results for writing and mathematics in 2007 show:

- Level 4 in writing was reached by 59 per cent of boys in the 'all maintained' school category compared to 81 per cent in 'independent' schools – a gap of 22 per cent;
- the equivalent gap for girls was 17 per cent;
- Level 5 in mathematics is achieved by 60 per cent of boys in independent schools against 35 per cent in all maintained schools – a gap of 25 per cent;
- 29 per cent of girls in the 'all maintained sector' achieved Level 5 for mathematics, compared to 57 per cent in independent schools, a 28 per cent gap. (DCSF, 2007d)

Similar patterns reflecting gender, ethnicity and socio-economic status can be seen at KS3 with the gender gap for English increasing from 9 per cent at KS1 to 15 per cent at KS3. Between 2004 and 2006, GCSE results show a 10 per cent gender gap for those achieving five A★–C grades and a 9 per cent gap in 2007; this has been fairly consistent since 1995. The interactive effect of ethnicity and gender can be seen starkly in the 2006 data in that 36 per cent of Black Caribbean boys achieved five A★–C passes, compared to 84 per cent of Chinese girls. (DCSF, 2007d, 2007e)

The gender and ethnicity gaps are again less than the socio-economic gap represented by eligibility for free school meals. In 2007 the FSM gap for those gaining five A★–C GCSEs is 27 per cent for boys and girls, confirming the significance of socio-economic factors in educational achievement (DCSF, 2007f).

At A level the patterns change to some extent although girls are more likely than boys to stay in full-time education and, in a change over the last ten years, girls perform better in terms of the percentage gaining A★ grades. The new dimension visible with A levels is the degree to which students still make stereotyped choices. Boys are more than three times as likely to take physics, 50 per cent more take mathematics and twice as many as girls take further mathematics. But this gap has decreased since 2001–2. In computer studies, while the numbers are small for both male and female students, 12 times as many males take this subject. More than twice as many males take economics. Male subject choices cluster around physics, mathematics, computer studies and economics.

Women still predominate in the arts and social sciences. There are nearly three times as many female students taking psychology and just over three times taking sociology. In the areas of art and design, drama, English, French, Spanish and religious studies there are over twice as many female than male students. Applied A-level examination results show even greater differences. Applied engineering was taken by 181 males compared to 13 females, while health and social care was taken by 162 males compared to 4054 female students (DCSF, 2007g). The data show differences in achievement but less pronounced than for KS1–4. The overall pass rate by subject and gender shows very little difference between boys and girls. But in those achieving grade A, a trend over the last ten years is for female students to perform better than male students with 22. 8 per cent of males and 25. 1 per cent of females gaining grade A in 2006.

English at this level shows no difference between boys and girls and mathematics has reversed a historical trend with a 4 per cent gender gap in the girls' favour. Some subjects show significant differences in the percentages achieving grade A:

- physics: males 28, females, 36;
- geography: males 22, females 31;
- psychology: males 11, females 20. 5;
- sociology: 16. 7 to 22;
- art and design: 25 to 30.

The exception to this trend is in modern languages. In German 41 per cent of males to 35 per cent females and in Spanish 42 per cent compared to 35 per cent females attained an A grade. One area that is at first sight unexpected is physical education where twice as many females achieved an A grade: 20 per cent compared to 10 per cent for males. At the other end of the scale the pattern is reversed in that in most subjects there is a higher percentage of males achieving grade E. Again there is an exception in modern languages, although the differences here are very small (DCSF, 2007g).

This confirms a different set of choices for boys and girls at A level, although girls are increasing their participation in such stereotypical male areas as mathematics and physics. These are important choices as they help determine access to degree courses, which can significantly affect the opportunities available within the job market (Francis, 2002).

The data suggest that differences in attainment appear to be smaller between genders compared to those for ethnic origin and social class background. One further indicator of the impact of social class can be seen in the highest qualification level achieved by 18-year-olds in 2006. 66 per cent of pupils with parents identified as higher professional achieved Level 3 and above, while only 25 per cent of pupils with parents identified as in routine occupations reach the same level (DCSF, 2007i). The differences in achievement between ethnic groups also continue with the average points awarded to black boys achieving Level 3 qualifications being 30 points below Chinese boys (DCSF, 2007g).

Gender, class and ethnic identity undoubtedly interact with one another: ethnic inequalities remain even when controlling for gender and class (Gillborn and Mirza, 2000; DfES IPPR, 2006) and socio-economic status measurements show the greatest differences in pupil achievements. This is worth remembering in all the fuss about boys' underachievement.

EXPLANATIONS OF THE GENDER GAP

Having placed the gender gap in that wider context, there are consistent gender differences in achievement that need to be understood. The rest of the chapter offers explanations for differences in achievement associated with gender with references to class and ethnicity where relevant.

Children do not enter the classroom as a blank sheet but bring with them a wide range of expectations about how it is appropriate to behave and what is expected of them. Children at the age of three learn the sort of behaviour approved by parents and teachers. Research into three-year-olds playing with Lego showed significant gender differences in both the process and the actual constructions made, with girls building houses and boys, cars and guns (Browne and Ross, 1991). Schools have an important role in either countering such stereotypes or helping to reinforce them. But children also resist and challenge the expectations they encounter and select what they chose to adopt and act on in their own lives. The variety of teachers and experiences that pupils encounter, and the interaction of ethnicity and social class, make a complex mix in gender formation.

However we understand the complexity of gender differences and its interrelationship with class and ethnicity, there has been considerable focus on boys' underachievement. Some writers, such as Mac an Ghaill (1994), have set this within wider debates about changing patterns of masculinity. He argues that the loss of working-class manual occupations has undermined traditional models of masculinity, which in turn has led to an erosion of confidence and a sense that education lacks relevance and value. This helps explain what has become known as the 'laddish' culture, which rejects educational success and gives status to achievements in sport (Francis, 1999). This negative approach to education is indicated by greater rates of truancy and exclusion (Ofsted, 1996). Teachers report that male students exhibit greater behaviour problems within the classroom and have a group culture that gives power to the idea that education is undesirable. A five-year study by Davies and Brember (2001) shows that issues associated with discipline and authority should be given far more attention when considering boys' academic achievement.

Girls' higher achievement may relate to the fact that women now expect to have a job and to continue in the labour market after they have children. A greater emphasis upon a career as the focus of gender identity now informs young women's educational aspirations, motivation and achievements. The labour market itself has grown in those areas of clerical and service work that have traditionally been women's work. While these jobs are not well paid and women still remain underrepresented in positions of power and management, there has been a shift in the expectation that young women have of themselves. However, males remain advantaged in employment opportunities and levels of pay. A recent Higher Education Statistics Agency (HESA) report found that this held even for graduates where the median salary of full-time first degree male graduates was £1,000 higher than that of equivalent female graduates (HESA, 2007). The Institute of Chartered Management found the pay gap has recently widened slightly (Chartered Management Institute, 2007).

Within the school the curriculum, assessment techniques, teaching styles, teacher expectations, differences in learning styles, behaviour management and the organisation of teaching groups all contribute to gender differences. Girls do better at open-ended tasks and boys are more responsive to memorizing abstract facts (Howe, 1997). In Scotland girls seem to do well in coursework and essays, whereas boys do better at multiple choice questions (Powney, 1996). Different teaching styles and a range of teaching strategies may be needed to address the differences in preference between boys and girls (Younger et al., 2005).

Within gender cultures girls concentrate and focus on schoolwork and boys engage in the disruptive behaviour that gives status within the male peer group. Ofsted (1996) suggested that definitions of pupils' ability appeared to relate more to teacher expectations and behaviour than academic performance. Such expectations are transmitted in the classroom, in the corridors and through the many organisational aspects of the school. These expectations are crucial given that, throughout their school career, pupils are actively engaged in constructing their gender identities and responding to the expectations of others. Strand's analysis of national tests also highlights the significance of pupil behaviour and teachers' perceptions of pupil behaviour in understanding the attainment gap for Black Caribbean pupils (Strand, 2007: 5).

The same issue of self-identity and expectations emerges in trying to understand social deprivation and educational achievement. A review of recent research by the Joseph Rowntree Foundation suggests 'that children from less advantaged backgrounds are more likely to feel a lack of control over and less involvement in their learning and so have a greater tendency to become reluctant recipients of the taught curriculum' (Hirsch, 2007: 9). Cassen and Kingdon's (2007) research into low achievement shows that children in poverty are also aware of the way poverty reduces their educational prospects and affects their own view of themselves within the education system. A cluster of recent reports for the Rowntree Foundation shows children in poverty are more likely to have negative experiences of school, are less likely to have space within which to do their homework or parents able to help them. These reports, summarised by Hirsch (2007), locate the experiences of pupils within the wider social and economic conditions of the community.

GENDER IDENTITY AND EDUCATIONAL ACHIEVEMENT

One of the most consistent explanations of gender and educational attainment lies in the social construction of gender and how models of masculinity and femininity develop amongst pupils and their peer groups (Connell, 2000). Pupils' expectations of their roles are informed by the patterns of gender that they see within both the labour market and the family. Expectations of future domestic responsibility are a major factor in working–class females' expectations of themselves (Lees, 1993) and help shape the way education is perceived. For secondary pupils their sexual identity contributes to expectations of themselves (Younger *et al.*,   2005).

Recognising the constraints and culture within which young people develop does not have to lead to a deterministic position: pupils do challenge traditional stereotypes. The present author's research into a primary playground supports studies that have shown how gender relations and ideologies are actively negotiated and resisted (Eden, 1995). Pupils moved in and out of gender groupings and on occasions actively intervened to enter into the other gender domain, particularly with regard to playing football. But even though gender stereotypes were resisted there were clear signs in the primary playground of boys dominating the physical space and frequently subjecting girls to sexual harassment. The subordination of femininity was acted out through the dominance of football and fighting within the playground environs, with girls often sitting on walls acting as cheerleaders and vying for attention. Within the secondary context a number of research studies have shown that, while girls resist and construct their own lives and femininity, they are nevertheless constantly subjected to language and behaviour from the boys, which places them in an oppressed position or one where they have to constantly challenge the boys' behaviour (Haywood and Mac an Ghaill, 2001).

The complex definitions of masculinity that young males have to deal with make it easy to become reluctant learners. Frosh *et al.* (2002) have shown the competitive hierarchy amongst boys and their concerns about being seen as feminine. These worries place consistent pressures on young men to distance themselves from the ways in which girls respond to the educational system. The need to redefine what is seen as acceptable male behaviour within young male peer groups is one of the areas that schools need to address if boys' achievement is to match girls' performance over recent years.

This might also allow the inequalities that affect girls within the labour and domestic spheres to become part of the debate. As attention has shifted to boys' educational achievements, inequalities have become 'privatised': about individual choice rather than part of the structures of inequality in society. The issue of how women can balance family demands and career expectations is one that schools do not address. Without this perspective females will continue to find themselves confronting inequalities in the labour market and within the domestic sphere. The emphasis on male underachievement takes attention away from what are still profound inequalities associated with gender. There is little evidence that success at school translates into success, power and prestige for women in the labour market. Until that happens we should still be addressing the needs of girls and their future opportunities as much as those of boys. The increase in women working has not been accompanied by any radical shift in the responsibilities that men and women, particularly working-class women, take for childcare responsibilities and domestic tasks. Young girls still see themselves tied to a future that gives them the main responsibility for childcare.

CONCLUSION

The emphasis on boys' underachievement obscures such inequalities and their interaction with social class and ethnicity. The research cited in this chapter makes it clear that improvements in female achievement are not shared by all girls and are not across all subjects. Connolly (2006) has argued that recognising the way gender identity interacts with social class and ethnicity produces 'differing and enduring' forms of identity and requires that any programme of intervention be applicable to all boys and all girls'. Debates about inequality may therefore be more appropriately focused on which particular categories of boys and girls are underachieving. Addressing gaps in achievement requires that the three dimensions discussed here are recognised and monitored to ensure appropriate strategies are developed to challenge ethnic, class and gender inequalities.

SUMMARY POINTS

- The evidence demonstrates that gender is a significant factor in educational achievement and is reflected across different ethnic groups and social classes.
- The emphasis on gender has to some extent obscured the fact that social class is a greater influence on attainment.
- All ethnic groups show differences in attainment between genders, but there is variation in the extent of the gender gap.
- Debates about boys' underachievement need to be set within wider debates about access to power and influence in the labour market and their place within future childcare responsibilities.
- Explanations for the gender gap need to recognise the significance of the social construction of masculinity and femininity in influencing expectations and educational achievement.
- Addressing inequalities in achievement requires strategies that challenge ethnic, class and gender divisions.

QUESTIONS FOR DISCUSSION

1   How do gender, social class and ethnicity interact in relation to educational achievement?
2   How can a 'laddish' culture be challenged to both support boys' achievement and greater gender equality in society?
3   What experiences have you had that help you understand the importance of teacher expectations?
4   In what ways do notions of masculinity and femininity impact on attitudes to learning?
5   Think of the women you know in positions of power. Are women translating their educational achievements into the labour market?

FURTHER READING

Connolly, P. (2006) Effects of social class and ethnicity on gender differences, *British Educational Research Journal*, 32(1): 3–23. A careful and precise analysis of the nature of the relationship between social class, ethnicity and gender.

DfES (2005) *Ethnicity and Education: The Evidence on Minority Ethnic Pupils*. Online. Available http://www.dfes.gov.uk/research/programmeofresearch/projectinformation.cfm?projectid=14488&resultspage=1 (Accessed 10 September 2007). A research report that brings together a range of data and explanations about the achievement of a range of minority ethnic groups.

DfES (2007) *Gender and Education: The Evidence on Pupils in England*. Online. Available http://www.dfes.gov.uk/research/data/uploadfiles/RTP01-07.pdf (Accessed 12 September 2007). Summarises data on subject choice and attainment, drawing on a wide range of literature to account for gender differences in attainment.

DfES 'The Standards Site' has a section on gender and achievement, which gives references to books and journal articles, resources and links. Online. Available http://www.standards.dfes.gov.uk/genderandachievement/ (Accessed 4 April 2008).

Skelton, C., Francis, B., and Valkanova, Y. (2007) *Breaking Down the Stereotypes: Gender and Achievement in Schools*. London, EOC. Online. Available http://www.equalityhumanrights.com/Documents/Gender/Research/

Breaking%20down%20the%20stereotypes%20Gender%20and%20achievement%20in%20schools%20EOC%20 research.doc (Accessed 10 October 2007). A detailed review of a wide range of research and data with suggestions for a range of strategies to address the gender gap in achievement.

REFERENCES

Arnot, M., Gray, J., James, M. and Rudduck, J. (1998) *A Review of Recent Research on Gender and Educational Performance*, Ofsted Research Series, London: The Stationery Office.

Browne, N. and Ross, C. (1991) Girls' stuff, boys' stuff: Young children talking and playing' in N. Browne (ed.) *Science and Technology in the Early Years*, Milton Keynes: Oxford University Press.

Cassen, R. and Kingdon, G. (2007) *Tackling Low Educational Achievement*, Report for Joseph Rowntree Foundation. Online. Available http://www.jrf.org.uk/bookshop/details.asp?pubID=901 (Accessed 31 October 2007).

Chartered Management Institute (2007) *Female Resignations Hit New High Despite Rapid Promotion and Bonus Payouts*. Online. Available http://www.managers.org.uk/listing_media_1.aspx?id=10: 347&id=10: 138&id=10: 11&doc=10: 3364 (Accessed 20 October 2007).

Connell, R. W. (2000) *The Men and the Boys*, Cambridge: Polity Press.

Connolly, P. (2006) Effects of social class and ethnicity on gender differences, *British Educational Research Journal*, 32(1): 3–23.

Council for Education (England) (1959) *15–18, (Crowther Report)*, London: HMSO.

Davies, J. and Brember, I. (2001) *Closing The Gap in Attitudes Between Boys and Girls: A Five Year Longitudinal Study*, Manchester: University of Manchester School of Education.

DCSF (2007a) *National Curriculum Assessments at Key Stage 1 in England 2007*. Online. Available http://www.dfes. gov.uk/rsgateway/DB/SFR/s000740/sfr26-2007.pdf (Accessed 10 October 2007).

DCSF (2007b) *National Curriculum Assessment, GCSE and Equivalent Attainment and Post-16 Attainment by Pupil Characteristics in England 2005/06 (Provisional)*. Online. Available http://www.dfes.gov.uk/rsgateway/DB/SFR/ s000693/SFR46_2006_tables.xls (Accessed 10 October 2007).

DCSF (2007c) *National Curriculum Assessments at Key Stage 2 in England, 2007 (Provisional)*. Online. Available http:// www.dfes.gov.uk/rsgateway/DB/SFR/s000737/SFR24_2007_nat.xls. (Accessed 10 October 2007)

DCSF (2007d) *National Curriculum Assessment, GCSE and Equivalent Attainment and Post-16 Attainment by Pupil Characteristics, in England 2006/07*. Online. Available http://www.dfes.gov.uk/rsgateway/DB/SFR/s000759/ SFR38_2007_Tables.xls (Accessed 28 November 2007).

DCSF (2007e) *National Curriculum Assessments, GCSE and Equivalent Attainment and Post-16 Attainment by Pupil Characteristics, in England 2005/06*. SFR 04/2007. Online. Available http://www.dfes.gov.uk/rsgateway/DB/ SFR/s000708/index.shtml (Accessed 18 October 2007).

DCSF (2007f) *National Curriculum Assessment, GCSE and Equivalent Attainment and Post-16 Attainment by Pupil Characteristics, in England 2006/07*. Online. Available http://www.dfes.gov.uk/rsgateway/DB/SFR/s000755/ SFR35_2007_All_ (Accessed 30 November 2007).

DCSF (2007g) *GCE/VCEA/AS and Equivalent Examination Results in England, 2005/06 (Revised)*. Online. Available http://www.dfes.gov.uk/rsgateway/DB/SFR/s000703/index.shtml (Accessed 18 October 2007).

DCSF (2007h) *The Activities and Experiences of 18 Year Olds: England and Wales 2006*. Online. Available http://www. dfes.gov.uk/rsgateway/DB/SFR/s000695/Addition1.xls (Accessed 20 October 2007).

Department of Education and Science (England) (1963) *Half Our Future (Newsom Report)*, London: HMSO.

DfES IPPR (2006) *Social Mobility: Narrowing Social Class Attainment Gap*. Online. Available http://www.dfes.gov. uk/rsgateway/DB/STA/t000657/SocialMobility26Apr06.pdf (Accessed 14 September 2007).

Eden, C. (1995) Gender in the playground, Paper presented at the British Education Research Conference, University of Bath, September, 1995.

Francis, B. (1999) Lads, lasses and (New) Labour: 14–16 year old students' responses to the laddish behaviour and boys' underachievement debate, *British Journal of Sociology of Education*, 20(3): 355–71.

Francis, B. (2002) Is the future really female? The impact and implications of gender for 14–16 year olds' career choices, *Journal of Education and Work*, 15: 75–87.

Frosh, S., Phoenix, A. and Pattman, R. (2002) *Young Masculinities*, London: Palgrave.

Gillborn, D. and Mirza, H. S. (2000) *Education Inequality – Mapping Race, Class and Gender: A Synthesis of Research Evidence*, Report for the Office for Standards in Education, London: HMSO.

Haywood, C. and Mac an Ghaill, M. (2001) The significance of teaching English boys: exploring social change, modern schooling and the making of masculinities, in W. Martino, and B. Meyenn(eds) *What About the Boys?* Buckingham: Open University Press.

HESA (2007) *Career Progression of Graduates*. Online. Available http://www.hesa.ac.uk/index.php/content/view/888/161/ (Accessed 31 October 2007).

Hirsch, D. (2007) *Experiences of Poverty and Educational Disadvantage*, Joseph Rowntree Foundation. Online. Available http://www.jrf.org.uk/knowledge/findings/socialpolicy/2123.asp (Accessed 31 October 2007).

Howe, C. (1997) *Gender and Classroom Interaction: A Research Review*, Edinburgh; SCRE.

Lees, S. (1993) *Sugar and Spice: Sexuality and Adolescent Girls*, London: Penguin.

Mac an Ghaill, M. (1994) *The Making of Men: Masculinities, Sexualities and Schooling*, Buckingham: Open University Press.

Ofsted (1996) *Exclusions from Secondary Schools*, London: HMSO

Powney, J. (1996) *Gender and Attainment: A Review*, Edinburgh: The Scottish Council for Research in Education.

Strand, S. (2007) *Minority Ethnic Pupils in the Longtitudinal Study of Young people in England (LSYPE)*, DCSF Research Report. Online. Available: http://www.dfes.gov.uk/research/data/uploadfiles/DCSF-RB002.pdf (Accessed 29 October 2007).

Younger, M., Warrington, M. and McLellan, R. (2005) *Raising Boys' Achievements in Secondary School: Issues, Dilemmas and Opportunities*, Maidenhead: Open University Press/McGraw Hill.

4 Social and Educational Inclusion

Tilly Mortimore

INTRODUCTION

Are your school days a time you like to remember or something you'd rather forget? Think back to those days and what was good about them: games in the playground? Having a laugh with your friends? It is likely that your most positive memories are connected with being an accepted member of a group, feeling good about yourself, being included. Were you ever the one chosen last, the one with whom others wouldn't work, never shared secrets with, the one who walked home alone? This is exclusion at its simplest, most fundamental level and the associated stress and anxiety affects children's ability to learn and to thrive.

This chapter explores the life-long impact of exclusion/inclusion. It examines ways in which mechanisms in society increase the likelihood that certain groups and individuals will be excluded, how exclusion manifests itself at broader levels throughout society, and how a range of factors can reduce or increase the likelihood of people being denied the benefits that contemporary society can offer.

DEFINITIONS

We need to move beyond personal memories of being included or left out, towards an understanding of 'inclusion' as applied within the fields of education or sociology. The term 'inclusion' is frequently linked with education:

> Inclusive education is part of a human rights approach to social relations and conditions. The intentions and values involved relate to a vision of the whole society of which education is a part. Issues of social justice, equity and choice are central to the demands for inclusive education.
>
> (Morris, 2001, p. 59).

However this 'rights' approach is equally applicable to social inclusion. Nind and her colleagues (2003) state:

> If we wish to develop inclusion we need to accept all individuals having control of their own lives, having a say in the running of organisations that represent them and affecting the processes of the institutions that dominate much that happens to them and around them (p. 6).

In education, this means:

> ... valuing all children irrespective of the type or degree of impairment; ... restructuring the institution to remove barriers so teaching and learning take place so all children can be valued for who they are, participate, interact and develop their potential.
>
> (Rieser, 2001, p. 175)

This calls for radical reappraisal of the structure of schools and colleges and, by extension, of policy and institutions. Inclusive thinking is radical thinking and exclusion/inclusion is now at the heart of government social policy. The government set up the Social Exclusion Task Force in 2006 to create a more inclusive society and extend those opportunities available to the majority to others who suffer exclusion and deprivation. The Task Force's activities are driven by its own definition of social exclusion:

> Social exclusion is about more than income poverty. ... [It] is an extreme consequence of what happens when people don't get a fair deal throughout their lives, often because of disadvantage they face at birth, and this disadvantage can be transmitted from one generation to the next.
>
> (Cabinet Office, 2007)

WHO IS AT RISK?

The range of categories of people at risk of exclusion includes:

- people living in poverty, at risk of violence, abuse or illness within the family, affected by environmental degradation or by war;
- children at risk of violence or abuse, oppressed minorities whose mother tongue is not the dominant language, 'looked after' children, child labourers or travellers;
- people who are pregnant or caring for relatives or young children;
- girls;
- people with disabilities;
- learners whose schools, curricula or teaching is inadequate or unsuitable. (Booth, 1999)

Some categories apply only to specific individuals; others, such as old age, are open to almost anyone. In addition, exclusion is dynamic: changes in circumstance mean that many people fall into one of the categories at some stage in their lives; children can become homeless through family breakdown or can get into trouble with the law. Such circumstances can lead to school exclusion, which contributes to the high incidence of illiteracy current among the population in young offenders' institutions and prisons. The slope towards exclusion is a slippery one. Percy-Smith (2000) cites seven factors; any one, or combination, can trigger the slide:

1   economic;
2   social difficulties;
3   the political sphere, having little power or voice;
4   environment, deprived or decaying neighbourhoods;

5   individual aspects such as disability, ill health or learning differences;
6   spatial dimensions where excluded groups are in close proximity with each other in degraded surroundings;
7   group membership of one of the 'at risk' groups.

The Equalities Review (2007) highlights the significance of particular combinations of group membership and specific trigger points, such as the transition to school or taking on a caring role for a baby or relative. It aims to establish how individuals can be helped to become resilient in these circumstances. An exploration of how exclusion might work for a single group, and the experiences this group might have in common with others, will help us to appreciate what exclusion can mean for individuals. For example, the changing experiences of many disabled people provide a rich picture. Exploring the nature and experience of disability can show how mechanisms within society have operated to oppress and disempower particular people and to exclude them from the social and economic benefits of contemporary life. The emerging human rights agenda makes all people equally entitled to human and material resources (see Chapter 10). This has politicised and liberated many disabled individuals and their stories reflect the experience of other excluded groups, such as women or black people. The changes have affected the world of education: ways of thinking, working and teaching. There are implications for training and research and unresolved controversies throughout policy and practice.

DISABILITY AND INCLUSION

This section examines different models of philosophical, ethical, social and political approaches to disability. Two things have affected current thinking. First the impact of the struggle for emancipation throughout the later twentieth century by three important oppressed groups: black people through the Civil Rights movement; women via the rise of feminism; and gay and lesbian groups through the celebration of Gay Pride (see Chapter 3). Second, disability studies emerged as an academic discipline, driven and informed by the experiences of disabled activists and academics and of those who had worked to further the interests of vulnerable learners. This established disability as a legitimate focus for academic consideration. Thinkers such as Foucault (1980), Barton (1996) and Shakespeare (1998) explored the ways disability is perceived, constructed and represented, and how the current model of disability reflects thinking about disability and how it impacts upon the expectations and treatment of people with impairments.

A 'model' is a representation of reality through which we interpret the world. It includes ideas, pictures, practices and systems constructed in such a way as to encourage shared understanding. For example, Elizabethans represented their world in the 'Great Chain of Being' created out of chaos by the Christian God.

God sat firmly at the top and each stratum had power over the one below. If the order was threatened, the world would return to chaos. This worldview informed much of the imagery and ideas of Shakespeare's plays: in Macbeth, the killing of the king results in unnatural happenings throughout the world of people, animals and the elements alike. The world was 'theocentric', the social order was preordained and aspirations beyond one's 'place' meant danger for all. The model shaped and restricted the ways in which things and people could be seen.

Models of disability have influenced its depiction in the western world. A crucial element of this model was the distinction between what is 'normal' and what is 'other' – what is like me, and therefore 'family', what is not and therefore 'alien'. This 'normal'/'other' distinction also plays a part in shaping our

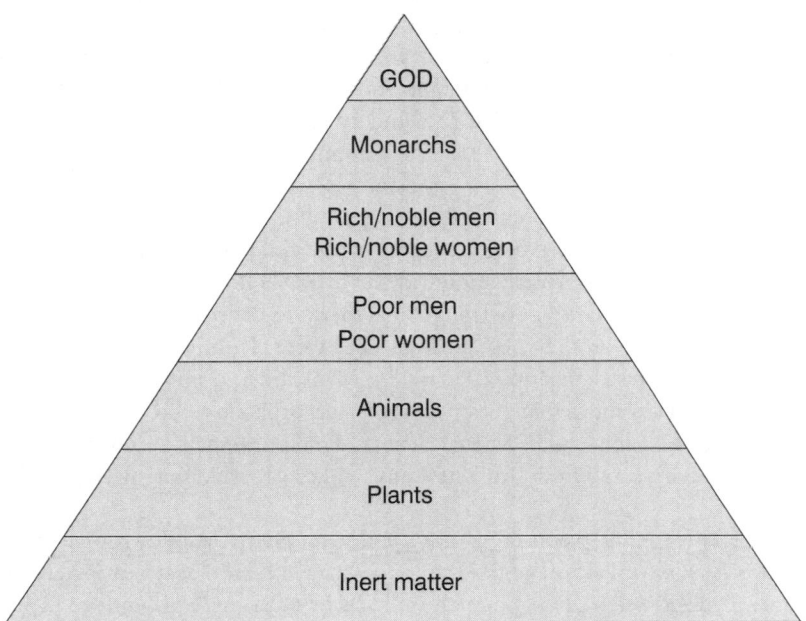

Figure 4. 1 Simplified version of the Great Chain of Being as a pyramid.

responses to excluded groups, such as refugees, travellers or other ethnic minorities who subsequently become dehumanised and less worthy of sharing in our prosperity.

Barnes (1996) explored cultural attitudes to disability throughout history. There is archaeological evidence of the existence of disability from the Neanderthal period and one utilitarian argument suggests that, in societies where survival is precarious, any individual unable to contribute would be seen as a liability and disposed of. However, Barnes provides examples of societies where people with impairments are both cared for and valued. He suggests that prejudice against people with impairments is not universal and that responses were culturally produced by a complex relationship between the beliefs of the society and its social and economical structure.

The war-like, slave-based society of the Ancient Greeks glorified the physical toughness and perfection expressed in Greek statuary and the Olympic Games. Its obsession with bodily perfection introduced an ongoing bias against people with impairments in Western society. Those with disabilities received little help in Roman or Greek society. Charity developed haphazardly through the Christian church in Europe, which took the view that any individual not created in the perfect image of God was the product of the Devil and a punishment for sins of mankind (Barnes, 1998). The notion was popularised through folk tales about changelings, dwarves, giants and ugly sisters and epitomised in the works of Shakespeare and other writers whose depiction of the impaired body created an impression of abnormality, damage and powerlessness or focused upon the hidden impairment of the 'diseased' mind. Think of the fate of Victor Hugo's *Hunchback of Notre Dame*, Shakespeare's black-hearted hunchbacked *Richard III*, the hook-handed Captain Hook in *Peter Pan* or the blinded and dependent Mr. Rochester in *Jane Eyre*.

Disability frequently signified moral ambivalence, evil, or childlike dependency. Dwarves and the 'feeble-minded' were the butt of jokes. Visits to Bedlam or the 'lunatic asylum' became entertainment and, by the Victorian era, the freak show was flourishing. Terms such as 'spastic' and 'moron' became

insults. Darwin's theories of evolution, natural selection and the survival of the fittest produced Social Darwinism: the philosophy of sending the weak to the wall to benefit the majority. The Eugenics movement linked idiocy, poverty and criminality to heredity and argued that these 'degenerates' threatened society, should be kept separate to avoid contamination and sterilised to prevent their reproduction. These ideas were taken to the logical extreme by the Nazi party in Germany.

In the UK in 1870 the introduction of universal compulsory schooling increased pressure on schools through an influx of children from poorer families. Copeland (2003) points out that the Egerton Royal Commissions (1886; 1889) suggested 5 per cent of urban children were incapable of coping with elementary education and the school population was thus divided into two unequal groups. 'Exceptional children' or 'the dull and deficient' (Copeland, 2003, 45) were defined as 'imbeciles', condemned to pass their limited capabilities onto their descendants. They were identified by medical examination and placed in special schools with strictly limited curricula. Many did have impairments, but contemporary surveys suggested that disadvantages such as poverty, being orphaned, and being infected with heart and lung diseases affected many more. Their learning 'disabilities' sprang from the social, economic and environmental exclusion and from brutal teaching and classroom discipline, rather than from their own impairment.

The treatment of these children epitomises the 'medical model' of disability rooted in the individual's biology. It regards personal impairment and the individual's failure to adapt to society as the cause of disability. People are diagnosed by experts, usually medical or quasi-medical, who see all difficulties from the perspective of proposed treatments for patients. Disabled people are allocated the permanent sick role (Oliver, 1990), denied a voice, and relieved of responsibility and expectations. They are rendered dependent on 'experts' and forced to play the 'victim'. Experts make decisions about where they are educated, where they live, their employment, support or benefits available, and whether they can have children. The individual is pressured to cooperate, to abandon an impaired state that is regarded as 'less than human', to be rehabilitated into 'normal' functions or to be dismissed as 'incurable', dehumanised, identified by the disability, regarded as 'other' and punished by being excluded from ordinary life. This model is oppressive, frequently involving dominance and absence of choice. Up to ten years ago, people with disabilities were routinely excluded from the preparation of their own community care plans. The model also imposes both practical disadvantages and a 'discourse of disadvantage' onto people with disabilities. It is sometimes termed the 'disadvantage' model.

The medical model is constructed from a non-disabled or 'normal' standpoint and results in a society that segregates and establishes 'special' facilities away from community life, encouraging patronising attitudes, pity and fear. It has fuelled the market for the 'disability industry' (Barnes, 1996), particularly evident within education. It has encouraged the media representation of people with disabilities as 'other', dependent and of low social account. Some charities highlight this representation to incite a mixture of pity and guilt in potential donors, creating a dependent relationship between the (usually) non-disabled charity helpers and the disabled 'helped' and reducing the need for the state to be the prime mover in enabling people with disabilities to reach their potential.

The medical model became the approach to the provision of services throughout much of the twentieth century. Although still dominant within NHS thinking, education and social service professions, it has been robustly challenged. The 1960s and 1970s saw struggles for civil liberties, in which people with disabilities increasingly participated. Social and economic structures began to be seen as contributing to the oppression of people with impairments. In the UK, the Union of Physically Impaired People Against Segregation (UPIAS, 1976) insisted that disabled people should speak for themselves and rejected the idea of 'experts' pronouncing on their behalf. UPIAS highlighted ways in which disabled people are discriminated against both by their exclusion from the material benefits of education and the economy and by the prejudice arising from cultural representations of disabled people as 'other'.

The emergence of post-modern theories and the work of philosophers such as Foucault (1980) sharpened awareness of the destructive nature of the current 'representations' of disability. Barton (1996) states that 'Disabled people's history needs to be viewed as part of an increasing struggle to establish and maintain positive self-identities' (p. 58). He distinguishes between the impairment, physical or mental, possessed by an individual and the nature of disability and quotes the statement of Fundamental Principles of Disability taken from UPIAS and the Disability Alliance.

> In our view, it is society which disables physically impaired people. Disability is something *imposed* on top of our impairment by the way we are unnecessarily isolated and excluded from full participation in society. Disabled people are therefore an oppressed group in society.
>
> Thus we define *impairment* as lacking part or all of a limb, organ or mechanism of the body; and *disability* as the disadvantage or restriction of activity caused by a contemporary social organisation which takes no or little account of people who have physical impairments and thus excludes them from participation in the mainstream of social activities. Physical impairment is therefore a particular form of social oppression.
>
> (p. 14, in Barton, 1996, p. 56)

This is the 'social model', which represents a radical shift in perspective. It removes the 'problem' from the impaired individual and places it firmly with the way society is organised. It highlights the social and individual attitudes and behaviours that produce the physical and conceptual barriers that oppress disabled people. The social model has been emancipatory: it focuses upon the dismantling of barriers and grants individuals the power and responsibility to make decisions about their future. It also emphasises that current representations of disabled people as 'other', tragic or helpless victims are learned prejudices rather than rational responses. Morris (1992) highlights the role played by 'rights' in the social model: 'Our vision is of a society which recognizes our rights and our value as equal citizens rather than merely treating us as the recipient of other people's good will' (p. 10).

But this is not the last word. The social model has been criticised for reducing everything to economics, neglecting the stories and voices of disabled people and taking little account of the physical experience of living with the kind of impairments that cannot be solved by social manipulation. The social and medical models have been diametrically opposed in the way that they see disability and some suggest that placing the lived experiences of people with disabilities back in the picture risks reinforcing a 'medical tragedy' perspective. However, the voice of disabled people is increasingly being heard.

A further 'affirmative' model (Swain and French, 2000) has emerged, inspired in particular by the Disability Arts Movement. This offers a positive identity, focusing upon the benefits of lifestyle and experience of being impaired, and challenges notions of 'normality and otherness'. It promotes the building of a positive collective identity through membership of campaigning groups such as the Disabled People's Movement. In common with other affirmative models, such as Black Power, it can be expressed by the slogan 'proud, angry and strong' (ibid, p. 573).

DISABILITY LEGISLATION

The medical model is now challenged by the social model, which has informed a raft of recent legislation. The Disability Discrimination Act (1995) made discrimination in the workplace and public life illegal and recent legislation ensures that people with impairments receive the same opportunities as the rest of the population. In 2001 the Disability Discrimination Act (Part IV) brought education and training providers into line with other groups by placing a legal responsibility upon institutions to raise staff awareness, to find out about an individual's disability and to take reasonable steps not to treat any disabled student less favourably for any reason relating to his or her disability. The SEN Code of Practice (2001), which accompanied the Act, gave further guidelines on avoiding unlawful discrimination.

Disability has now been defined in Article 14 of the Human Rights Act 1998 as physical or mental impairment that has a substantial and long-term adverse impact on the person's ability to carry out normal day-to-day activities.

THE IMPACT OF THE SOCIAL MODEL ON EDUCATION IN THE UK

The Warnock Report (Warnock Committee, 1978) was a milestone for change in education and disability. It shifted the emphasis away from 'in-child' medicalised difficulties towards the individual's educational needs, acknowledging the barriers currently preventing children from participating in a rich educational experience alongside their peers. It underpinned legislation that introduced the concept and reality of the inclusive school.

In 2001 the SEN Code of Practice (DfES, 2001), endorsed the principles of equal opportunity clarified in the Salamanca Statement (UNESCO, 1994). It stated that a child with special educational needs should have his or her needs met, normally in mainstream schools or settings and be offered full access to a broad, balanced and relevant education. It should include the National Curriculum and an appropriate curriculum for the foundation stage. The child's views should be taken into account and parents should play a vital role.

Policy documents such as *Every Child Matters* (DfES, 2004a) and *Removing Barriers to Achievement* (DfES, 2004b) continue to promote support for children. The policies of the Labour government indicate a firm commitment to the introduction of an inclusive form of education that will allow all students to be educated together in mainstream schools.

INCLUSIVE EDUCATION

'Inclusion', however, is not an easy option. Bailey (1998) suggests that inclusive education is 'being in an ordinary school with other students following the same curriculum at the same time, in the same classroom, with the full acceptance of all, and in a way that makes the student feel no different to other students' (p. 179). Rieser (2001) reminds us that there are profound differences between 'integration' and 'inclusion'. Integration is simply a matter of locating a child in a mainstream school and expecting him or her to change and adapt to school life. Inclusion requires the institution to be reframed to 'remove barriers so teaching and learning take place so all children can be valued for who they are, participate, interact and develop their potential' (p. 175). It is a radical concept that demands a rethink of the ways in which school life, teaching and the curriculum are organised and delivered to create suitable learning support for the whole student population. There are implications for governors, managers, teachers, support staff, parents and children.

The government has encouraged change. The Qualifications and Curriculum Authority (QCA, 2000) requires inclusive practices to be structured into the curriculum. In 2004 Ofsted imposed mandatory training in inclusion for all its inspectors. All schools in England received the *Index for Inclusion* (Booth and Ainscow, 2002), enabling schools to review their progress along the road to inclusion. However, any examination of the reality of contemporary school life (Nind *et al.*, 2003; Cigman, 2007) reveals that, despite the drive for inclusion and the rise in the number of children with disabilities in mainstream schools, changes are partial and inconsistent.

There are three reasons for this. First, the drive towards inclusion coincides with increased emphasis on competition, consumerism and individual choice, generated by successive Conservative administrations and continued under New Labour (see Chapter 1). Concern to raise standards and test scores has fuelled the move away from child-centred approaches towards a test-driven 'standards' agenda. Teachers are being asked to celebrate diversity in the classroom at the same time as being castigated if their test results compare unfavourably with other schools in the league tables.

Second, even if we can define what is meant by 'raising standards', another contested issue is whether students with disabilities benefit academically from full inclusion. Despite evidence from Jordan and Goodey (1996) that general standards of educational achievement are improved by the changes in teaching strategies, students with disabilities do not necessarily benefit. Research reviewed by Hornby *et al.* (1997) presents an uncertain picture. The only clear conclusion is the role played by appropriate training for teachers. Studies exploring the attitudes of teachers towards inclusion have indicated a lack of confidence in their own abilities and underlying prejudices against disabled people.

Third, and most striking, in 2005 Baroness Warnock herself expressed doubts about fully inclusive provision. Research (Cigman, 2007) suggests that some children can be as disadvantaged by compulsory placement in mainstream schooling as they were by segregation. This is echoed by parents of children with and without disabilities who are not wholly in favour of inclusion and by some senior management in schools or local authorities whose 'standards' agendas may not be compatible with full inclusion. There is also, in some quarters, a genuine concern that the development of a perspective that downplays individual assessment of a child's profile may well reduce the existence of specialist knowledge available to support individuals with a range of impairments. Pressure groups frequently promote the interests of individual children with a 'type' or label to their difficulty. This is illustrated graphically in the case of some children with Specific Learning Difficulties or dyslexia. Although there is agreement over the radical nature of true 'inclusive education', much remains contested. Is inclusion compatible with the maintenance of specialised schools? Can the medical and social models be reconciled? Does inclusion raise standards for all? Does inclusion really lead to rights for all?

A major question in special education is that of the 'dilemma of difference' (Warnock, 2005). Cigman (2007) explains:

> We either treat all children as essentially the same, which means treating them as fairly as possible but with the risk of neglecting individual differences, or we treat them differently, with the consequence that some are better off than they would otherwise have been, but there is a risk of being unfair by devoting more resources or expertise to some than others (p. xxii).

CONCLUSION

Education is one of the prime factors in preventing exclusion, but not the only one. The Every Child Matters agenda acknowledges the full spectrum of circumstances underpinning exclusion/inclusion and recognises the need to improve access, engagement and participation by creating stronger links across education, social and health care. The aim is to strengthen inter-professional links, understanding and cooperation to prevent vulnerable individuals falling through the cracks. This agenda draws upon the ideas implicit in the models discussed here to train professionals in the type of cooperative thinking and working that can remove barriers to participation for the full range of vulnerable individuals. This is a recent initiative and the jury is still out over whether policy can be realised in practice and what impact it will have upon thinking, training, research and the experience of the people it aims to reach (see Chapter 2.).

SUMMARY POINTS

- Inclusion means valuing all people alike, regardless of their situation or group membership, and restructuring social and economic institutions to remove barriers, allowing all to be valued, to participate, to interact and to develop their potential.
- Inclusion means developing a critical awareness of how certain groups can be represented as 'other' and lose their right to access the fruits of our society.
- Particular 'triggers' might put an individual temporarily or permanently into a group that is likely to be excluded.
- The impact of constructed models representing particular groups, such as those with disabilities, contributes to the risk that members will be excluded.
- Current government policies, legislation, resources and practices aim ostensibly to develop a more inclusive society where professional groups can cooperate closely; yet there are many tensions that threaten to undermine the outcomes.

QUESTIONS FOR DISCUSSION

1   What are the most crucial triggers affecting those at risk of exclusion?
2   Can medical and social models of disability truly be reconciled?
3   Can educational inclusion work?
4   How can we deal with the 'dilemma of difference'?
5   What are the barriers to the implementation of Every Child Matters?

FURTHER READING

Barton, L. (ed.) (1996) *Disability and Society: Emerging Issues and Insights*, Harlow: Addison Wesley Longman. A fascinating and accessible selection of chapters by leading thinkers across the disability studies arena.

Booth, T. and Ainscow, M. (2002) *Index for Inclusion: Developing Learning and Participation in Schools*, Bristol: Centre for Studies in Inclusive Education (CSIE). Practical guidance on implementation of inclusive practices.

Cigman, R. (ed.) (2007) *Included or Excluded. The challenge of the Mainstream for Some SEN Children*, Oxon: Routledge. A collection of recent essays exploring some of the more contested areas around educational inclusion.

Nind, M., Rix, J., Sheehy, K. and Simmons, K (eds.) (2003) *Inclusive Education: Diverse Perspectives*, London: David Fulton. Contains the voices of many stakeholders within this debate; accessible and challenging.

REFERENCES

Bailey, J. (1998) Australia: inclusion through categorisation, in T. Booth and M. Ainscow (eds) *From Them to Us: An International Study of Inclusion in Education*, London: Routledge.

Barnes, C. (1996) Theories of disability and the origins of the oppression of disabled people in Western societies, in L. Barton (ed.) *Disability and Society: Emerging Issues and Insights*, Harlow: Addison Wesley Longman.

Barnes, C. (1998) The social model of disability: a sociological phenomenon ignored by sociologists? in T. Shakespeare (ed.) *The Disability Reader: Social Science Perspectives*, London: Cassell.

Barton, L. (ed.) (1996) *Disability and Society: Emerging Issues and Insights*, Harlow: Addison Wesley Longman.

Booth, T. (1999) Viewing inclusions from a distance: gaining perspective from comparative study, *Support for Learning*, 14(4): 164–8.

Booth, T. and Ainscow, M. (2002) *Index for Inclusion: Developing Learning and Participation in Schools*, Bristol: Centre for Studies in Inclusive Education (CSIE).

Cabinet office (2007) *Context for Social Exclusion Work*. Online. Available http://www.cabinetoffice.gov.uk/social_exclusion_task_force/context/ (accessed 15 October, 2007).

Cigman, R. (2007) *Included or Excluded. The Challenge of the Mainstream for Some SEN Children*, Oxon: Routledge.

Copeland, I. C. (2003) Integration versus segregation: the early struggle, in M. Nind, J. Rix, K. Sheehy and K. Simmons (eds) *Inclusive Education: Diverse Perspectives*, London: David Fulton.

DfES (2001) *Special Educational Needs: Code of Practice of Schools, Early Education Practitioners and Other Interested Parties*, London: DfES.

DfES (2004a) *Every Child Matters: Change for Children*, Nottingham: DfES.

DfES (2004b) *Removing Barriers to Achievement*, Nottingham: DfES.

The Equalities Review (2007) *Fairness and Freedom: The Final Report of the Equalities Review*. Online. Available http://www.theequalitiesreview.org.uk/equality_review.pdf (accessed 11 November, 2007).

Foucault, M. (1980) The politics of health in the eighteenth century, in C. Gordon (ed.) *Michel Foucault: Power/knowledge*, Brighton: Harvester.

Hornby, G., Atkinson, M. and Howard, J. (1997) *Controversial Issues in Special Education*, London: David Fulton.

Jordan, L. and Goodey, C. (1996) *Human Rights and Social Change: The Newham Story*, Bristol: CSIE.

Morris, J. (1992) *Disabled Lives: Many Voices, One Message*, London: BBC.

Morris, J. (2001) *Having a Say, That Kind of Life: Social Exclusion and Young Disabled People with High Levels of Support Needs*, London: Scope.

Nind, M., Rix, J., Sheehy, K. and Simmons, K. (eds) (2003) *Inclusive Education: Diverse Perspectives*, London: David Fulton.

Oliver, M. (1990) *The Politics of Disablement*, Basingstoke: Macmillan.

Percy-Smith, J. (ed.) (2000) *Policy Responses to Social Exclusion: Towards Inclusion*, Buckingham: Open University Press.

QCA (2000) *Curriculum 2000 Appendix on General Inclusion Statement*, London: QCA.

Rieser, F. (2001) The struggle for inclusion: the growth of a movement, in L. Barton (ed.) *Disability, Politics and the Struggle for Change*, London: David Fulton.

Shakespeare, T. (ed.) (1998) *The Disability Reader: Social Science Perspectives*, London: Cassell.

Swain, J. and French, S. (2000) Towards an affirmation model of disability, *Disability and Society*, 15, 4, 569–82.

UNESCO (1994) *The Salamanca Statement: A Framework for Action*, Salamanca: UNESCO.

UPIAS (1975) *Fundamental Principles of Disability*, London: Disability Alliance.

Warnock Committee (1978) *Special Educational Needs: The Warnock Report*, London: DES.

Warnock, M. (2005) *Special Educational Needs: A New Look*, London: Philosophy of Education Society of Great Britain.

5   Religion and Cultural Plurality in Education

Denise Cush

INTRODUCTION – RELIGIOUS AND CULTURAL PLURALITY?

In the four years since the first edition of this book, awareness of religious and cultural plurality in education has become if anything even more important. Religion continues to make news headlines, the number of students in England taking GCSEs and A levels in religious studies has increased, the Ajegbo Report in 2007 (DfES, 2007) added a fourth strand of ethnic, cultural and religious diversity to the Citizenship agenda, and research in religion and education has become increasingly international.

Human beings do not agree on fundamental issues concerned with the meaning and purpose of our lives, human nature and destiny, the nature of reality, reliable authorities and sources of knowledge, and the purpose of education. We also disagree on ethical issues from war to abortion. Our customs and practices, values and priorities differ from culture to culture, family to family, individual to individual. Global communications have made us more aware of cultural differences and increased the complexity of both shared human experience and the countless segmentary sub-worlds we inhabit. Geir Skeie (1995:84) has usefully distinguished between 'plurality' as a descriptive term for this situation and 'pluralism', which is used to refer to a prescriptive or evaluative position (usually positive) on the fact of plurality. This chapter concentrates on religious and cultural plurality and discusses how education systems can respond.

CULTURE AND RELIGION

'Cultural' and 'religious' plurality are closely linked and sometimes indistinguishable. The terms 'culture' and 'religion' are in common use, but there is no agreement as to what these words mean, whether they refer to the same dimension of human experience or two distinct areas, or whether they are useful terms at all. They also become mixed up with concepts like 'ethnicity', 'nationality', 'community' and 'identity'. Some have suggested that the word 'religion' could be replaced by 'culture' (Fitzgerald, 1995) as both can refer to the beliefs, values and customs of particular groups. However, as 'cultures' are usually viewed as human constructs, this would be difficult for adherents to accept. From a believer's point of view, a clear distinction can be made between 'religion' (the eternal truths) and 'culture' (the changeable social context). It does make sense to talk of 'religions' adapting to different 'cultures' or making changes in what is merely 'cultural'. Yet in practice there is often no agreement as to what counts as 'religion', and what as 'culture'. For example, ordaining women as priests, monogamy, not cutting one's hair, honouring ancestor spirits and local gods, and female circumcision may all be viewed as religion or as culture by different people, or the distinction may not make sense to them.

'Culture' tends to be defined as the learned aspects of being human. It includes language, customs and beliefs, and is passed from one generation to the next by means of socialisation and education. The way in which we use the word 'culture' can suggest that there are distinct 'sets' of language/customs/beliefs to which an individual 'belongs', or is even 'torn between' two of them. 'Cultures' can be seen as having different educational needs. This can (and did, in South Africa under apartheid) lead to separate provision for the different categories of pupils. On the other hand, 'cultures' can be viewed as fluid, internally diverse and contested, influenced by and influencing other cultural streams (Jackson, 1997). An individual therefore does not so much 'belong' to 'a culture', but is influenced by and engaged with a number of cultural streams. A culture is in this view more like a language you learn than something you 'are'. Cultures are not only challenged and changed by interactions with other cultures, but may be criticised from within (the concept of 'counter-culture'). Jackson's (1997) research with young Hindus in Britain reveals them, not as negatively 'caught between two cultures', but as having the 'multiple cultural competence' to navigate multiple cultural streams successfully (p. 83).

'Religion' is notoriously difficult to define. Definitions focusing on belief in God or the supernatural leave many traditions out. Westerners, influenced by Christianity, Protestantism and the Enlightenment, tend to think of religion as being about 'beliefs', but in other contexts people focus more on practice or identity. Similarly, the division of the beliefs and practices of peoples into clearly distinguished 'isms' – Buddhism, Hinduism, Christianity, Islam – is seen by many as an artificial construct of nineteenth-century western thinking (Jackson, 1997). In reality 'religions' are internally diverse, and the dividing lines between them are not clear, particularly in non-Western (e.g. Indian) traditions or postmodern manifestations of religion such as 'new age'. In many non-European languages (e.g. African languages such as Setswana), there is no word that translates into the English 'religion', or way of distinguishing between 'religious' and 'non-religious'; there is just how people live their lives. Thus the current trend in academic circles is to take what is called a 'non-essentialist' view of the term religion: 'religion' tends to be viewed as an artefact of the academy (Smith, 1998: 281), a tool for analysis, rather than having any relationship to reality 'out there'.

A further problem with the term 'religion' is that for many people in Britain today it has negative overtones, associated with controlling authorities, 'meaningless ritual', and fanatical terrorists. Or they may be afraid of 'religion', of venturing into an area where it is easy to cause offence. Misunderstandings occur between those who view religion as a matter of belief and opinion that can be a topic for debate, and those for whom religion is a crucial part of identity – so that what for one person is a critical (or even idle) questioning of an idea is for the other a vicious personal attack. 'Spirituality' tends to be seen as less threatening and it has been suggested (Heelas and Woodhead 2005) that there has been a 'spiritual revolution' in society, meaning a turn from 'organised religion' to individual, subjective spirituality. Be that as it may, recent research with young people (Cush 2007a; Blaylock and Williams, 2007) reveals that for those who identify with a tradition it is most importantly an expression of identity, and that for those who do not the most common attitude is a tolerant acceptance of other people's beliefs and customs based on a strong attachment to human rights.

RESPONSES TO CULTURAL AND RELIGIOUS PLURALITY: MULTICULTURAL/ INTERCULTURAL EDUCATION

The term 'multicultural education' can refer to any attempt on the part of education to respond to cultural plurality, or particular approaches that can then be contrasted with other approaches such as 'anti-racist'. The basic idea behind 'multicultural education' – much discussed in the 1970s and 1980s – was that cultural diversity should be appreciated and reflected in the school curriculum. Music, art and literature should include examples of African, Indian and Chinese origin, as well as European; history, geography and religious studies should be worldwide not just national; mathematics and science should emphasise the contributions of non-Western peoples such as 'Arabic' numerals. 'Multicultural education' has been criticised for being superficial and for failing to address the real roots of racism and discrimination, and sometimes for making relationships between different groups worse by stressing differences and reinforcing stereotypes. The term 'multicultural society' might suggest that several discrete cultures exist in competition. Instead the term 'intercultural' has become popular, to reflect the fact that 'cultures' are fluid, changing and interacting, with exciting new 'hybrids' emerging all the time. The debates about 'multiculturalism' were overshadowed in the UK throughout the 1990s by the priorities of the National Curriculum: literacy, numeracy and ICT. Recently, however, both the new stress on 'diversity' in Citizenship (see Chapter 6) and plans for a more flexible and creative New Secondary Curriculum 2007–8 may produce a favourable climate for exploring cultural and religious plurality.

INTERNATIONAL DIVERSITY OF RELIGION IN EDUCATION

Worldwide, the response by state-funded education systems to the plurality of 'religious' and 'non-religious' beliefs, values and customs is varied, but can be summarised into three basic options – the 'secular', the 'confessional' and the 'non-confessional'. Simply put, this means either having no religious education, having religious education whose primary aim is to nurture children in the religion of their heritage, and religious education that aims to be open, multi-faith and unbiased.

The word 'secular' has different meanings, but is used here to mean that the education system does not officially include consideration of religions. It is not a subject on the timetable. This does not imply that pupils, teachers and parents are not themselves religious. The most powerful country in the world, the USA, takes this secular option in state-funded schools, in spite of being one of the most 'religious' countries in the world in terms of people's self-identity in surveys (roughly 80 per cent 'religious'). Other countries that currently take the 'secular' option in state-funded schools include France (except Alsace and part of Lorraine), Russia, Albania, China and Japan. Some of the most common arguments given for excluding religion from the curriculum are:

- it is too personal and private and should be left to the family and community;
- it is impossible for teachers to be impartial in such a contested area;
- students may be open to proselytising by teachers, persuaded to adopt a particular religious, anti-religious or agnostic stance;
- any study risks highlighting areas of difference and conflict between people;
- academic evaluation might seem to criticise pupils' religious and cultural heritage;
- any presentation in school is bound to be so simplified that it misrepresents and stereotypes the tradition in question;
- religions may include views unacceptable to the values underpinning liberal education.

In the USA the major consideration is that the First Amendment to the 1787 Constitution sought to protect religious freedom by instituting a complete separation between 'church' and 'state' so that there was 'no establishment' of religion. This has been interpreted as meaning that no public funds can be used for teaching about religions in schools, and thus no religious education. However, this clause was interpreted differently in different eras, and in different states. An important ruling in 1963 made it clear that it is only promoting a particular religion that is ruled out, rather than teaching about religion. The increasing awareness of plurality has led several states, such as California, to include teaching about religions in the history or social studies syllabus (Cush, 2007b). However, there are no teachers specially qualified to teach religious studies, and many teachers leave religion out as too controversial. Nevertheless, some argue that the much-vaunted religious freedom of the USA is only really guaranteed by education that includes learning about religions. In France, similar suggestions are being made. Pupils need to understand Islam to understand national and world affairs. So 'religion' increasingly finds some place in a general humanities curriculum, though not as a discrete subject. Even in China, religion is now dealt with as an aspect of geography (Nandu, 2008), and it could be argued that the teaching of Marxist beliefs is a form of confessional education.

Most of the countries of Europe take the confessional approach to religious education. This means that schools contribute to the nurturing of children within the particular faith tradition of their family, or what is deemed to be the heritage of the country. There are many variations. Religious education can be compulsory or optional, the syllabus can be decided by the state or the churches/groups concerned or a partnership of both. There may or may not be an alternative subject, such as 'ethics', for the 'non-religious'. It can be taught by the ordinary class teacher or by paid or unpaid church workers coming into school. Where one particular tradition forms part of the dominant construction of national identity – Catholicism in Poland, Orthodoxy in Romania or Greece – that tradition forms the basis of the syllabus. Where there is more awareness of diversity, separate religious education classes may be offered for the main groups represented. For example in the majority of German Länder there is choice between Protestant and Catholic religious education, and in Finland there is a choice between Lutheran or Orthodox religious education and 'ethics' for the non-religious. In spite of the confessional label, many European educators in practice take a more open approach as they seek to connect with the actual worldviews and experience of their pupils (see Larsson and Gustavsson, 2004).

A growing minority of countries take the 'non-confessional' approach and provide a religious education that is open, balanced and impartial, seeking to educate children about religion rather than promote a particular religion or religion in general. The countries with the longest experience of this are Sweden, England, Wales and Scotland, which have pioneered non-confessional multi-faith religious education since the late 1960s. More recently, they have been joined by Norway, South Africa and Namibia, and for students over 16 ('upper secondary') in Denmark and Finland. South Africa, which made the decision to take the non-confessional route in 2000, has decided to call the subject 'religion education' to emphasise that it does not have the aim of 'making people religious'.

Some of the most common arguments for including religion in the curriculum are:

- the majority of people in the world are 'religious', it is crucial to understand this important component of their identity, and religions are very powerful forces in world affairs;
- religion is intertwined with culture, so it is impossible to appreciate history, art, music, architecture, laws, customs, morality without understanding religion;
- ignorance is often the root of prejudice and conflict, knowledge assists understanding and appreciation of diversity;
- students need the opportunity to reflect on their own beliefs and values, and a vocabulary with which to do so;

- students need the opportunity to critically evaluate their inherited beliefs and values and conditioning by society;
- if religion is omitted there is an implicit anti-religious bias to the curriculum, causing children from religious backgrounds to feel excluded;
- one (or more) religions may be the truth.

It is possible to construct arguments in favour of the secular, the confessional and the non-confessional approaches to education as being the best way to ensure freedom of religious belief and promote harmony rather than conflict. However, ignorance is a dangerous option. An increasingly plural world calls for a positive approach to plurality of beliefs and values.

POSITIVE PLURALISM

'Positive pluralism' is a term coined by the author in 1991, to describe an approach that sees the plurality of religious and non-religious beliefs, values and customs as a positive resource for the human race, rather than a problem. It is outlined in Cush and Francis (2001) and was developed from practical experience in an English context. The positive pluralist approach is based upon 'epistemological humility' – having your own sincerely and deeply held views, beliefs, values and customs need not mean that you have nothing to learn from others, even when their views differ greatly. Plurality is to be welcomed and respected. Schools should respect the religious and cultural backgrounds of all pupils, whether religious or not, but also accept that these perspectives are open to debate and critical evaluation in the *public* forum that is education. This is *not* to maintain that all views/beliefs/traditions are 'equally valid', a position that no one really holds when pressed, or to teach 'universalism' – the belief that all religions are the same really, just different paths to the same goal, as these are themselves confessional positions.

It is argued here that religious education should take a non-confessional, multi-faith (and non-faith) approach, which attempts to be as far as is humanly possible impartial and empathetic, where all children are taught together, and where no one tradition is privileged in terms of its truth claims. Plurality within the so-called 'religions', and interactions and hybridity between them need to be recognised. The non-confessional approach means learning *about* religions and non-religious views rather than learning *to be* 'religious'. It does not rule out, and indeed encourages and facilitates, students exploring and developing their own perspectives on religious issues and questions, whether or not these perspectives turn out to be the same as their family/community heritage or any previously recognised worldview.

RELIGIOUS EDUCATION IN ENGLAND

In England non-confessional religious education is well established, and was an early advocate and location for multicultural education. Religious education has been a compulsory subject in the school curriculum since 1944. It was established as non-confessional in 1971 (Schools Council, 1971), and reinforced as part of the 'basic curriculum' in 1988. The 1988 Education Act, repeated in the 1996 Education Act, requires religious education to 'reflect the fact that the religious traditions in Great Britain are in the main Christian, while taking account of the other principal religions represented in Great Britain' (1996 Education Act, section 375. 3). This is open to a variety of interpretations as to which religions are included and what proportion of the syllabus is spent on each. Religious education is not technically part of the National Curriculum, as each local authority must produce an 'Agreed Syllabus' for use in its schools. The parties agreeing the syllabus are the Church of England, other faiths and other Christian denominations, teachers' representatives and elected members of the local authority. The *local* nature of the syllabus allows for considerable 'grass roots' involvement, and the local Standing Advisory Council on Religious Education (SACRE) has been a forum for different faith communities to meet and get to know each other. In Bradford a student version of the SACRE has allowed young people from different faith communities to meet and get to know each other in an area where demographic patterns tend to make some schools mono-religious or mono-cultural. Religious education is a subject from which parents can withdraw their children on grounds of conscience, a right seen by some as anachronistic, and does not apply to other subjects to which parents may have conscientious objections, such as ICT.

Recently there have been moves towards more national uniformity. In 1994 two 'Model Syllabuses' were produced as guidance for local syllabuses (SCAA, 1994); in 2000 National Expectations for Attainment in RE were published, and in 2004 the Non-Statutory Framework for Religious Education (QCA, 2004) appeared, and was welcomed by the vast majority of the 'RE community' including faith communities with their own schools, and some Humanist organisations. This document recognises the importance of including non-religious perspectives and traditions other than the 'major world religions'. It has ambitious learning objectives, which stress critical thinking and links with other subjects and global issues.

In 2007 there were important developments. The Religious Education Council produced a report (REC, 2007) on the strengths and weaknesses of current provision for RE in schools, initial teacher training and continued professional development, with recommendations for improvement. Although the subject is flourishing and popular, weaknesses included a shortage of specialist RE teachers in secondary schools, insufficient preparation of primary trainee teachers for RE and religious diversity, and lack of opportunities for post-qualification professional development. Ofsted (2007) underlined similar weaknesses, especially with regard to provision of challenging learning and appropriate assessment. The REC have produced a National Strategy for RE and considerable resources have been provided for the inclusion of RE in the implementation of the New Secondary Curriculum (2007).

The situation in England is complicated by the presence of state-funded 'schools with a religious character', one category of which is allowed to provide its own confessional religious education. This provides a case study of the complexities that arise in the area of religion, culture and education.

THE 'FAITH SCHOOLS' DEBATE

Internationally, Christian churches and religious organisations such as Buddhist monasteries pioneered education for the poor as well as the rich. Many countries, including Great Britain, have private schools independently funded by religious groups. However the history of education in England has given rise to the existence of state-funded 'faith-based' schools. In 1870, when state education was introduced, it supplemented rather than replaced the voluntary provision by religious groups, and some state assistance was given to allow the voluntary schools to survive and meet basic standards. This is known as the 'dual system'. The 1944 Education Act established two categories of state-funded voluntary schools, a distinction that still persists today, with the addition of a third numerically small category of 'foundation schools'. The two important categories are the 'voluntary controlled' (VC) and 'voluntary aided' (VA) schools. The former is controlled by the local authority from which it receives all its funding. These schools must follow the non-confessional Locally Agreed Syllabus for religious education, but as a reflection of their original foundation may conduct denominational worship. The voluntary aided category receives the majority of its funding from the LA, but, in return for providing some of the funding itself, the religious body is allowed to provide religious education of a confessional, denominational nature, as well as worship in the tradition to which its belongs.

'Faith-based' schools have become controversial in recent years. Both the Church of England and the Labour government are in favour of increasing the number of such schools. They are popular with parents and perceived as obtaining good academic results. Since 1998 seven Muslim and two Sikh schools have gained voluntary aided status. Racism, and in particular Islamophobia, colour the discussions in the media. Far more people opposed separate Muslim schools than separate 'Church' schools (43 per cent to 27 per cent in a 2001 MORI poll), expressing fears that separate Muslim schools might be training grounds for terrorists.

DCSF figures for the year 2007 show that state-funded faith-based schools account for roughly one third of primary schools (6,255 of 17,361) and one sixth of secondary schools (587 of 3,343). Of the total, 4,642 are Church of England and 2,038 Roman Catholic, the rest being counted in single figures or tens and the next largest group being Jewish schools at 37. Arguments for and against state-funded faith-based schools can be found in Cush (2003), Jackson (2003), Gardner *et al.* (2005) and Parker-Jenkins *et al.* (2005).

If the system was started from scratch, perhaps the fully comprehensive pluralist community school would work best. However, as a substantial faith-based school system exists, perhaps what matters is the way such schools approach religious and cultural plurality. Many faith-based schools are trying to make up for the disadvantages of segregation by making links with other schools, and by following multi-faith and multi-cultural curricula. In 2005 all the 'major faith communities' made a written agreement with the Department for Education and Skills (DfES) that it was important for schools with a religious character to teach about faiths other than their own. The voluntary controlled option, where the school can have a faith foundation but must follow a non-confessional syllabus for religious education 'agreed' by all the local faith communities, is one that could perhaps be explored further.

RELATED AREAS: MORAL EDUCATION, CITIZENSHIP, WORSHIP

Other areas of school provision that need to take account of cultural and religious plurality are spiritual development, moral education, personal and social education, health education and citizenship education. Often these are attempted without thinking through the full implications of cultural and religious diversity and real disagreement on fundamental issues. There is also the issue of the practice of prayer and worship in school. In England, the attempt to provide non-confessional religious education is compromised by the legal requirement for community schools to provide daily 'collective worship' that is 'wholly or mainly of a broadly Christian character'. There is the possibility of parental withdrawal from this and complex ways in which schools can be exempted from this requirement, but it remains a tricky area.

CONCLUSION

There are many ways in which religious and cultural plurality impact upon education and there needs to be a subject in the school curriculum to deal directly with this area of human experience (see Cush, 2007b). It should allow students to learn about and respect the beliefs, values and customs of others and to develop their own, either within a heritage tradition or in critical opposition to it. It is currently called 'religious education', but it possibly needs a new name. It is unlikely to be achieved as a small part of another subject such as history, social studies or citizenship and needs to be taught by specialist teachers knowledgeable about the traditions and skilled in appropriate pedagogies. In the words of Peter Schreiner (2001), talking about Europe, but applicable to the world:

RE can elaborate a critical potential in a civil society through its international, ecumenical and inter-religious dimension. This would contribute to a sustainable Europe in which the diversity of religions and cultures is not a burden but an enrichment to co-habitation. (p. 266)

SUMMARY POINTS

- It has become increasingly recognised that it is important to address religious and cultural plurality in education.
- There is a complex and contested relationship between 'religion' and 'culture'.
- Educational provision worldwide takes different approaches to addressing religious and cultural diversity; an approach through 'positive pluralism' is suggested as a way forward.
- Religious education policy in England is outlined up to 2007.
- The question of whether the state should fund faith-based schools is addressed as an example of a current issue at the interface between religion and education.

QUESTIONS FOR DISCUSSION

1   What is the relationship between religion and culture? Can religious education contribute to intercultural education?
2   What is the place of faith-based schools in a plural democracy? Should the state fund such schools?
3   How can schools ensure that pupils from all religious/non-religious/cultural backgrounds feel included?
4   Should religious education be included in the school curriculum? If so, what should be its aims, content and methods?

FURTHER READING

Copley, T. (1997) *Teaching Religion: Fifty Years of Religious Education in England and Wales*, Exeter: University of Exeter Press. A comprehensive history of religious education in England and Wales.

Grimmitt, M. (ed.) (2000) *Pedagogies of Religious Education*, London: McCrimmons. A useful collection, with a critique of the major pedagogies of religious education in Britain today.

Jackson, R. (1997) *Religious Education: An Interpretive Approach*, London: Hodder. One of the best theoretical discussions of religious education, from one of the leading UK professors, with much on religion and culture.

Jackson, R. (2004) *Rethinking Religious Education and Plurality Issues in Diversity and Pedagogy*, Oxon: RoutledgeFalmer. Addresses many of the issues in this chapter as well as examining current pedagogies.

QCA (2004) *Religious Education: The Non-Statutory National Framework*, London: QCA. Although 'non-statutory' for reasons of local accountability explained above, this gives a widely shared picture of religious education in England.

References

Blaylock, L. and Williams, P. (2007) Explaining the beliefs of 16–19 year olds. Respect, spirituality, human rights, life after death, *Journal of Chaplaincy in Further Education*, 3(1): 17–29.

Cush, D. (2003) Should the state fund 'schools with a religious character'? *Resource*, 25: 10–15.

Cush, D. (2007a) Should religious studies be part of the state school curriculum? *British Journal of Religious Education*, 29(3): 217–27.

Cush, D. (2007b) Engaging with young people's spirituality: what teenage interest in witchcraft can tell us about the task for RE and SMSC at 16–19, *Journal of Chaplaincy in Further Education*, 3(2): 4–12.

Cush, D. and Francis, D. (2001) Positive pluralism to awareness, mystery and value: a case study in RE curriculum development, *British Journal of Religious Education*, 24: 52–67.

DfES (2007) *Diversity and Citizenship Curriculum Review*, London: DfES.

Fitzgerald,T. (1995) Religious studies as cultural studies: a philosophical and anthropological critiques of the concept of religion, *Diskus* 3. 1. Online. Available http://web.uni-marburg.de/religionswissenschaft/journal/diskus/fitzgerald.html (Accessed 1 April 2008).

Gardner, R. , Cairns, J. and Lawton, D. (2005) *Faith Schools: Consensus or Conflict?* London: RoutledgeFalmer.

Heelas, P. and Woodhead, L. (2005) *The Spiritual Revolution: Why Religions is Giving Way to Spirituality*, Oxford: Blackwell.

Jackson, R. (1997) *Religious Education: An Interpretive Approach*, London: Hodder.

Jackson, R. (2003) The faith-based schools debate, special edition of *British Journal of Religious Education*, 25(2): 89–102.

Larsson, R. and Gustavsson, C. (eds) (2004) *Towards a European Perspective on Religious Education*, Uppsala: Artos.

Nandu, H. (2008, forthcoming) Religion in Chinese education: from denial to cooperation, *British Journal of Religious Education*, 30: 3.

Ofsted (2007) *Making Sense of Religion: A Report on Religious Education in Schools and the Impact of Locally Agreed Syllabuses*, London: Ofsted.

Parker-Jenkins, M. , Dimitras, H. and Irving, B.A. (2005) *In Good Faith: Schools, Religion and Public Funding*, Aldershot: Ashgate.

QCA (2004) *Religious Education: The Non-Statutory National Framework*, London: QCA.

REC (2007) *Religious Education Teaching and Training in England: Current Provision and Future Improvement. The Report of the REC's RE Teaching and Training Commission*, London: REC.

SCAA (1994) *Religious Education: Model Syllabuses*, London: SCAA.

Schools Council (1971) *Religious Education in Secondary Schools* (Working Paper 36), London: Evans

Schreiner, P. (2001) Towards a European oriented Religious Education, in H. Heimbrock, C. Scheilke and P. Schreiner (eds) *Towards Religious Competence: Diversity as a Challenge for Education in Europe*, Münster: Comenius Institute.

Skeie, G. (1995) Plurality and pluralism: a challenge for religious education, *British Journal of Religious Education*, 17: 84–91.

Smith, J. Z. (1998) Religion, religions, religious, in M. C. Taylor (ed.) *Critical Terms for Religious Studies*, Chicago: Chicago University Press.

6 Education for democracy and citizenship

Howard Gibson and Don Harrison

INTRODUCTION

This chapter provides an overview of the arrival of citizenship education in England and confirms the importance of Bernard Crick's report in 1998 (QCA, 1998). It then explains the backdrop to New Labour's initiative and tries to locate the particular form that citizenship education took within a historical context. We attribute its qualities to a neoliberal economic agenda associated with social policies that seek to increase the 'responsibility' of individuals. They are also to ensure that schools become sites for social regeneration and civic renewal and so counter the worrying trend towards political apathy. It is suggested that if this *is* the role given to schools by citizenship education they may be charged with an insurmountable task. Many of the problems facing democracy may actually come from a deficit of trust in politicians, the decline in power of the nation state and the problem of defining a common social identity in a multicultural nation.

THE BIRTH OF CITIZENSHIP EDUCATION IN ENGLAND

While citizenship education may be a recent addition in English schools, it has long, historic roots. During the early part of the twentieth century the Moral Instruction League tried to influence government provision for state education. Between the two world wars the Association of Education in Citizenship lobbied with a similar purpose, as did the Council for Education in World Citizenship. In response to such pressure the Ministry of Education published a pamphlet in 1949 entitled *Citizens Growing Up: At Home, in School and After* (HMSO, 1949). However, not until the 1980s, when the speaker of the House of Commons, Bernard Wetherill, called for a Commission on Citizenship, was there added the cross-curricular 'theme' of Citizenship to the National Curriculum for England. In practice it was largely neglected by schools because it was non-statutory. Only in 2002 when the Advisory Group on

Citizenship under Bernard Crick had reported did the subject achieve its official recognition in the school curriculum (QCA, 1998, 2002).

The 1998 Crick Report (QCA, 1998), *Education for Citizenship and the Teaching of Democracy in Schools*, in many ways mirrored T. H. Marshall's model of civil, political and social rights for citizenship (Marshall, 1950). The Crick model comprised three aspects: *social and moral responsibility*, *community involvement* and *political literacy*, which could be described more simply as the learning of values, social action and politics. The model provided the underlying rationale for the 2002 statutory *Programme of Study for Citizenship* in secondary schools and for the optional primary *Guidelines for PSHE and Citizenship*, that have recently been revised by the QCA to augment both its economic and global dimensions of learning (QCA, 2007).

But although there has been much enthusiasm to strengthen the social and political commitment of young people, the form of citizenship education current in English schools has been seen by many teachers, parents and commentators not to be fully coherent. For example, there have been debates about whether GCSE short courses should more properly be called 'Citizenship' or 'Citizenship Studies', and Ofsted have reported that many pupils have not been aware that they have been learning the subject at all because of its absorption within PSHE, religion or history, and that provision was inadequate in a quarter of schools (Ofsted, 2006). Perhaps such concerns are to be expected from the rapid introduction of a new area of learning, with an initial shortage of trained teachers and appropriate learning materials. But much of this apparently muddled thinking about citizenship education can possibly be traced to the political pragmatism behind its creation and to issues that make questionable its very assumptions. In Scotland and Wales and in other parts of the world, other forms of citizenship education have emerged that place greater emphasis on the community and upon curriculum provision for all stages of primary and secondary education. In the next section we explain the specific cultural and political backdrop to the particular form of citizenship education now statutory in English schools.

NEOLIBERALISM, SOCIAL REGULATION AND CITIZENSHIP

Clues are to be found in the policies of Margaret Thatcher during her long period in office as prime minister (1979–90). In an interview with *Woman's Own* (1987) magazine she had declared: 'There is no such thing as society: there are individual men and women, and there are families. ' For some observers her declaration seemed to encapsulate the age, the individualism of self-seeking consumers and the Hobbesian belief that life was 'nasty, brutish and short' for the unsuccessful. Such philosophical underpinnings were combined with policies that would 'roll back the state', that is, diminish the role it had played since the end of the Second World War in providing services like public transport, unemployment benefit or free health care. It would now rely more upon the abilities of individuals to survive and for the market to provide solutions to individual needs (see Chapter 1). For those who were unfortunate or without sufficient wit to understand the nature of the game, there would always be a minimum of state provision and, as in Dickensian times, charity. In essence then, some commentators epitomised the age as one dominated by self-seeking, wealth-creating adventurers whose concern as citizens for society seemed limited to voluntary and occasional acts of compassion:

> The active citizen of Thatcherism was a law abiding, materially successfully individual who was willing and able to exploit the opportunities created by the promotion of market rights, while demonstrating occasional compassion for those less fortunate than themselves – charity rather than democratic citizenship was to be the main instrument of 'active citizenship'.
>
> (Faulks, 2006, p. 125)

The election of Tony Blair as the Labour Party prime minister (1997–2007) changed little regarding the assumptions about the benefits of a 'modern dynamic economy' (Blair, 1998) and only extended neoliberal economic policies. Blair coined the phrase 'the Third Way' in an attempt to position his government in the centre of politics. It should not be too far to the left, where it had been traditional for the state to intervene in people's lives for reasons of social equity by taxing the rich to pay for the needs of the poor. It should neither be too far to the right, where it might be accused of identifying too closely with his former ideological enemies in the Conservative Party who seemed to deny that 'society' existed independently of competing individuals. Thus the Third Way was to gain credence from the broadest political footing, and a new concept of citizenship was said to be central to the programme:

> Rebuilding Britain as a strong community, with a modern notion of citizenship at its heart, is the political objective for the new age. Labour must transform itself into a credible vehicle for achieving it.

> (Blair, 1993, p. 11).

Behind the rhetoric were two fundamental policies: an economic one associated with neoliberalism, and a social one that emerged in a series of political discourses on individual responsibility, opportunity and citizenship. The neoliberal economic one was essentially a development of Thatcherism and included the promotion of free competition as the most effective basis for market forces to ensure quality and efficiency. This included the deregulation of labour markets and the reduction in the role of law and the state to optimise productivity and generate new markets. It meant privatisation, in which the public sector was sold off or joined in public–private partnerships so that the state was diminished as a provider of goods and services to both business and the community. This led to the construction of market proxies in the residual public sector with the aim of encouraging market forces, so that schools, for example, would compete for pupils and funding. It also meant free trade beyond the nation's borders to encourage the mobility of capital and labour, as well as the abolition of tariffs, subsidies and control on foreign investments in order to stimulate global market forces. And, to enable individuals to make choices, the move toward indirect taxation and the reduction in basic income tax in the 2007 budget (see Chapter 1).

The social regulatory part of the Third Way was closely linked with the economic one and designed primarily to prepare citizens for the move from a historical over-dependency on the welfare state. Because of its apparent cost, inefficiency and failure to eliminate poverty, the goal was to move people from the old 'welfare state'. Instead there would be a 'workfare' one in which people were trained in the necessary skills and given incentives to find employment, or, rather, *disincentives* if they didn't. The press described the policy as 'a hand up rather than a hand out'. At the same time there was a move towards emphasising 'personal empowerment', 'opportunity' and 'individual responsibility' for, it was stressed, there are 'no rights without responsibilities' (Giddens, 1998, p. 65). In essence, the Keynesian welfare state was gradually being replaced by a regime where the state's role was to create the necessary economic and social structures for the successful operation of the market, one where individuals would increasingly compete and plan for themselves as individuals, take opportunities where they found them and become more active and responsible with regard to their civic obligations.

School curricula emerging from central government have mirrored these policy objectives. On the one hand *Personal Financial Capability* (DfEE, 2000) and *Enterprise and Entrepreneurial Education* (Davies, 2002) have addressed the requirement that pupils be taught the skills necessary for survival within a neoliberal economy. On the other hand *citizenship education* has helped carry the social regulatory part of the policy. For some such curriculum initiatives have been an appropriate and upbeat response to pressures upon the nation state whereby the renewal of civic virtues would start the process of addressing concerns such as the rise in crime, social disorder and political apathy.

For others, however, citizenship education has been yet another example of the state using the school curriculum as a tool for social engineering. In 1921, for example, in the wake of the First World War and its economic legacy, together with high unemployment and burgeoning class warfare, the government commissioned the Board of Education to consider ways in which the English curriculum could be used to reunite 'a divided nation':

> An education fundamentally English would, we believe, at any rate bridge, if not close, this chasm of separation. The English people might learn as a whole to read their own language, first with respect, and then with a genuine feeling of pride and affection. More than any mere symbol it is actually a part of England: to maltreat it or deliberately to debase it would be seen to be an outrage; to become sensible of its significance and splendour would be to step upon a higher level . . . Such a feeling for our own native language would be a bond of union between classes, and would beget the right kind of national pride. Even more certainly should pride and joy in the national literature serve as such a bond.
>
> (Board of Education, 1921, p. 22)

In more recent times there has been a similar recognition of the need to use education to deal with social ills, to tackle the growing disillusionment with politics and the political process. Citizens have become increasingly apathetic as voters and are said to be disenchanted with political parties and cynical about the sleaze and sound bites from those in public office. Some have seen the rise of citizenship education as part of the quest for 'social glue' (Gold, 2000), a desire to try and stick together an increasingly fragmented society where 'social capital' – the range of connections and networks that underpin connectivity between people cooperating and working together in society – has been dwindling. But if this is the function of citizenship education, schools acting as agents of social regeneration and civic renewal face a daunting, if not insurmountable, task.

EXPLAINING CITIZENS' DISENGAGEMENT WITH POLITICS

Is citizenship education an appropriate response to national apathy with political life? Despite clear evidence to suggest that voter turnout is historically low and that the political parties have been haemorrhaging members for the last fifty years, some have disputed the assumption that the populace *is* apathetic. This was just the approach an influential pressure group funded by the Rowntree Charitable Trust took in 2006. Helena Kennedy QC, Chair of the *Power Inquiry*, agreed with the government that low participation in formal politics was 'a serious problem threatening to undermine our democracy', but strongly disagreed about the interpretation of the evidence. She argued:

> When a government presides over two of the lowest general election turnouts and the two biggest street demonstrations since 1945, it's time to start asking and answering hard questions about why politics is failing to engage with the people of Britain through the traditional channels.
>
> (Kennedy, 2006)

The *Power Inquiry* reported:

> Contrary to much of the public debate around political disengagement, the British public are not apathetic. There is now a great deal of research evidence to show that very large numbers of citizens are engaged in community and charity work outside of politics. There is also clear evidence that involvement in pressure politics – such as signing petitions, supporting consumer

boycotts, joining campaign groups – has been growing significantly for many years. In addition, research shows that interest in 'political issues' is high.

(Power Inquiry, 2006, p. 16)

It concluded by suggesting that disengagement with politics 'is NOT caused by an apathetic and uninterested public with a weak sense of civic duty' (ibid. , p. 17) but, rather, by the convergence of political parties upon the centre ground and by citizens feeling that the processes of formal democracy fail to offer them sufficient influence over political decisions because of the incremental growth in the power of the executive.

Secondly, and linked to this, political disengagement may be inversely related to the public's perception of an increase in 'sleaze', 'spin', the 'sound bite' and 'dumbing down' commonly associated with British political life in recent years: 'There is evidence that the increasing number of people abstaining from the electoral process do so less out of a disengagement with politics than with a contempt for politicians' (Lewis *et al.* , 2005, p. 3). The *Power Inquiry* concluded that the level of animosity felt towards politicians, the main political parties and the key institutions of the political system was 'extremely high and widespread' (2006, p. 16). Furedi (2004) too has suggested that spoon-feeding the British public with synthetic 'sound bites' is counterproductive, and that the attempt to augment postal voting during general elections has been merely a substitute for genuine participation.

Thirdly, the effects of globalisation and of industrial capitalism upon democracy have not been dealt with properly in the government documents on citizenship education. Bottery (2003), for example, has argued that the more the state is withdrawn under the banner of neoliberalism, the less citizens feel a sense of commitment to it. Anderson has suggested that globalisation has challenged the traditional territorial bases of liberal democracies and that this makes them vulnerable:

> Globalisation is putting democracy in question and is itself being questioned as undemocratic. Its border crossings are undermining the traditional territorial basis of democracy and creating new political spaces which need democratizing. 'Global forces' are disrupting the supposedly independent, sovereign states and national communities which have provided democracy's main framework. And these 'global forces' are apparently beyond control or, more specifically, beyond democratic control. The political implications are wide reaching and far from clear.
>
> (2002, p. 6)

In short, one of the consequences of globalisation has been the decline in the economic, political and social effectiveness of nation states. As private multinational corporations have become more powerful they have affected the success or otherwise of national economies. Nation states have lost at least some of their autonomy as their power has been usurped by multinational corporations and supra-state political institutions like the EU or the International Monetary Fund (IMF), and economic power has outrun political power and political control has been lost to global markets. Hertz (2001) has argued that modern democracies are now resigned to the fact that multinational companies are taking the place of elected governments. Businesses are so dependent upon the loyalty of their customers that shopping may be now more effective than voting in effecting political change. 'None of it is good for democracy', she adds (p. 7).

A fourth factor that may explain political disengagement is the complex nature of British identity today. Because of globalisation, post-colonial migration and increasing population mobility, many citizens now have multiple identities (see Kymlicka, 2003). Today, for example, one can be English, British, Muslim, a member of the EU, and have a commitment to another country by birth or marriage simultaneously. In consequence, suggests Parekh (2002), the state today is too plural and diverse to consist of a single people:

Since it is constantly exposed to external influences and its members do not share a moral and cultural consensus, it cannot aspire to be a single cultural unit and base its unity on the cultural homogeneity of its citizens. It cannot claim to embody and legitimate itself in terms of their sense of collective identity either, both because many of them no longer place much emphasis on their national identity or privilege it over their other identities, and because some of them increasingly have and cherish transnational ties and identities (p. 53).

The consequence is sometimes fundamental for democracy in a literal sense. For example, one of the effects of the publication of Salman Rushdie's *The Satanic Verses* (1988) was a *fatwa* being placed upon the author together with book burnings and demonstrations around the UK concerning his allegedly blasphemous text. It also confirmed the juxtaposition of different ideologies and the fragility of formerly self-evident 'British principles': freedom of speech versus blasphemy.

CONCLUSION

Trust in politics and politicians remains at the 'lowest levels' according to surveys of pupils' attitudes to citizenship education (Cleaver *et al.* , 2005). To understand this one would need to set aside simplistic invective regarding the duty of young citizens to participate in their local community and become more active, responsible and charitable (QCA, 1998, par. 2. 11). Instead, there would need to be a curriculum for citizenship that gave pupils an understanding of the complex causes of political disengagement, such as the seeming antipathy (rather than apathy) to what politicians currently stand for; the deficit of trust and seeming lack of genuine encounter in the discussion of their policies from taking the nation to war to finding solutions to global warming; an understanding of the relationship of the media to a modern democracy; the effects of globalisation on the power of democracies to be authoritative on the international stage in the presence of dominant multinational companies; and the changing, complex nature of British identity and what it might mean to be a citizen of this country today.

While there are many sectors of British society that support values education, community involvement and the regeneration of political awareness, global citizenship has been a weaker aspect of the project and largely relegated to the work of non-government organisations (NGOs) and development education sectors such as Oxfam (see Chapter 9). Recently there have been optimistic signs, however, such as a joint enterprise with the DfES and the Department for International Development (DfID) and the publication of a position paper on the global dimension of learning aimed at boosting this area. The crux of the debate has been: how effective can young people be as active, global citizens? A citizen's allegiance to a local community and a nation state is more apparent than a global identity. For this reason, the Crick Report and the subsequent QCA Programme of Study prescribed learning for action at levels up to the European Parliament but offered a far vaguer concept of global responsibility beyond that. Many students and teachers of citizenship, however, are excited by possibilities for learning about, and participating in, global change, whether environmental or social and economic. The surge of support for the NGO-inspired 'Make Poverty History' campaign is possibly evidence for that. Therefore one of the future challenges of citizenship education may be to embed this global dimension more centrally in national curriculum policy and give it a more central place for all age levels (see Chapter 9).

SUMMARY POINTS

- Bernard Crick was commissioned by David Blunkett MP, Minister of Education at the time, to report on *Citizenship and the Teaching of Democracy in Schools* (QCA, 1998). This led to the addition of citizenship education as a statutory part of the secondary school curriculum in September 2002.
- Reports from Ofsted suggest that the quality of teaching of citizenship education is at best patchy. Studies from the National Foundation for Educational Research (NFER) show that pupils' trust in politicians is still low and that their 'active involvement' in political or civic activities is at best uneven or inconsistent.
- Accounting for the historical rise of citizenship education in England is interesting because it helps set the policy within the broader remit of a move to neoliberal economics and an accompanying social agenda that emphasises 'individual responsibility' and 'civic duty'. It may be that schools facing the challenge of social regeneration and civic renewal may find it not only ideologically unsound, but an insurmountable goal.
- For some the international arena seems like an important concern that is currently emaciated within the citizenship curriculum in English schools. And yet, because of the effect of globalisation upon the diminishing authority of nation states, this is possibly where the focus should be in order to deal with serious international issues such as global warming and inequality.

QUESTIONS FOR DISCUSSION

1   How might a teacher stimulate pupils' awareness of global warming and manage to escape the brickbats of 'modern puritanism', 'scaremongering' or 'political bias' from ideological enemies, some of whom might be parents? More than that, if citizenship education is clearly said to be about taking *action*, based upon their understanding of the issues and their commitment to a cause, how far would you want your pupils to go?

2   The Crick Report refers to a distinction between 'justice' and the 'law'. Unfortunately his committee didn't expand on the ramifications of this distinction. You try. Say your pupils wished to march to parliament to demonstrate about the government's 'unjust' involvement in the Afghanistan war, would you let them? It's illegal for them to abscond from school – it's truanting – but *you* could give them permission if you were a teacher. Would you?

FURTHER READING

Breslin, T. and Dufour, B. (eds) (2007) *Developing Citizenship: A Comprehensive Introduction to Effective Citizenship Education in the Secondary School*, London: Hodder Murray. A good overview of how citizenship education is taught in English secondary schools.

Citizenship Foundation. Online. http://www.citizenshipfoundation.org.uk (accessed 7 March, 2008). An important website supported by the Law Society that raises questions like 'What is citizenship and why teach it?', although you may dispute its suggestions.

Crick, B. (2007) Citizenship: the political and the democratic, *British Journal of Educational Studies* 55(3): 235–48. One of Crick's many papers since his 1998 report. In this one he expands on the nature of democracy.

Faulks, K. (2006) Education for citizenship in England's secondary schools: a critique of current principle and practice, *Journal of Education Policy* 21(1): 59–74. A well-developed critique of current policy and the curriculum for citizenship education.

REFERENCES

Anderson, J. (2002) Questions of democracy, territoriality and globalisation, in J. Anderson (ed.) *Transnational Democracy: Political Spaces and Border Crossings*, London: Routledge.

Blair, T. (1993) Why modernisation matters, *Renewal* 1(4).

Blair, T. (1998) *The Third Way: New Politics for the New Century*, Fabian Pamphlet 588, London.

Board of Education (1921) *The Teaching of English in England* (The Newbolt Report), London: HMSO.

Bottery, M. (2003) The end of citizenship? The nation state, threats to its legitimacy, and citizenship education in the twenty-first century, *Cambridge Journal of Education* 33(1): 101–22.

Cleaver, E., Ireland, E., Kerr, D. and Lopes, E. (2005) *Citizenship Education Longitudinal Study: Second Cross-Sectional Survey 2004. Listening to Young People: Citizenship Education in England*, London: National Foundation for Educational Research.

Davies, H. (2002) *A Review of Enterprise and the Economy in Education*, London: HMSO.

DfEE (2000) *Financial Capability Through Personal Financial Education: Guidance for Schools at Key Stages 1 and 2*, London: DfEE/QCA.

Faulks, K. (2006) Rethinking citizenship education in England: some lessons from contemporary social and political theory, *Education, Citizenship and Social Justice* 1(2): 123–40.

Furedi, F. (2004) *Where Have all the Intellectuals Gone? Confronting 21st Century Philistinism*, London: Continuum.

Gold, K. (2000) Stick with Blunkett's belief in social glue, *Times Educational Supplement*, 29 December.

Hertz, N. (2001) *The Silent Takeover: Global Capitalism and the Death of Democracy*, London: Heinemann.

HMSO (1949) *Citizens Growing Up: At Home, in School and After*, Ministry of Education Pamphlet No. 16.

Kennedy, H. (2006) Announcement at launch of Power Inquiry report. Online. Available http://www.powerinquiry.org/press/documents/youngcommissioner.pdf (accessed 20 March 2006).

Kymlicka, W. (2003) Two dilemmas of citizenship education in pluralist societies, in A. Lockyer, B. Crick and J. Annette (eds) *Education for Democratic Citizenship: Issues in Theory and Practice*, Aldershot: Ashgate.

Lewis, J., Inthrorn, S. and Wahl-Jorgensen, K. (2005) *Citizens or Consumers? What the Media Tell Us About Political Participation*, Maidenhead: Open University Press.

Marshall, T. H. (1950) *Citizenship and Social Class and Other Essays*, Cambridge: Cambridge University Press.

Ofsted (2006) *Citizenship is Improving But There Remains Wide Variation in Quality With Inadequate Provision Seen in a Quarter of the Schools Surveyed*. Online. Available http://www.ofsted.gov.uk (accessed 15 October, 2007).

Parekh, B. (2002) Reconstituting the modern state, in J. Anderson (ed.) *Transnational Democracy: Political Spaces and Border Crossings*, London: Routledge.

Power Inquiry (2006) *Power to the People – The Report of Power: An Independent Report into Britain's Democracy*, York: The Power Inquiry/Rowntree Trust.

QCA (1998) *Education for Citizenship and the Teaching of Democracy in Schools: Final Report of the Advisory Group on Citizenship* (Crick Report), London: QCA.

QCA (2002) *Programme of Study for Citizenship*, London: QCA.

QCA (2007) *Programme of Study for Citizenship*. Online. Available http://www.qca.org.uk (accessed 7 March 2008).

Rushdie, S. (1988) *The Satanic Verses*, London: Penguin.

Woman's Own (1987) 31 October.

Part II

Global and Environmental Education

7 The Global Dimension in Education

David Hicks

INTRODUCTION

Why do teachers need to know about global issues, events and trends? How can we help young people understand the rapidly changing world in which they live? What resources are available to assist in teaching about such matters? This chapter sets out to answer questions such as these and, in particular, explores:

- the rationale for a global dimension in the curriculum;
- two frameworks for implementing such a dimension;
- how this relates to selected areas of the curriculum.

RATIONALE FOR THE GLOBAL DIMENSION

We cannot fully understand life today in our own communities unless this is set in the wider global context. What happens elsewhere in the world constantly impacts on our daily lives even if we may not be aware of it. We need therefore to know something about the 'state of the world'. Some current global trends (Worldwatch Institute, 2007) include:

- increased impact of climate change on both people and environment;
- use of wind and solar energy growing rapidly;
- the global economy and strain on the environment continue to grow;
- child labour is harming the lives of many children in the world;
- socially responsible investment is growing rapidly.

Issues relating to climate change, energy use, economic growth, wealth and poverty, and violent conflict also affect our local communities and day-to-day living. A useful source of information on such issues is the annual publication *Vital Signs: The Trends Which are Shaping our Future* from the Worldwatch

Institute. Many of the risks that society faces in the early twenty-first century are now global in nature. Whilst once science was seen as having all the answers, science and technology are now also seen as contributing to contemporary problems, from the storage of nuclear waste to carbon emissions as a key factor in global warming. Similarly the forces of globalisation, engineered by the rich world, are being more fiercely resisted than ever, since they raise all sorts of questions about the need for more ethical lifestyles (Clark, 2006).

Clearly many of these matters are a cause for concern. However, because they are sometimes uncomfortable to look at people often prefer to act as if they did not exist. This is called the 'psychology of denial' – if I pretend something isn't happening it may just go away. In reality, of course, any problem (whether personal or global) that we choose to ignore may as a result only get worse. The truth is that every person who chooses to act for change does in fact make a difference, especially if they join with others to do so. 'But', you may say, 'I still don't really see what this has got to do with education.' Well it is something that educators in the UK have been concerned about since the 1920s. Progressive teachers at that time felt that education needed to be both more child-centred and more world-minded. By the latter they meant not only knowing more about the world but the need for greater tolerance and respect between both groups and countries.

Richardson (1990) aptly captures the contemporary importance of these two long-standing educational traditions when he writes:

> The one tradition is concerned with learner-centred education, and the development and fulfilment of individuals. This tradition is humanistic and optimistic, and has a basic trust in the capacity and will of human beings to create healthy and empowering systems and structures … The second tradition is concerned with building equality, and with resisting the trend for education merely to reflect and replicate inequalities in wider society of race, gender and class; it is broadly pessimistic in its assumption that inequalities are the norm wherever and whenever they are not consciously and strenuously resisted.
>
> Both traditions are concerned with wholeness and holistic thinking, but neither, arguably, is complete without the other. There cannot be wholeness in individuals independently of strenuous attempts to heal rifts and contradictions in wider society and in the education system. Conversely, political struggle to create wholeness in society – that is, equality and justice in dealings and relationships between social classes, between countries, between ethnic groups, between women and men – is doomed to no more than a partial success and hollow victories, at best, if it is not accompanied by, and if it does not in its turn strengthen and sustain, the search for wholeness and integration in individuals (p. 7).

Recently there has been considerable renewed interest in the need for a global dimension in the school curriculum. For example, two thirds of 14 year olds in a study by Holden (2007) felt that it's important to learn about global issues at school in order to make better choices about how they might lead their lives. Official support for this is given in the DfES (2005) document *Developing the Global Dimension in the School Curriculum* and NGOs (non-governmental organisations) such as Oxfam (2006) have espoused the need for an emphasis on 'global citizenship' in both primary and secondary schools. The Development Education Association (DEA) (2007) stresses the importance of 'global perspectives in education' and networks such as TIDE (Teachers in Development Education) (2007) provide resources and support to schools on teaching about global issues.

A number of different terms may be used when referring to the need for a global dimension in the curriculum but they do not all mean the same thing (Hicks, 2007). Table 7.1 clarifies the meaning of some of these key terms.

Table 7.1 Clarifying 'global' terminology

Global education	The term used internationally to designate the academic field concerned with teaching and learning about global issues, events and perspectives. NB. During the 1970s–1980s this field was known as world studies in the UK.
Development education	Originated with the work of NGOs that were concerned about issues of development and North–South relationships. Focus of concern has widened to embrace other global issues but development remains the core concept.
Global dimension	Refers to the curriculum taken as a whole and the ethos of a school; those subject elements and cross-curricular concerns that focus on global interdependence, issues and events.
Global perspective(s)	What we want students to achieve as a result of having a global dimension in the curriculum; in the plural refers to the fact that there are different cultural and political perspectives on global matters.
International dimension	Literally 'between countries' – as in international relationships; also refers to the study of a particular concern, e.g. education, as it manifests in different countries. NB. International refers to the 'parts' and 'global' to the whole.
Global citizenship	That part of the citizenship curriculum that refers to global issues, events and perspectives; also being or feeling a citizen of the global community (as well as cultural or national communities).
Globalisation	The innumerable interconnections – economic, cultural, technological, political – that bind the local and national into a global community; the consequence of neoliberal economic policies that see everything, including education, as a commodity to be sold in the global market place.

I will be using the term 'global education' as shorthand for the concerns of this chapter. Sometimes these terms get used as if they were interchangeable but, given that they each have their own distinct meanings, this can then lead to a general fuzziness about global education. Having a link with a school elsewhere in the world or taking a school trip abroad is not necessarily an example of good practice in global education. Neither necessarily is teaching about global warming or the war in Iraq. A number of key components have to be present before one can properly use the term global education or argue that there is a global dimension in the curriculum.

PLANNING

The field of global education has a long history in the UK and as a result has developed a range of tried and tested principles for introducing a global dimension into the curriculum (Hicks and Holden, 2007). Two of the best known frameworks for planning such a dimension will be considered here. The first comes from the work of Graham Pike and David Selby (2000) and the second from Oxfam (2006). Both frameworks have been successfully used by teachers in a number of ways.

Pike and Selby: global education

Figure 7.1 is taken from Pike and Selby (1999/2000) and, as you will see, this model has four crucial components. These, it is argued, are the 'irreducible minimum' that needs to be present in order for the curriculum to have a global dimension. The four components are briefly described in my own words in Table 7.2.

The place to begin is with the particular global issues, trends and events that young people need to understand in order to make sense of their lives today. These may be selected from the news because they are very topical and pressing or they may relate to what is already present in curriculum subjects, such as geography, history, RE or English. Most global issues fall into the four broad problem areas cited above: wealth and poverty, human rights, peace and conflict, the environment. These issues are of course present in our own countries and communities: they are both local *and* global in nature.

In particular it is important not to overwhelm pupils with the extent of particular *problems* as this will lead to their disengagement and feelings of disempowerment. Whilst they need to become more knowledgeable about the nature of particular problems they equally need to learn about the various practical *solutions* that can contribute to resolving them. It is exploring case studies of action for change and the experience of being able to contribute to this that actually empowers young people.

Table 7.2   The four components of global education

Issues dimension	There are four broad problem areas that need to be explored. These are issues of wealth and poverty, human rights, peace and conflict, and the environment. Not only do pupils need to understand specific examples from each of the problem areas they also need to study a range of solutions to such problems.
Spatial dimension	This involves exploration of the innumerable interconnections that exist between the local and the global. It focuses on the concept of interdependence between issues, people, places and countries, whilst also exploring the nature of dependency, i.e. the fact that many such connections are inequitable ones.
Temporal dimension	This involves exploration of the innumerable connections that exist between past, present and future. In particular it focuses on the need to think more critically and creatively about the future impact of local–global issues and thus investigates the nature of possible, probable and preferable futures.
Inner dimension	This relates to one's own personal growth and development. It is about the personal and interpersonal skills that are needed in order to work cooperatively with others. It is also about the forms of teaching and learning that are most appropriate for the exploration of global issues, events and trends. In particular this requires a holistic and participatory approach that focuses on differing values perspectives and political literacy.

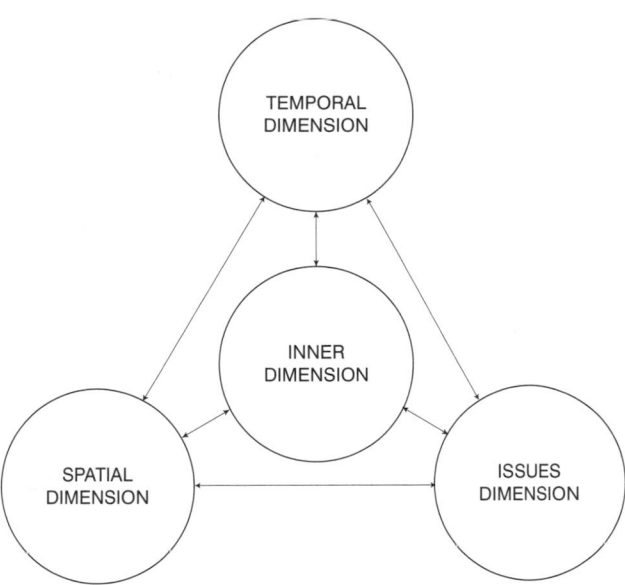

Figure 7.1   The four dimensions of global education (Pike and Selby, 1999/2000)

Table 7.3 shows in more detail what Pike and Selby see as essential within each of the four components. The key ideas for each component are listed in the second column followed by a familiar subdivision for teachers, a breakdown into knowledge, attitudes and skills. Detailed examples of classroom activities can be found in Pike and Selby (1999/2000).

Oxfam: global citizenship

Many NGOs in Britain, e.g. Oxfam, Greenpeace, Amnesty International, are concerned about the state of the world. Some of these NGOs have long-established education programmes run by staff with considerable experience of schools. The resources they produce for teachers are often directly tailored to the needs of the national curriculum and are often of a very high quality. Vitally important in the context of this chapter is Oxfam's (2006) *A Curriculum for Global Citizenship*, which has been widely used by educators in the UK. There is, of course, no separate subject called 'global citizenship' but a key element of citizenship, whether at primary or secondary level, is the wider global scene. Educators with an interest in global education or development education feel that this element of citizenship should be particularly highlighted.

The main features of the Oxfam framework for planning are shown in Figure 7.2. You will notice a familiar three-fold breakdown into knowledge and understanding, skills, values and attitudes. A brief paragraph elaborates on each of the subheadings. This is followed by three tables (Table 7.4, 7.5 and 7.6), which then give further details on each of these in relation to key stages in England and Scotland. Detailed examples of classroom activities can be found in Young and Commins (2002) and at Oxfam's (2007) website.

These two frameworks for planning, whilst coming from different sources, clearly have much in common. Either of them will provide a sound template for auditing what goes on in school and for planning detailed lessons across the curriculum that taken together make up the global dimension. One difference that you will notice between the two frameworks is that Pike and Selby are very explicit about

Table 7.3 The four dimensions of global education (Pike and Selby, 2000)

	Key ideas	Knowledge	Skills	Attitudes
Spatial dimension	• Interdependence • local ↔ global • systems	• of local/global connections and dependencies • of global systems • of the nature and function of a system • of connections between areas of knowledge • of the common needs of all humans and other species • of oneself as a whole person	• relational thinking (seeing patterns and connections) • systems thinking (understanding the impact of change in a system) • interpersonal relationships • cooperation	• flexibility in adaptation to change • willingness to learn from and teach others • willingness to work as a team member • consideration of the common good • sense of solidarity with other people and their problems
Issues direction	• local/global issues • interconnections between issues • perspectives	• of critical issues at interpersonal through global levels • of interconnections between issues, events and trends • of a range of perspectives on issues • of how perspectives are shaped	• research and enquiry • evaluating, organising and presenting information • analysing trends • personal judgement and decision making	• curiosity about issues, trends and the global dimension • receptivity to, and critical examination of, other perspectives and points of view • empathy with/respect for other peoples and cultures
Temporal dimension	• phases of time as interactive • alternative futures • action	• of the relationship between past, present and future • of a range of futures including possible, probable and preferred • of sustainable development • of potential for action, at personal to global levels	• coping with change and uncertainty • extrapolation and prediction • creative and lateral thinking • problem solving • taking personal action	• tolerance of ambiguity and uncertainty • preparedness to consider long-term consequences • preparedness to utilise imagination and intuition • commitment to personal and social action
Inner dimension	• journey inwards • teaching/learning processes • medium and message	• of oneself – identity, strengths, weaknesses and potential • of one's perspectives, values and worldview • of incongruities between professed beliefs and personal actions	• personal reflection and analysis • personal growth – emotional, intellectual, physical, spiritual • learning flexibility (learning within a variety of contexts and in a variety of ways)	• belief in own abilities and potential • recognising learning as a lifelong process • genuineness – presenting the real person • preparedness to take risks • trust

Knowledge and understanding

Social justice and equity
Understanding of inequality and injustice within and between societies. Knowledge of basic human needs and rights and our responsibilities as global citizens.

Globalisation and interdependence
Knowledge about the world and its affairs: the links between countries, power relationships and different political systems. An understanding of the complexities of global issues.

Peace and conflict
Understanding of historical and present day conflicts and conflict mediation and prevention.

Sustainable development
Knowledge of how to take care of things. A recognition that the Earth's resources are finite, precious and unequally used. An understanding of the global imperative of sustainable development.

Diversity
Understanding of cultural and other diversity within societies and how the lives of others can enrich our own. Knowledge of the nature of prejudice towards diversity and how it can be combated.

Skills

Critical thinking
Ability to assess viewpoints and information in an open-minded and critical way and to be able to change one's opinions, challenge one's own assumptions and make ethical judgements as a result.

Ability to challenge injustice and inequalities
Ability to recognise injustice and inequality in whatever forms they are met and to select appropriate action.

Ability to argue effectively
Ability to find out information and to present an informed, persuasive argument based on reason.

Cooperation and conflict resolution
Ability to share and to work with others effectively, to analyse conflicts objectively and to find resolutions acceptable to all sides.

Values and attitudes

Empathy
Sensitivity to the feelings, needs and lives of others in the world; a sense of common humanity and common needs and rights; a capacity for compassion.

Sense of identity and self-esteem
A feeling of one's own value and individuality.

Belief that people can make a difference
A realisation that individuals can act to improve situations and a desire to participate and take action.

Value and respect for diversity
Appreciation that everyone is different but equal and that we can learn from each other.

Concern for the environment and commitment to sustainable development
Respect and concern for the environment and all life within it. A willingness to consider the needs of future generations and act responsibly.

Commitment to social justice and equity
An interest in and concern about global issues; commitment to fairness and readiness to work for a more just world.

Figure 7.2   Key elements for global citizenship (Oxfam, 2006)

Table 7.4 Global citizenship: knowledge and understanding (Oxfam, 2006)

Knowledge and understanding	Pre KS1 Pre stages P1–P3	KS1 Stages P1–P3	KS2 Stages P4–P6	KS3 Stages P7–S2	KS4 S3–Standard grade	16–19
Social justice and equity	what is fair/unfair what is right and wrong	awareness of rich and poor	fairness between groups causes and effects of inequality	inequalities within and between societies basic rights and responsibilities	causes of poverty different views on the eradication of poverty role as global citizen	understanding of global debates
Diversity	awareness of others in relation to self awareness of similarities and differences between people	greater awareness of similarities and differences between people	contribution of different cultures, values and beliefs to our lives nature of prejudice and the way to combat it	understanding of issues of diversity	deeper understanding of different cultures and societies	
Globalization and independence	sense of immediate and local environment awareness of different places	sense of the wider world links and connections between different places	trade between countries fair trade	awareness of interdependence of our political system and others	power relationships North/South world economic and political systems ethical consumerism	complexity of global systems
Sustainable development	living things and their needs how to take care of things sense of the future	our impact on the environment awareness of the past and the future	relationship between people and environment awareness of finite resources our potential to change things	different views of economic and social development, locally and globally understanding concepts of possible and preferable futures	global imperative of sustainable development lifestyles for a sustainable world	understanding of key issues of Agenda 21
Peace and conflict	our actions have consequences	conflicts past and present in our society and others causes of conflict and conflict resolution – personal level	causes of conflict impact of conflict strategies for tackling conflict and for conflict prevention	causes and effects of conflict, locally and globally relationship between conflict and peace	conditions conducive to peace	complexity of conflict issues and conflict resolution

Table 7.5 Global citizenship: skills (Oxfam, 20006)

Skills	Pre KS1 Pre stages P1–P3	KS1 Stages P1–P3	KS2 Stages P4–P6	KS3 Stages P7–S2	KS4 S3–Standard grade	16–19
Critical thinking	listening to others asking questions	looking at different viewpoints developing an enquiring mind	detecting bias, opinion and stereotypes assessing different viewpoints	media literacy making informed decisions	critically analysing information making ethical judgement	handling contentious and complex issues
Ability to argue effectively	expressing a view	beginning to state an opinion based on evidence	finding and selecting evidence beginning to present a reasoned case	learning to develop/ change position through reasoned argument	arguing rationally and persuasively from an informed position	political literacy participating in relevant political processes
Ability to challenge injustice and inequalities	beginning to identify unfairness and taking appropriate action ⟶		recognising and starting to challenge unfairness	starting to challenge viewpoints that perpetuate inequality	selecting appropriate action to take against inequality	campaigning for a more just and equitable world
Respect for people and things	starting to take care of things – animate and inanimate starting to think of others	empathising and responding to the needs of others making links between our lives and the lives of others	making choices and recognising the consequences of choices	growing ability to take care of things – animate and inanimate	following a personal lifestyle for a sustainable world ⟶	
Cooperation and conflict resolution	cooperating sharing starting to look at resolving arguments peacefully starting to participate	tact and diplomacy involving/including society and others	accepting and acting on group decisions compromising	negotiation ⟶	mediation	conflict resolution

Table 7.6 Global citizenship: values and attitudes (Oxfam, 2006)

Values and attitudes	Pre KS1 Pre stages P1–P3	KS1 Stages P1–P3	KS2 Stages P4–P6	KS3 Stages P7–S2	KS4 S3–Standard grade	16–19
Sense of identity and self-esteem	sense of identity and self-worth	awareness of and pride in individuality	sense of importance of individual worth	open-mindedness	→	→
Empathy and sense of common humanity	concern for others in immediate circle	interest and concern for others in wider sphere	empathy towards others locally and globally	compassion sensitivity to the needs and rights of others	sense of common humanity and common needs	sense of individual and collective responsibility
Commitment to social justice and equity	sense of fair play	sense of personal indignation willingness to speak up for others	growing interest in world events sense of justice	concern for injustice and inequality willingness to take action against inequality	commitment to social justice and equity	commitment to the eradication of poverty
Valuing and respecting diversity	positive attitude towards difference and diversity	valuing others as equal and different willingness to learn from the experience of others	growing respect for difference and diversity	respecting rights of all to have a point of view	valuing all people as equal and different →	→
Concern for the environment and commitment to sustainable development	appreciation of own environment and living things sense of wonder and curiosity	concern for the wider environment beginning to value resources willingness to care for the environment	sense of responsibility for the environment and the use of resources	concern about the effects of our lifestyles on people and the environment	concern for the future of the planet and future generations commitment to a lifestyle for a sustainable world	commitment to sustainable development
Belief that people can make a difference	willingness to admit to and learn from mistakes	awareness that our actions have consequences willingness to cooperate and participate	belief that things can be better and that individuals can make a difference	willingness to take a stand on global issues	willingness to work towards a more equitable future →	→

the need to help children think critically and creatively about the future whilst this is merely implicit in the Oxfam framework. Detailed examples of how to develop a futures perspective can be found in Chapter 12 of this book.

PRACTICE

It is important to note that *all* subjects can contribute to a global dimension and a wide range of resources exists to support this endeavour. Here I will briefly make reference to three different areas of the curriculum and highlight some possibilities.

Early years

There is a common and erroneous belief that younger children are unaware of the wider world and that consideration of such matters should really be left to Key Stage 2. However, younger children are very aware of the world in their own way. Fountain (1990) points out that nursery and infant children regularly:

- Call each other names (prejudice).
- Arbitrarily exclude others from their play (discrimination).
- Argue over materials (resource discrimination).
- Protest that rules are not fair (human rights).
- Quarrel and fight (peace and conflict).
- Waste consumable materials (environmental awareness).
- Find that more can be accomplished by working together (interdependence).

So some of the key concerns of global education are there in the classroom from the beginning and how the teacher deals with these is of crucial importance. For younger children 'the world' is not construed in the same way as older children – but it is still the world, *their* world. This may relate to the family, the street, the park, the shops, going to town, going on holiday, places seen on TV. Their sense of the world is generally very immediate and often local. At the same time:

> Young children do not need to understand where people and places are in order to develop ideas and concerns about them. Indeed, it could be considered irresponsible of us to ignore these developing ideas and the attitudes and values associated with them, some of which might be stereotypes that lead to prejudice and bias … the ideas and attitudes pupils hold about 'otherness' or diversity will have a profound impact on how they respond to global issues and change in the future.
>
> (Martin, 2007, pp. 164–5)

So developing children's self-esteem, their empathy for others, respect for diversity, concern for the environment and ability to resolve conflicts fairly needs to begin at a very early age. Excellent resources are available to this end such as *Growing Up Global: Early Years Global Education Handbook* (RISC, 2006).

Citizenship

The presence of citizenship in the curriculum is of crucial importance for it offers a variety of contexts for children to think about their place in the local and global community. It should always be remembered that local and global are two sides of the same coin and thus inextricably bound together. Questions about the nature of good citizenship are being discussed not only in the UK but in a large number of other countries too. In their nine-country study Cogan and Derricott (2000) found that the following qualities were seen as vital for 'effective citizenship' in the twenty-first century.

- See problems in a global context.
- Work cooperatively and responsibly.
- Accept cultural differences.
- Critical and systemic thinking.
- Solve problems non-violently.
- Follow an environmental lifestyle
- Defend human rights.
- Participate in politics.

The list was not drawn up by teachers but by people with an interest in the nature of good citizenship. Teachers, however, readily recognise most of these characteristics as behaviours that they actively seek to promote in the classroom. It should be noted that the term 'politics' is used here in its widest sense, i.e. questions to do with the distribution of power in local and global society and how people gain it and use it. One can thus talk about the politics of the family, a relationship or an institution. Understanding the difference between 'power over' and 'power with' is one of the most valuable distinctions that can be made in citizenship.

One of the most interesting aspects of citizenship is that it seeks to develop skills of participation and responsible action. It is thus legitimate not only to learn about the world but also to act to change it. This involves identifying possible 'projects for change', whether in the school, local or global community, and working with others to achieve particular positive goals. It is just such active involvement in daily life that gives young people a sense of purpose and hope. Both pupils and teachers are often surprised to find just how many local and national groups there are working for change. The focus ranges from the environment, homelessness and human rights to globalisation, animal rights and transport. There are many excellent classroom resources that look at different aspects of global citizenship. These include Clough and Holden (2002), Young and Commins (2002), and websites such as Global Dimension (2007) and Oxfam (2007).

Science

An excellent example of the possibilities in science is set out in *Science: The Global Dimension*, one of a series of subject booklets published by the Development Education Association. Part of the rationale given for such a dimension in science is that it 'offers pupils opportunities to explore real issues with real solutions where there are clear social, moral and ethical choices made by scientists and all those involved in the journey from scientific principle and research to practical application' (Brownlie, 2003, p. 4). Amongst the issues that could be discussed in science at key stages 3 and 4 are the following statements:

- Fast food shops in our high streets are to blame for deforestation in Latin America
- It is easier to get funding for research into obesity and slimming treatments than it is for malaria

- Poverty is the most environmentally destructive force on the planet
- The promotion of baby formula milks has improved infant survival and health
- Terminator gene technologies benefit farmers in India
- Nuclear power is clean, safe and easy to use.

(Brownlie 2003, p. 7)

Such an approach to science education has many benefits for pupils. It makes it easier for them to appreciate the relevance of science to their own lives, to find science more interesting and motivating, to develop informed opinions and take appropriate action about scientific matters, and to understand their own role in global society.

CONCLUSION

This chapter has set out the rationale for a global dimension in the curriculum by referring to current global trends and also to official DCSF requirements. It offers two different models for planning such a global dimension – from the work of Pike and Selby and from Oxfam – both of which offer practical ideas for curriculum implementation. All curriculum subjects can contribute in different ways to the global dimension and three examples have been used to illustrate this from early years, citizenship and science.

SUMMARY POINTS

- All teachers today need some understanding of contemporary global issues.
- All such issues have an impact in different ways on our local communities.
- There is a long-standing tradition of 'global education' for teachers to draw on.
- It is an official requirement for there to be a global dimension in the curriculum.
- Using expert frameworks for planning will enhance such work in the classroom.

QUESTIONS FOR DISCUSSION

1   Which of the two frameworks for planning do you prefer and why?
2   Take a school subject you are familiar with. How can it contribute to the global dimension?
3   Which of the classroom resources listed do you find valuable and why?

FURTHER READING

Claire, H. and Holden, C. (eds) (2007) *The Challenge of Teaching Controversial Issues*, Stoke-on-Trent: Trentham Books. Looks at why global and local issues are often controversial in nature and provides case studies of how these may be dealt with in the classroom.

DfES (2005) *Developing a Global Dimension in the School Curriculum*, London: DfES. The brief but key official document that argues that the global dimension is a vital element in all school curricula.

Hicks, D. and Holden, C. (eds) (2007) *Teaching the Global Dimension: Key Principles and Effective Practice*, Oxon: Routledge. An authoritative text in which leading global educators explore key themes in detail and their implications for the classroom.

Pike, G. and Selby, D. (1999/2000) *In the Global Classroom*, 2 vols, Toronto: Pippin Publishing. An excellent classroom resource for teachers, full of practical and lively ideas for use in the classroom.

Young, M. and Commins, E. (2002) *Global Citizenship: The Handbook for Primary Teaching*, Cambridge: Chris Kington/Oxford: Oxfam. A most useful and practical resource book for exploring the nature of global citizenship in the classroom.

REFERENCES

Brownlie, A. (2003) *Science: The Global Dimension*, London: Development Education Association.

Clark, D. (2006) *The Rough Guide to Ethical Living*, London: Rough Guides Ltd.

Clough, N. and Holden, C. (2002) *Education for Citizenship: Ideas into Action*, London: RoutledgeFalmer.

Cogan, C. and Derricott, R. (2000) *Citizenship for the 21st Century*, London: Kogan Page

DEA (2007) Development Education Association. Online. Available http://www.dea.org.uk (accessed 20 September 2007).

DfES (2005) *Developing the Global Dimension in the School Curriculum*, London: DfES.

Fountain, S. (1990) *Learning Together: Global Education 4–7*, Cheltenham: Stanley Thornes.

Global Dimension. Online. Available http://www.globaldimension.org.uk (accessed 13 September 2007).

Hicks, D. (2007) Principles and precedents, in D. Hicks and C. Holden (eds) *Teaching the Global Dimension*, Oxon: Routledge.

Hicks, D. and Holden, C. (eds) (2007) *Teaching the Global Dimension: Key Principles and Effective Practice*, Oxon: Routledge.

Holden, C. (2007) Young people's concerns, in D. Hicks and C. Holden (eds) *Teaching the Global Dimension*, Oxon: Routledge.

Martin, F. (2007) The wider world in the primary school, in D. Hicks and C. Holden (eds) *Teaching the Global Dimension*, Oxon: Routledge.

Oxfam (2006) *A Curriculum for Global Citizenship*, Oxford: Oxfam's Development Education Programme. Online. Available at: http://www/oxfam.org.uk/coolplanet (accessed 13 September 2007).

Pike, G. and Selby, D. (1999/2000) *In the Global Classroom*, 2 vols, Toronto: Pippin Publishing.

Richardson, R. (1990) *Daring to be a Teacher*, Stoke-on-Trent: Trentham Books.

RISC (2006) *Growing up Global: Early Years Global Education Handbook*, Reading: Reading International Solidarity Centre.

Teachers in Development Education (TIDE). Online. Available http://www.tidec.org (accessed 13 September 2007).

Worldwatch Institute (2007) *Vital Signs: The Trends That are Shaping our Future 2007–2008*, New York: W. W. Norton.

Young, M. and Commins, E. (2002) *Global Citizenship: The Handbook for Primary Teaching*, Cambridge: Chris Kington/Oxford: Oxfam.

8 European Education Systems: Convergence and Difference

David Coulby

INTRODUCTION

Europe as a whole is tending to come together politically, economically and culturally. Within the social sciences, not least in Education Studies, Europe is increasingly being used as the unit of analysis and description, rather than that of individual states. Europe, in the current lexicon, is seen and analysed as an educational space (Novoa and Lawn, 2002). This coming together of Europe is happening in an exceedingly complex and conflicted way. Furthermore, any convergence in matters of education is at least matched by areas of stubborn isolationism as states and more local levels seek to retain control over educational institutions and practices.

This chapter describes and explains three trends:

- the trend towards European unification;
- the move towards conversion in matters of educational policy and practice;
- areas of radical difference between education systems in Europe.

THE TREND TOWARDS EUROPEAN UNIFICATION

The trend towards European unification is complex because it involves two main international bodies, the European Union (EU) and the North Atlantic Treaty Organisation (NATO), as well as many other organisations. The nature of these two bodies in terms of membership and policy is also complex and fractured, raising the vexed question of which states actually belong to Europe. This section examines these issues by considering firstly the EU and then NATO.

The EU at the time of writing consists of twenty-seven member states: Belgium, the Netherlands, Luxembourg, Germany, France, Italy, Ireland, Denmark, the United Kingdom, Spain, Portugal, Greece, Finland, Sweden, Austria, Poland, Hungary, the Czech Republic, Slovakia, Cyprus, Slovenia, Latvia,

Estonia, Lithuania, Malta, Romania and Bulgaria. Turkey has been agreed accession in principle but controversially no timetable has yet been agreed. Other countries, including those of former Yugoslavia and of the southern Mediterranean littoral, have expressed interest in eventual membership and, in the case of Croatia, this has been agreed in principle.

EU membership then does not include the whole of Europe. Norway, perhaps on the basis of confidence in its own oil wealth, and Switzerland, on the basis of banking wealth and the tangible gains of the policy of neutrality during the twentieth century, have consciously opted not to be members. Some of the European mini-states, with advantageous tax and banking regimes (Liechtenstein, Monaco), remain beyond EU control. The movement of the EU to the east, following the fall of communism in Eastern Europe in 1989 and the break up of the Soviet Union in 1991, has been painfully slow. The EU could hardly be said to have raced to embrace and assist the new democracies. The more impoverished and politically suspect states of former Yugoslavia remain beyond the pale. The question of the eventual entry of other former Soviet states (apart from the three Baltic countries) remains to be addressed: Ukraine, Belarus and indeed Russia itself.

Even within itself the EU is divided with some states subscribing to some policies, for example on immigration, and some states not (Budge and Newton, 1997). This is referred to as the multi-track Europe. Critically there is no unified policy on foreign affairs and defence (considered in the discussion of NATO below) or on the common currency. Possibly the most potent symbol of European unification and the greatest achievement of the EU, the euro, is progressively becoming the currency of most EU states though Sweden, as well as the UK, have notably retained their own currencies. Already the euro has become a preferred international currency for those states that, for economic or often political reasons, wish to avoid using the dollar. It is possible to predict that the euro will soon replace the dollar as the international trading currency of choice. The UK's reluctance to join the euro zone remains, however, significant. The UK has the second largest population and the second largest gross domestic product (wealth) of any of the EU countries. (The first in both cases is Germany.) London has by far Europe's largest financial sector. It is a nuclear power and a highly significant member of NATO. Opinion polls continually suggest an overwhelming majority against euro membership. This represents an apparent vote of no confidence in the common currency and perhaps even the European project as a whole.

Beyond the euro the successes of the EU are open to question. It has singly failed to achieve a unified foreign policy. Most recently this was evident in the split that emerged over the desirability of the 2003 invasion of Iraq. An even more fatal division occurred over policy with regard to the break-up of former Yugoslavia. Here, historically conditioned policies by Germany over the early recognition of Croatia and, most fatally, by the UK's inability, under the Conservatives, to take a critical stance against Serbia, played a significant part in the initiation and prolongation of the bloodshed. It was only decisive action by the USA over Bosnia and, with the UK, over Kosovo that averted the strong threat of genocide in Europe (Simms, 2001). (The role of education in these conflicts has been significant. The treatment of minorities by states throughout Europe can test the boundaries between education and warfare (Coulby and Jones, 2001).)

The EU's main policy and the one that absorbs nearly half of its not inconsiderable budget is the common agricultural policy (CAP). This policy provides subsidies for inefficient (in terms of world competition) farmers, especially in France and the other Mediterranean countries. One of its effects is to make it difficult for non-subsidised farmers in the majority of the world to compete in exporting food to the lucrative European market. It is one of the major areas of the EU's non-compliance with the terms of the World Trade Organisation (WTO). There has been strong pressure from both the European Commission itself and from the states of northern Europe to reduce or abolish the CAP. An important deal between France and Germany in Nice in 2002 guaranteed the continuation of the CAP at close to current levels as well as probably presaging the wider breach in the EU that subsequently emerged over Iraq. Whether the CAP can survive in the face of international hostility, the opposition of the UK and the pressure of the new member states, where agriculture is an important economic dimension, remains to be seen.

To cavil at waste, ineffectiveness and divisiveness within the EU is, in one way, to miss the point. The EU emerged as part of the post-World War II settlement in Europe. It provided a mechanism for the peaceful coexistence of France and Germany. The alliance between these two states remains the cornerstone of the EU to this day. The EU has undoubtedly played a major role in preserving peace between states in Europe for nearly sixty years. The other, major international organisation in Europe, NATO, has played an even more active role in the preservation of European peace.

NATO does not have the same membership as the EU. The USA, the world's only superpower, is a member of NATO as is Canada. Many of the EU countries belong to NATO but not all. Ireland and Austria are not part of NATO. Norway belongs to NATO but not the EU. France, Europe's second nuclear power, although currently a full member of NATO, has had an uneasy relationship with the organisation, especially with its perceived Anglo–American leadership. Turkey, persistently kept at arm's length by the EU, is a full member of NATO. It has borders with Iraq and the former Soviet Union.

Turkey has a rapidly expanding population, which is already at the same level as Germany's. It has two mega-cities, Ankara and Istanbul; the latter may be seen to be one the most important cities in the history of Europe as a whole. Istanbul controls the entrance to the Black Sea. It is a democracy though with a looming military presence. It is a secular state, though the influence of Islam is on the increase not least in politics and education. It has a rapidly developing and vibrant economy based in part on trade with Eastern Europe and the Turkic states of the former Soviet Union (the now independent countries of Kazakhstan, Turkmenistan, Uzbekistan, Tajikistan and Kyrgyzstan). It has a significant Kurdish population in eastern Anatolia, which it has so far preferred to deal with militarily rather than politically. It has an uneasy relationship with Greece, its neighbour and co-member of NATO, which periodically flares up into military standoffs. It is in military occupation of the northern part of EU member Cyprus. There are significant Turkish minorities in many cities of the EU, in Belgium and the Netherlands as well as Germany. Geographically, it is perceived to be split between two continents with Istanbul (Constantinople, Byzantium, I Polis) on the European side of the straights and the vast bulk of Anatolia on the Asian side. It is not hard to see that Turkey presents the EU with a sequence of challenges. The crude rejections of a timetable for Turkish membership by France's Chirac in 2002, repeated by the new President Sarkovsky in 2007, represent perhaps an inability to come to terms with Islam and people of a darker complexion rather than a sustained political evaluation. Whether the EU and Turkey can come to an accommodation will be a severe test of the commitment to internationalism, democracy and interculturalism on the part of both parties.

Many states in the EU, especially France, see NATO as an organisation whose time has past. The Cold War is over and the UK and USA have pulled back from their camps in Germany. Such states would like to see it gradually superseded by a European Defence Force. Given the commitment of the UK to NATO and given the partiality of many states, not least those of Eastern Europe, to having their integrity guaranteed by the military might of the USA, this is unlikely to happen in the near future. It is within this framework then that progress towards European unification remains complex and contested.

CONVERGENCE IN EDUCATIONAL POLICY AND PRACTICE

It is the explicit policy of the EU, as well as less powerful organisations such as the Council of Europe (European Commission, 1996, 2002) to shift to greater convergence between the European states in terms of education. An example of this in action would be the inclusion of a 'European theme' in school and university curricula at all levels. The EU has energetically advocated and financed this policy. It has been adopted by states with varying degrees of enthusiasm. It conflicts with the nationalist versions of history and culture so often promoted by European curricular systems. Germany and Poland still cannot agree a school version of their shared history. The states of Spain cannot even agree a school version of national history, as between Castile and Catalonia, to take but one example. In Cyprus the Turkish invasion of 1974 and its aftermath remains an important and separate curriculum subject. In this context it is likely to take a considerable time for states to accept a version of European history and culture that matches the EU's agenda of progress towards civilisation, harmony and unity.

Actual areas of convergence have occurred more as a common response to changes in the wider political and economic climate than as a result of centralist EU policy. An important example here would be the shift towards English as the first foreign language for all education systems in Europe. There are minor reservations on this generalisation, not least with regard to France, but it conveys the wider picture. Spain and Portugal abandoned French in favour of English as part of their liberalisation in the 1970s. The Eastern European and former Soviet Baltic States enthusiastically relegated Russian and adopted English in 1989 and 1991 respectively. The adoption of English in many states has been wholesale and successful. English is effectively the second language of the Netherlands. Courses at university level taught in English are to be found in, for example, Finland, Denmark and Spain. In most European countries there is a vigorous industry providing supplementary, evening and vacation courses in English. The EU has not advocated this trend, preferring to stress a three-language policy and to advocate the lesser-spoken languages of the Union. Nor has the EU yet acknowledged English as its common language. There is an unofficial policy of three big languages, English, German and French. Meanwhile much of the Union's diabolised bureaucracy is actually a translation factory, ensuring that documentation is available in all the recognised languages.

The spread of English throughout European education systems is far from a matter for Anglo–Saxon self-satisfaction. The spread of English represents one component of cultural imperialism, which is accompanying globalisation. In educational terms it may put in jeopardy not the lesser official languages of the Union, which will be well protected by their states, but rather the minority languages of the European nations, for example, Catalan, Friesian, Breton, Vlach, Welsh and Sami. Fortunately many states, including France, Spain and the UK, have belatedly come to see the importance of their national languages. Nevertheless, some European languages such as Gaelic, Sami and Livonian appear to be on the brink of extinction.

Still at school level, another area of convergence has been the increase in the number of years of compulsory schooling. In some states this results from continuing schooling to an older age; in others it results from an earlier start with schooling gradually replacing kindergarten. The emerging pattern is for schooling to continue to the age of eighteen either as a result of state compulsion or economic necessity. This leads to the key school examination at or around this age: *licencio*, *Abitur*, baccalaureate, licence, A levels. The key characteristic of this exam is that, by simply passing or by achieving a specific grade, it allows entrance to a place at university. In most states, though not really in Germany, the better the performance in this exam the higher the status of the university and the degree programme that the student can access.

It is at university level that there is the greatest amount of actual and potential convergence. Across Europe before and after the break-up of the Soviet Union in 1991 there has been a great increase in higher education both in terms of student numbers and in terms of the range of subjects that can be studied to degree level. New universities and other higher educational institutions (*hogeschools*) have been opened. Older universities have expanded. New courses in social and technical sciences have proliferated and more areas of vocational work have been brought to university level, not least the education of teachers. Research and higher degrees have also flourished with universities developing specialist areas of knowledge that they then go on to teach at undergraduate level. In this way universities are key players in the emerging knowledge economy. They tend to be prioritised by the state to the extent to which it is engaged in this knowledge economy; both Finland and the UK being well advanced in this respect. University education, from being the privilege of the elite sixty years ago, is becoming the expectation of the majority. The UK is leading the way in this respect as it is raising the percentage of the age cohort in higher education to 50 per cent by 2010.

The final area of convergence also concerns higher education, in this case with regard to the duration and pattern of study. Given the expenditure necessitated by university expansion, it is not surprising that the far-reaching changes being advocated by the proponents of harmonisation concern particularly the length and level of the first and second degrees. These were the key structural policies accepted by the signatories of the Bologna Declaration (European Ministers in Charge of Higher Education, 1999). In this Declaration the Ministers accepted a model of higher education that involves a three-year undergraduate degree, followed by a two-year Masters degree. This is sometimes referred to as the BA-MA model and is, to some extent, derived from the structure of degrees in England and the USA. However, the attractiveness of this model for the Ministers of Education was not some fond, positive view of English universities. Far from it. English universities offer the shortest and therefore the cheapest undergraduate degrees in Europe. Some European countries, such as the Netherlands, had already been looking for ways to shorten the amount of time students spent on their first degrees. The Bologna Declaration facilitates and legitimates this process. As well as harmonisation then the process is driven by the much less lofty ideal of reducing the cost to the state of each graduate.

Obviously the implementation of these changes is happening differentially within the twenty-seven countries and beyond. The UK Secretary of State signed the Declaration knowing that little change would be needed in universities in England, though the implications for Scotland may be more far-reaching. Italy initially appeared to have found the changes to the structure of the degree courses unproblematic. A law of 1999 specified for a three-year *laurea* to be followed by a two-year *laurea specialistica*. The implementation of this scheme has, however, proved problematic. In the Netherlands politicians would have welcomed the Declaration because it allowed them to push through the shortening of the first degree, which had proved a far from popular policy. Unlike the UK which transformed all its polytechnics into universities by the fiat of the 1992 Education Act, the Netherlands have so far not addressed the issue of the bipartite education system. Despite changes in title, the *hogeschools* have not become universities. The bipartite system remains also in Scandinavia, Belgium, Greece and Germany.

In Finland reforms initiated in the 1990s have resulted in the universities shifting to a three plus two model in most subjects. However, a first degree taken in a polytechnic can still need a minimum of three and a half to four and a half years of full-time study to complete. In Germany the shift to the three plus two model has been facilitated by legislation. But the adoption of the new model is at the discretion of the individual institutions. There is thus a dual system with some higher education institutions offering Bologna-style degrees and some preferring the traditional pattern. German universities, like the rest of the education system, are decentralised and controlled at the level of the Land. They also enjoy considerable autonomy. In order to meet the requirements of Bologna, and thereby reduce unit costs, the central state is playing a more active role in higher education reform. In Greece, despite popular opposition and the resistance of the universities, the bipartite system is being eroded. Legislation (2001) has made the Technological Institutes part of the higher education system but without giving them the full status of universities. Again Bologna has been used as a pretext to justify politically desirable or expedient changes.

The continuation of bipartite higher education in so many European states could be seen to represent both the strength of entrenched university interests and the persistence of an elitist structure. To this extent the post-1992 changes in the UK might be seen as egalitarian as well as widening participation. But this is not the case. In practice the universities in the UK are organised in a highly hierarchical way with Oxbridge and London at the top and the large urban ex-polytechnics at the bottom. This is reflected in both student choice and arcane funding arrangements, which favour the elite universities. The focus of the chapter now shifts from convergence to differences in European education.

DIFFERENCES BETWEEN EUROPEAN EDUCATION SYSTEMS

The first section of this chapter highlighted some of the ways in which the UK is an anomaly in Europe. This is also the case with regard to education. The UK has far more private schooling than other European countries, over 8 per cent of the cohort attending such schools. This schooling has a status that is unusual in other countries and it is linked to the elite universities (about half of all Oxford and Cambridge students come from private schools) in a way that would be unthinkable elsewhere. In the UK, especially in England, as far as the rich and the powerful are concerned, the publicly provided school system is for other people's children. This partly explains its chronic lack of funding and the way that it has been treated as the guinea pig for the wilder side of policy experimentation by both political parties since at least 1987.

The extent to which religious institutions are involved in the control and curricular content of schools and universities differs widely across Europe. In France there are a few private, religious schools, but that is the total extent of religious involvement in the education system of a state that prides itself on the integrity of its laity. By contrast in the Netherlands, Belgium and the UK there are distinct religious schooling systems up to and including university level. These systems also differentiate in terms of the actual religions and denominations. In the UK there are state schools; there are also Church of England (Protestant) and Catholic schools. Both these denominations are represented in sufficient numbers to constitute a separate system. There are also a few Jewish, Islamic and Greek Orthodox schools. Gloucestershire University, as well as many smaller higher education institutions, is a Church of England university. The extent to which religion penetrates the school curriculum also differs between countries. Not all systems have a daily act of collective worship, though this is compulsory in the UK, which also boasts at least one school that teaches biblical rather than Darwinian theories of evolution. In Greece, not only is Greek Orthodox religion a compulsory subject, most teachers in public schools are followers of this religion. In all twenty-seven of the EU countries, religious education means education in or about Christianity. Attitudes to Islamic Turkey may well be far from benign in such a context. The ultimate response to Turkey's EU-entry bid will be a severe test for the intercultural toleration and celebration ostensibly espoused by the EU states.

It is probably in terms of curricular content that the greatest differences exist between European systems at school level. This results from the historical role that schools have played in 'nation-building'. In all states in Europe, though much more in Greece, Latvia, Romania and the UK and much less in Norway and Finland, the teaching of history, national language and social and cultural subjects is infused with nationalism (Coulby, 2000). History in the school curriculum is all too often the story (legend, myth) of the heroic struggle of the nation to escape foreign oppression; of the glorious unifications of all parts of the nation under one monarch/republic; of the spread of the nation's civilisation to all other parts of a benighted world. The teaching of literature and culture can be equally triumphalistic as schools celebrate the richness of the nation's cultural products and activities and either ignore or denigrate those of other nations. Schools in Norway teach children to be citizens of Norway and the world, schools in England teach children to be citizens of England, confident that that means of the world; schools in Latvia teach children to be citizens of Latvia in contradistinction to the world. These are fundamental differences and contribute hugely to the contrasting national identities that are found in Europe. National and nationalist curricular systems at school level remain the most intractable divergence in education between states.

Selection of pupils at secondary level according to their perceived abilities is a practice that is perhaps dying out in Europe, but only slowly. Bipartite and tripartite secondary education systems remain in some regions and some states. In most of the German Länder, selection at secondary level continues to be the largely uncontested norm with middle class children attending the Gymnasium and progressing via the Abitur to university. There are usually two further types of school in subservience to the Gymnasium. In Transylvania there are grammar schools and non-grammar. Here the pattern is complicated by the fact that both tiers exist as Romanian speaking and Hungarian speaking (in some cities German speaking also). In England some local education authorities such as Kent and Wiltshire retain secondary selection despite the fact that the evidence has been incontestable for decades that school performance overall is better in non-selective systems. In the Netherlands secondary stratification is more by curriculum than institutions. There, in secondary schools, pupils may be following three distinct curricula each with its own exam and destination in higher education or the workplace. Progress towards the common school, taken for granted in France as well as the USA, remains slow, reflecting the vested political interests of middle class parents wishing to continue elite and socially exclusive secondary schooling for their children.

One of the benevolent effects of looking at education from an international or even a comparative perspective may be that it provides a shock with regard to anomalous practice in one's own system. This may well be the case for students in the UK with regard to the education of children and young people perceived to have special needs (Daniels and Garner, 1999). The whole industry of detailed categorisation (labelling) and separate, special provision (segregation) is absent in countries such as Italy and Norway. All children are educated together in the least restrictive environment with the maximum of social and curricular integration. The glacial progress towards inclusion in the UK reflects a society that too readily rejects and segregates children on the basis of perceived difference. The process tends to be self-perpetuating as those educated in non-special schools fail to develop the attitudes and skills that would allow them to integrate with those whom they perceive to be needy.

The differential access to higher education resulting from the extent of provision of university places was highlighted in the previous section. Given the increasing scope of the knowledge economy, the appetite of young people and their parents for university education and wider international trends (the USA and South Korea already exceed the UK target of 50 per cent of the age cohort in higher education), this is likely to be an area of educational provision where differences will gradually reduce over time.

In conclusion, it may be that convergence within European education systems, as perhaps at the political level of the continent as a whole, is largely illusory. Where it does occur, as in the spread of English as a second language, it is the result of wider economic and political forces, rather than of centralist diktat.

SUMMARY POINTS

- European convergence is a slow process.
- The European Union and the North Atlantic Treaty Organisation have different memberships.
- European schools and universities are not converging with any rapidity either in their structure or their curriculum material.
- Curricula remain inscribed by nationalism and, in many cases, religion.
- English as a first foreign language is one area of congruence but this is not as the result of a centralised policy.

QUESTIONS FOR DISCUSSION

1   In what areas of the school and university curriculum is convergence between European countries actually desirable?

2   Is the unification of Europe a desirable policy objective? If so, how can it be assisted by educational policies?

3   Churchill once advised De Gaulle never to put the UK in a position where it had to choose between Europe and the sea. Is the UK now in this position? Which way should it choose?

FURTHER READING

The World Yearbook of Education series provides good coverage of current issues in international education. There is usually a good deal of material on Europe. The titles listed below are relevant to the topics of this volume.

Bourne, J. and Reid, E. (eds) (2003) *World Yearbook of Education 2003: Language Education*. Series edited by Coulby, D. and Jones, C., London: Kogan Page.

Brown, A. and Davis, N. (eds) (2004) *World Yearbook of Education 2004. Digital Technology, Communities and Education*. Series edited by Coulby, D. and Jones, C., Oxon RoutledgeFalmer.

Coulby, D., Cowen, R. and Jones, C. (eds) (2000) *The World Yearbook of Education 2000: Education in Times of Transition*. Series edited by Coulby, D. and Jones, C., London: Kogan Page.

Coulby, D. and Zambeta, E. (eds) (2005) *World Yearbook of Education 2005: Education, Globalisation and Nationalism*. Series edited by Coulby, D. and Jones, C., Oxon RoutledgeFalmer.

Daniels, H. and Garner, P. (eds) (1999) *World Yearbook of Education 1999: Inclusive Education*. Series edited by Coulby, D. and Jones, C., London: Kogan Page.

REFERENCES

Budge, I. and Newton, K. (1997) *The Politics of the New Europe: Atlantic to Urals*, London: Longman.

Coulby, D. (2000) *Beyond the National Curriculum: Curricular Centralism and Cultural Diversity in Europe and the USA*, London and New York: RoutledgeFalmer.

Coulby, D. and Jones, C. (2001) *Education and Warfare in Europe*, Aldershot: Ashgate.

Daniels, H. and Garner, P. (eds) (1999) *World Yearbook of Education 1999: Inclusive Education*. Series edited by D. Coulby and C. Jones, London: Kogan Page.

European Commission (1996) *Teaching and Learning: Towards the Learning Society*, Brussels.

European Commission (2002) *A New Impetus for European Youth, White Paper*, Luxembourg: Office for Official Publications of the European Communities.

European Ministers in Charge of Higher Education (1999) *The Bologna Declaration: The European Higher Education Area*, Bologna.

Novoa, A. and Lawn, M. (eds) (2002) *Fabricating Europe: The Formation of an Education Space*, Dordrecht, Boston, London: Kluwer Academic Publishers.

Simms, B. (2001) *Unfinest Hour: Britain and the Destruction of Bosnia*, Harmondsworth: Penguin.

9 Education in Developing Countries

Elaine Lam

INTRODUCTION

Education in 'other' countries is an important area of study. Education in 'developing countries' leads to further questions surrounding aspects of international aid and curriculum change. For example, the United Nations (UN) initiative of Education for All by 2015 remains an elusive dream for some children due to politics surrounding funding and complex cultural issues of gender, ethnicity and social values. This chapter examines problematic terms such as the 'Third World', describes some factors impeding Education for All, and discusses some key challenges facing education in 'developing countries'.

What does education 'look' like in 'developing countries'? What exactly does the term 'development' mean? Single quotation marks are used around 'developing countries' because the phrase is contentious: it implies that places need to move forward and change, perhaps moving closer towards Western models of reform. Development is defined as 'having a relatively high level of industrialization and standard of living' (Merriam-Webster Online). The most industrialised countries are usually those in the West and the G8 countries – UK, the USA, Canada, France, Italy, Germany, Japan and Russia – usually sit at the top of this hierarchy. 'Developing countries' are places that are not considered industrialised. As this notion is both problematic and laden with assumptions and standards, phrases such as 'transitional states' are sometimes used. The term 'developing countries' is often preferred over 'Third World', which implies a hierarchal view of the world. In this chapter, the phrase 'developing countries' will be used as it is consistent with current literature. The whole act of 'development' has raised these issues and causes one to reflect on the assumption that education is always good. The process of 'development' will be examined as well as current initiatives such as Education for All (EFA), the Millennium Development Goals (MDGs) and the challenges associated with education in 'developing countries'. The chapter concludes with some implications for Education Studies and what can be learned from studying education and development.

'DEVELOPING COUNTRIES'

Stereotypically, 'developing countries' refer to those in the south, such as countries in Africa and South America, although this is a very limited picture. Countries in Asia, Eastern Europe, the Caribbean and the South Pacific are not typically classed as 'industrialised' either. Further, minority people groups in Western Europe, North America, Australia and New Zealand such as traveller groups, African-Americans, and indigenous peoples are marginalised. These marginalised groups in the so-called 'developed countries', and small states that are on the fringe of existence, are known as the 'Fourth' or 'Forgotten World'. They struggle for recognition and typically suffer from a lower quality of life. Although much more attention needs to be paid to the 'Forgotten World', this chapter is limited to the challenges facing 'developing countries'. It is essential to note that the poverty and debt in these countries are frequently a result of colonisation, unequal trade and policies by international organisations such as the World Bank. Sachs (1989) gives a historical account of international debt.

Education is one aspect among many in the process of development. Although discussions on development increasingly occur with a multi-sectoral approach involving transport, finance, health and families, education is the focus of this chapter. However, it is important to note that development is a significant field of study that encompasses the other sectors and focuses exclusively on the process, people and institutions involved in development. The term 'sustainable development' is often used to highlight the aim of development beyond a Band-Aid approach to hunger, disease, illiteracy and debt. The development of a nation state usually involves several key 'actors', significant groups or individuals. The first group are international government funding agencies such as the UK's Department for International Development (DfID), the United States Agency for International Development (USAID) and the Canadian International Development Agency (CIDA). There are many of these agencies in European countries and Japan's development agency is also well known. The next group are known as non-profit organisations, and frequently referred to as non-government organisations (NGOs). They are not run by governments and may be either faith based (such as Christian Aid) or local charities that operate out of a single office. The third group are civil society organisations (CSOs), which arise out of the local groups. Employee unions and support groups are good examples of CSOs. The last group are local governments, which play an instrumental role in setting the infrastructure and strategic planning.

KEY DEBATES

Development is often dependent on the strength of the local government and its involvement in the development progress. Successful sustainable development must involve local governments and CSOs. In fact, international involvement is not a prerequisite for development. Havter (1971, cited in Xue, 2005) argues that capitalist countries provide aid as a way of maintaining imperialist control over other nations and preserve the constructed divide between industrialised countries and the 'Third World'. The services and aid provided by non-profit organisations and international funding agencies may not be appropriate to the cultural context. For example, PEPFAR, the American president's fund, has been heavily criticised for its 'abstinence-only' campaigns among youth in 'developing countries' as a way of combating HIV/ AIDS (human immunodeficiency virus/acquired immune deficiency syndrome).

While HIV/AIDS is one of the biggest challenges facing development, ensuring education for all the world's children is often regarded as a cure-all panacea. Education is seen as a necessary step to alleviate the impact of natural disasters, ensure economic growth and produce healthier children. Sperling (2001) summarises research undertaken in the world's poorest countries. It was found that 'education boosts family income, and female education in particular leads to smaller, healthier families by lowering infant and maternal mortality and improving child nutrition' (p. 8). However, this approach of education for healthier futures has been critiqued. Robinson-Pant (2004: 473) notes this is a 'functional' reason and asserts the need to re-examine the values behind women's education and its sole association with schooling.

On the whole, however, most educationalists would argue that education is beneficial to 'developing countries' when it is culturally appropriate, is locally managed and does not cause harm to children. While the necessity of education in an appropriate cultural context may appear to be obvious, it should not be taken for granted. Indigenous languages face extinction as textbooks and resources to train teachers are often limited to mainstream languages. Small states that exist on the edge of powerful hierarchies ruled by the G8 countries are often pulled towards the dominant cultures of the USA and Europe. Local management is important for ensuring that programmes are sustainable and continue to develop. ICT equipment may be seen as a temporary blessing as there are limited personnel to repair and update equipment. New and innovative teaching approaches may be valuable but unsustainable over a long period of time unless leadership and professional development opportunities are available. Children may face danger in educational contexts such as teenage pregnancy and girls' safety when travelling to and from school. However, there are examples of good education initiatives: Wong and Balestino (2001) on Latin American community programmes for street children in Brazil and Sundersingh (2006) on children living with HIV/AIDS.

The process and product of development – the extent to which local groups are involved and where funding is placed – is a key debate. Another is prioritising 'investment' for improving education. Khaniya and Williams (2004) assert the importance of a safe and quiet instructional site, a trained and motivated teacher and appropriate instructional material. Dalin's (1994) widely read book supports in-service training for teachers and Fuller's (1986) work argues for more emphasis on instructional time. The debate is critical when considering where to place financial resources in cash-strapped 'developing countries'.

Financing development is yet another issue. First, international aid is at best inconsistent. Commitments from G8 countries have been disappointing, as illustrated by the failure of governments to act on their commitments to 'Make Poverty History'. The campaign placed public pressure on governments and 'led them to make some big promises – to increase aid, and cancel many poor countries' debts' (Make Poverty History, 2007). Secondly, international agencies and NGOs may have preconceived ideas about schooling and may impose conditions on countries such as the use of certain textbooks. This is often referred to as 'tied aid'. As a result, children may not benefit from the education process. Alternatively, communities may design a project with the assistance of outside consultants and find themselves deprived of the funds that were supposedly set aside for education but instead have disappeared into debt relief or other areas of the government. Thirdly, funding from outside agencies has had the effect of relieving governments from ownership of its education programmes and not funding them from their own Ministry of Education. Finally, the evaluation of aid has faced much criticism as it is difficult to measure the effectiveness of a school or centre for learning. Dissatisfied donors may withdraw funding until conditions are met that may be linked directly to the programme or to other areas of the government. Chambers (2000) writes about aid evaluation, 'What is perceived and reported cannot reflect accurately the complex and diverse realities of people and institutions' (p. 23).

The complex challenges associated with education and development such as financial planning, the roles of large organisations such as the IMF and historical accounts of poverty are beyond the scope of this chapter (see Sachs, 1989 in Further reading). The remainder of the chapter will focus on the current UN Education for All initiative and the Millennium Development Goals.

EDUCATION FOR ALL

In 1990, the leaders of the world met in Thailand and pledged to provide education for all of the world's children by the year 2000, an ambitious goal that was reaffirmed during the World Education Forum in Senegal ten years later. The current target year for Education for All (EFA) is now 2015. The project has six goals, including free universal primary education (ensuring access and enrolment for all school-aged children) and learning and life skills for youth and adult literacy (UNESCO, 2007a). According to the United Nations Educational, Scientific and Cultural Organization (UNESCO) (2007b), the United Nations arm for education, science and culture, 77 million children are out of school. While this number has dropped since 1990, researchers have identified the factors that prevent children from participating in schooling. Blasser (2000) states there are six marginalised groups: girls, children with disabilities, children in war, child labourers, children with disease and street children. UNESCO (2007b) gives four background factors on out-of-school children: gender, residence (urban or rural), household wealth and the mother's education. It concludes with the following:

> In Guinea, an urban boy with an educated mother belonging to the wealthiest quintile is 126 times more likely to attend school than a rural girl from the poorest quintile with an uneducated mother (p. 12).

While school enrolment and access to schools is a problem for 'developing countries', particularly those in rural areas, retention in schools is another problem. This is multifaceted, but centres on household finances and quality of education. UNESCO (2007b) estimates that in some countries, households contribute 40 per cent of education-related fees associated with uniforms, textbooks, transport and fees. In rural agricultural areas, children are considered a financial asset to the family as they provide labour. The actual cost to a household may be more than 40 per cent in education related costs and the loss of labour for family income may discourage parents from sending children to school. If a child is fortunate enough to attend school, the quality of education may be poor and thus perceived as irrelevant to the realities of a child's life.

Thus, retention rates are a serious concern for the EFA initiative. The recent Global Monitoring Report estimates that less than two thirds of children in Sub-Saharan Africa reach the last grade in school (UNESCO, 2007b): 'Once in school, poor education quality – manifest in overcrowded classrooms, poorly trained teachers, and shortages of learning materials – seriously hampers student achievement and increases the risk of dropout' (p. 12) The education children receive in 'developing countries' should be relevant, culturally appropriate and taught in their home language. However, curriculum reform is a difficult task for countries that have inherited a colonial curriculum and structure. (See below on the knowledge economy for an example from the Caribbean.) Teachers may be underqualified and poorly supported. Low and unpredictable receipt of wages contributes to teacher absenteeism, a complex problem that has been further exasperated by the impact of HIV/AIDS on teachers. Schooling in a language other than the child's home language, coupled with absent teachers and an irrelevant curriculum, can be obstacles to attending school.

Delivering good quality and accessible schooling requires coordination between international agencies that fund initiatives, local actors who must tailor programmes to the needs of the population and strong government leadership to promote the importance of education. It is important to note that both traditional formal school settings as well as non-formal structures have been instrumental in achieving EFA. There have been successful community-led projects that have innovative approaches such as REFLECT (Latin America and India), and SIMAC (Zambia). Such examples serve as case studies to highlight community involvement.

Regardless of whether education takes place in formal schools or informal settings, participation from all members of the population should be encouraged to implement and improve universal primary education. In some countries, plans for EFA have included a strategy to provide adult education in order to gain support from parents and community members who may have negative perceptions. Creating a fully literate population also has benefits for supporting the learning of younger children. The last point is particularly important. Girls are often marginalised from the schooling process for complicated reasons such as cultural beliefs about educated females, the need for girls to help with domestic tasks and girls' safety when commuting to and from school. In general, the higher the level of education, the more difficult it is to access (Belanger and Liu, 2004). In Asia and around the world secondary education is more difficult to access than primary schooling, which had a worldwide net enrolment of 86 per cent in 2004 (UNESCO, 2007b). Projects such as the Female Secondary Stipend Programme in Bangladesh, in which families receive financial compensation, place importance on gender equality (Unterhalter, 2005).

The issue of gender and its relevance to both EFA and development is particularly complex. The former Secretary General of the United Nations, Kofi Annan (2000) declared the importance of females to the development process in his proclamation: 'No women, no development'. However, the relationship between girls' education and empowerment is not simple. Often, there is an assumption that education will improve the quality of life. But countries such as Cuba and Sri Lanka are counter examples: they have high female literacy rates and high indicators for poverty and domestic violence. In short, while education generally benefits females, improving girls' education does not directly equate to empowerment and economic returns (see also Chapter 3). Jayaweera (1997) provides a detailed account of education in Asia and concludes that secondary education does not necessarily guarantee a higher net income. The argument reinforces the need for a multi-sectoral approach to development, in which education, industries, national initiatives and civil society work together. This is one of the principles underlying the MDGs.

MILLENNIUM DEVELOPMENT GOALS

As the new millennium approached, the world's leaders drafted a list of goals for the purpose of development. While the goals may appear to be aimed at 'developing countries', they are intended for all countries regardless of their stage of development. The goals are that by 2015 states should:

1   eradicate extreme poverty and hunger;
2   achieve universal primary education;
3   promote gender equality and empower women;
4   reduce child mortality;
5   improve maternal health;
6   combat HIV/AIDS, malaria and other diseases;
7   ensure environmental sustainability;
8   develop a global partnership for development. (United Nations, 2007)

The six EFA goals are intended to contribute to the eight overarching MDGs, such as goal numbers 2 and 3 relating to primary education and gender equality. Although both the EFA initiative and MDG are widely accepted as positive programmes, they have faced criticism for lack of appropriate support and funding. Yet they have also generated excitement and innovation in both education and development spheres. Jeffrey Sachs (2005), in his popular book *The End of Poverty*, describes several economic initiatives that may lead to growth and the fulfilment of some MDGs for 'developing countries'. The same author has also developed Millennium Villages in which all the available resources, personnel and funds are provided for a single village all at the same time to ensure a multi-sectoral approach to development and to lessen the delay between developing one sector before beginning a new project. As a result, such a village has access to clean water, health care, food production, education and infrastructure concurrently. While Sachs's organization, The Earth Institute at Columbia University, provides the necessary scientists and expert support, all initiatives are supposedly community led. The premise is as follows:

> The Millennium Villages are based on a single powerful idea: impoverished villages can transform themselves and meet the Millennium Development Goals by 2015 if they are empowered with proven, powerful, practical technologies.
>
> (Millennium Promise, 2007)

There are currently seventy-nine villages in twelve African countries operating or in the process of planning. While the sustainability of these villages is still in question, researchers such as Lewis (2005) report successful outcomes in the villages visited. While education plays only one part in this initiative, it is important to recognise the larger picture of development and the intersections with poverty and growth. Without coordination among the sectors, education alone cannot alleviate poverty.

FACTORS AFFECTING EDUCATION IN 'DEVELOPING COUNTRIES'

If Millennium Villages are the ideal for the future, what is the current state of education in 'developing countries'? This is a difficult question as each country is different and the factors that affect it vary. Yet there are some significant features that 'developing countries' may share with respect to education.

Colonisation

The remnants of colonisation can be felt in many 'developing countries'. In some cases, the country may still follow the curriculum of the coloniser; in other cases traditions exist. Teaching practices in some former English colonies may appear to be like Victorian English classrooms. Although the 11+ examination has long been eradicated in England, it still exists in former colonies, perhaps to the detriment of the country's EFA goals. Some western African countries formerly colonised by the French still follow aspects of the French system, such as repeating grades. An example is Togo, where repetition of grades may ensure academic quality for students who complete schooling, but may not be practical for pupils as the economy is weak and few opportunities exist for employment. Repeating grades is also a struggle for households that cannot afford to send their children to schools and may discourage children and families from education. Another classic example is school uniforms, costly for parents in 'developing countries' and a financial impediment to accessing and completing education.

The knowledge economy

A stronger force is the knowledge economy, which may be perceived as a form of 'neocolonialism'. Many countries still participate in Oxford and Cambridge GCSE and A level examinations, while others use examinations based on O levels or American SATs (American SATs are standardized tests required for entry to universities). These have a strong currency in the global market. As a result, schools in 'developing countries' may teach a foreign curriculum initially designed for English and Welsh pupils and not necessarily for pupils in 'developing countries'. The curriculum content is thus removed for pupils in such countries. It impacts on teacher training, on pupil motivation and perpetuates dependence on foreign powers. In addition, such examinations are costly. Moving away from such dependence comes at a price. Although the Caribbean Examination Council creates its own examinations for the English-speaking Caribbean region, there was initial resistance to local examinations. In fact, one educationalist accounts for the high standard demanded: 'We have always had to be a little higher than the rest on an international level to be recognised in the first place' (author's interview with Caribbean educationalist, January, 2007.) Countries attempting to create their own national curriculum face problems of international recognition. Trinidad, for example, is in the process of creating a national secondary curriculum, but prestigious schools are resisting the 'lowered' standards (author's conversation with Trinidadian head teacher, May, 2007). Students from 'developing countries' who complete secondary school may prefer larger international universities (such as those in the UK and the USA) and stay abroad for work after graduation. While autonomy may be paramount for students who wish to study and move abroad, such a trend further drains countries of valuable academic and professional human resources necessary for growth.

Impact of HIV/AIDS

With half of new infections occurring among youth, and over 12 million orphans in Sub-Saharan Africa, the impact of HIV/AIDS is the most serious problem facing education in 'developing countries' and threatens to reverse gains made by the EFA initiative. The lack of infrastructure to cope with the pandemic further exacerbates challenges faced by the EFA initiative. Infected teachers are often unsupported and are absent for long periods of time due to stigma and illness. Wambete (2006) recalls her experience as an HIV-infected teacher in which she was greeted by her students: 'Good morning madam HIV!' Education systems struggle to cope with HIV/AIDS orphans, sick teachers and little or no sexual health education. In some 'developing countries', governments inadequately address the problem. South Africa has been criticised for its slow reaction to the pandemic and the health minister has made unfounded statements encouraging a diet of fruit and vegetables over antiretroviral drugs, which are clinically proven to slow down the effects of the virus (Bevan, 2006). Governments and education systems are not prepared to cope with the problem and this is reflected in the lack of knowledge in pupils: only 33 per cent of males and 20 per cent of females between the ages of 15–24 were able to identify correct ways of HIV prevention and reject misconceptions of HIV transmission (UNAIDS, 2006) Although schools can barely cope with the enormous consequences of the HIV/AIDS pandemic, out-of-school children face an even greater risk as they are further marginalised from society. This is the single largest problem facing education and development and will continue to impact upon the EFA initiative and the MDGs.

IMPLICATIONS FOR EDUCATION STUDIES

Education in 'developing countries' is a vast topic that encompasses both political and economic spheres. By examining education in the context of development, one may pause and reflect upon their own education system and the values held and transported into another context. This strange reflection may result in critically questioning the purposes of education and the rationale for international aid. Learning about education in 'developing countries' opens up taken- for-granted notions of education and creates a global perspective of schools in various stages of development (see Chapter 7). It also reinforces the highly interconnected nature of education both inside and outside the systems of familiarity. By learning about the 'other', ethnocentrism – the tendency to view one's own cultural group as superior to others – is reduced. The 'other' becomes more accessible and no longer viewed as 'strange'. Instead, learning about education in developing countries becomes a practice of questioning long-held notions and critiquing values that become absorbed over time.

SUMMARY POINTS

- Development is a complex process and is highly contentious as it is laden with assumptions about what it means to be 'industrialised'.
- International aid is problematic as commitments are not kept and impositions are tied to aid. Local management and community-led initiatives are best practices for sustainable education development.
- The EFA initiative attempts to ensure access to education for 77 million school aged children. Background factors for out-of-school children are gender, residence (urban or rural), household wealth and mother's education.
- Retention of children in schools is a problem and this may be attributed to the low quality of education. Some aspects of quality education include use of home language and qualified teachers.
- Girls are marginalised from the education process due to cultural beliefs, household economics and concerns about safety. However, education and female empowerment is a complex relationship and one does not equate with the other.
- The Millennium Villages are a radical approach to the MDGs in which all aspects of development happen at once.
- Three factors affecting education in developing countries are colonisation, the knowledge economy and HIV/AIDS. HIV/AIDS poses the largest threat to the EFA initiative.

QUESTIONS FOR DISCUSSION

1   What is the goal of education in 'developing countries'? Is it to develop citizens who are able to participate fully in their societies?
2   When is international cooperation in education 'a good thing'?
3   Are there universal aspects to 'good' teaching that cross cultural and development borders?
4   Why do we fear the 'other'?

FURTHER READING

Knodel, J. (1997) The closing of the gender gap in schooling: the case of Thailand, *Comparative Education*, 33(1): 61–86. Provides a good account of girls' education in Thailand and has implications for the region of Asia.
Sachs, J. (1989) *Developing Country Debt and the World Economy*, Cambridge, MA: The National Bureau of Economic Research. Gives the background to the wider global economic issues.

REFERENCES

Annan, K. (2000) The future of this planet depends on women, *Inaugural address of the Secretary General of the United Nations*, June.

Belanger, D. and Liu, J. (2004) Social policy reforms and daughters' schooling in Vietnam, *International Journal of Educational Development*, 24(1): 23–38.

Bevan, S. (2006) Branson sees red over Dr Beetroot's Aids cure 'garbage', *The Guardian*, 29 October.

Blasser, M. (2000) Education and equity: new strategic directions for the excluded and marginalized, *Nine Years Since Jomtien: Is Education for all a Dream or Reality?* Proceedings from a one-day symposium at the Annual Conference of the Comparative and International Education Society, Office of Research on Education Policy, McGill University.

Chambers, R. (2000) Foreword to B. Cracknell, *Evaluating Development Aid: Issues, Problems, Solutions*, New Delhi: Sage Publications, pp. 21–4.

Dalin, P. (1994) *How Schools Improve: An International Report*, School Development Series, London: Cassell.

Fuller, B. (1986) *Raising School Quality in Developing Countries: What Investments Boost Learning*, Washington DC: World Bank.

Jayaweera, S. (1997) Women, education and empowerment in Asia, *Gender and Education*, 9(4): 411–23.

Khaniya, T. and Williams, J. (2004) Necessary but not sufficient: challenges to (implicit) theories of educational change: reform in Nepal's primary education system, *International Journal of Educational Development*, 24(3): 315–28.

Lewis, S. (2005) A gallery of alternatives: race against time. *Massey Lecture Series*, Autumn.

Make Poverty History campaign (2007) Make Poverty History Homepage. Online. Available http://www.makepovertyhistory.org (accessed 28 August 2007).

Merriam-Webster Online (2007) Merriam-Webster Online Dictionary. Online. Available http://www.m-w.com (accessed 26 August 2007).

Millennium Promise (2007) Millennium Promise homepage, Sect. Villages. Online. Available http://www.millenniumpromise.org/villages (accessed 28 August 2007).

Robinson-Pant, A. (2004) Education for women: whose values count? *Gender and Equality*, 16(4): 473–89.

Sachs, J. (1989) *Developing Country Debt and the World Economy*, Cambridge, MA: The National Bureau of Economic Research.

Sachs, J. (2005) *The End of Poverty: Economic Possibilities for our Time*, New York: Penguin Books.

Sperling, G. B. (2001) Toward universal education: making a promise, and keeping it, *Foreign Affairs*, 80(5): 7.

Sundersingh, J. (2006) Developing advocacy leaders among children orphaned by HIV and AIDS, *Asserting Children's Rights in the Era of HIV*, Rapporteur report by S. Msimang *16th International AIDS Conference*. Online. Available http://www.aids2006.org (accessed 4 December 2006).

UNESCO (2007a) United Nations Education Scientific and Cultural Organization. Sect. About EFA. Online. Available http://portal.unesco.org/education/en/ev.php-URL_ID=47044&URL_DO=DO_TOPIC&URL_SECTION=201.html (accessed 28 August 2007).

UNESCO (2007b) *Education for All Global Monitoring Report 2007: Strong Foundations Early Childhood Care and Education*, Summary. Online. Available http://www.efareport.unesco.org (accessed 28 August 2007).

United Nations (2007) UN Millennium Development Goals Homepage. Online. Available http://www.un.org/millenniumgoals (accessed 28 August 2007).

UNAIDS (2006) Figure 3.1: 2005 Country progress towards 2001 Commitment on HIV/AIDS global targets (low- and middle- income countries). *2006 Report on the Global AIDS Pandemic, Progress in Countries*. Online. Available http://www.unaids.org (accessed 5 September 2006).

Unterhalter, E. (2005) Global inequality, capabilities, social justice: the millennium development goal for gender equality in education, *International Journal of Education Development*, 25(2): 111–22.

Wambete, M. (2006) Capacity building for HIV positive teachers (KENEPOTE) in Kenya's education sector, *Education and AIDS: Challenges and Possibilities, 16th International AIDS Conference*. Online. Available http://www.aids2006.org (accessed 4 December 2006).

Wong, P. and Balestino, R. (2001) Prioritizing the education of marginalized young people in Brazil: a collaborative approach, *Journal of Education Policy*, 16(6): 597–618.

Xue, Y. (2005) Assessing educational aid: a critical analysis of the debate in basic education: global, national and local issues, Doctorate of Philosophy Transfer Paper. Oxford University, June.

10   Human Rights and Education

Heather Williamson

INTRODUCTION

We have a habit of thinking of human rights problems as other people's problems. Starvation in Africa is seen as a problem for Africans, not for us. We may sympathise and even telephone our credit card number to alleviate our conscience, but rarely do we see starvation as *our* problem. If we do recognise that in some ways we are partly responsible for such problems we tend to feel helpless given the quantity and scale of them. In reality it is the industrialised nations that hold the power to prolong or alleviate these problems. Frequently, instead of acknowledging their share of the responsibility for hunger, disease and conflict, they seem to abuse their power by continuing to work to their own advantage. If we believe in education we need to acknowledge that it has a role to play in helping us to understand our part in both the creation of these problems and their resolution.

This chapter is intended to help you to:

- understand the relationship between moral philosophy and the claim to human rights;
- recognise your own assumptions, and those of others about human rights;
- apply an understanding of human rights theory to education policy.

MORAL THEORIES

Before we look at the role of education we need to understand the moral philosophy that is used to justify the claim to human rights. Hudson (1980) argued that for a century philosophers had been torn between two overarching views of morality: a *utilitarian* one, now generally recognised as a consequentialist theory because it is rooted in the idea that we can only come to understand what is the morally right thing to do by assessing the consequences of our action, and an *intuitionist* one, which claims that there are at least some moral principles that cannot be subordinated to the principle of utility. Most moral philosophy is broadly either utilitarian or intuitionist.

In its simplest form, the principle of utility suggests that the morally right action is the one that provides for the 'greatest happiness of the greatest number of people' regardless of the consequences for individuals (John Stuart Mill, 1861). In contrast the intuitionist claims that there are some actions that should be forbidden however beneficial the consequences of such action might seem. Determinists argue that both intuitionists and utilitarians are wrong in assuming that human beings have free will and can choose what to do. They argue that all of our choices and actions are the result of factors beyond our control. While determinism is accepted by some people opponents claim that there remain arguments for believing that human beings can initiate change. The most common of these rests on an appeal to our subjective experience. It claims that as individuals we are constantly aware of being in a position where we must choose between alternatives. Our experience is reflected in our language. We talk of having *intentions* and failing to act in accordance with them.

We experience *regret* because we believe we could have behaved differently. If our choices were so predetermined that we could not initiate change then it would be logical to give up trying to overcome the problems we identify within society. Many people therefore prefer to hold on to the belief that they can make decisions to act to bring about change. They argue that people such as William Wilberforce (1759–1833) who campaigned against slavery succeed in initiating change.

Let us assume that we have at least some measure of free will and accept Hudson's broad distinction between utilitarians and intuitionists. How then should we judge the morality of an action? Should we judge it by its consequences or do we claim that some actions are always morally wrong, regardless of them appearing to result in beneficial consequences? There are problems with both suggestions. A committed utilitarian might want to argue that the Al Qaeda suspects imprisoned on Cuba in 2002 should have been tortured to release information. They might want to claim that access to this information would have resulted in the greatest happiness for the greatest number of people. The information collected could have been used to save many more lives than those lost when the twin towers were destroyed on 11 September 2001. The intuitionist would regard torture as morally wrong because the perpetrators would have been violating the *rights* of the prisoners. To put it in the terms of Immanuel Kant (1786) the prisoners would have been treated as a 'means to someone else's end' and not as 'ends in themselves'. The intuitionist would argue that we should not use other people for our own ends however beneficial the consequences may seem. Vlastos (1984) argues that we need to distinguish between merit and worth. Human beings, he claims, have worth regardless of how depraved their behaviour may be and society should not violate their fundamental rights to suit its own ends. Critics of this view who take an extreme utilitarian position would argue that the suggestion that human beings have rights, just because they are human beings, is an illusion. Rights can only be claimed in the context of a contract, which depends on the will of the majority. Whichever position we prefer to take up it is now common for people to assume they have rights and to seek recognition of these in the legal system.

WHAT DO WE MEAN BY RIGHTS?

In the seventeenth and eighteenth centuries the common people found it increasingly necessary to free themselves from the tyrannical power of dynastic monarchies exercised by virtue of belief in the divine right of kings. The English revolution (1642–9) led to the execution of Charles I so destroying the king and his absolute power. The philosopher John Locke (1690) argued that human beings should respect what he called the law of nature by recognising the rights of all individuals to their own life, liberty and property. Almost a century later in America the colony sought to exert its independence from George III. In 1776 Thomas Jefferson wrote in his preamble to the complaints of the colony against the king, 'We hold these truths self-evident that all men are created equal; that they are endowed by their creator with certain inalienable rights; that amongst these are life, liberty and the pursuit of happiness.' In France the revolution of 1789 aimed at establishing that all human beings had the right to liberty, equality and fraternity. Thomas Paine (1791) is often credited with fermenting many of the ideas that led to the movements to assert the liberty of the individual. He claims in *The Rights of Man* that sovereignty resides in human beings and is not bestowed by members of a class or nation.

Although in our own time many different prefixes to rights are used such as fundamental rights and universal rights the term 'human rights' remains appropriate because it draws attention to the essential point that rights are possessed by people by virtue of the fact that they are *human* beings. These rights are perceived as *universal* because all human beings have them and *natural* because they do not depend on institutions created by human societies. This allows them to be regarded as independent of governments and as a standard by which governments can be judged.

The rights to life, liberty and property are often regarded as *negative* rights. This is because these rights originate in the claim for freedom from interference by others. Some people believe that these are fundamental rights and the only ones with which we should concern ourselves. Even the claim to these rights is challenged in different ways and debates within society reflect these challenges. Whether any individual or group of individuals should own land is an example of such a debate. It can be argued that the Earth should belong to all creatures and no human being should claim dominion over a portion of it. *Positive* rights are those associated with maintaining a reasonable standard of living and are sometimes referred to as welfare, economic or social rights. These are rights that depend on society or institutions within society to assert and maintain. They include the right to work, to health care and to education.

Following the Second World War in 1948 the Universal Declaration of Human Rights (UDHR) was drawn up. Since then there has been a proliferation of declarations and conventions, clarifying and elaborating the clauses in the UDHR. These declarations may be nothing more than moral prescriptions. Their power as a moral force depends on who is prepared to sign them. Some sets of rights accepted by governments are incorporated into law and become *legal* rights. The European Convention of Human Rights (ECHR) was signed in Rome in 1950 and the UK was the first nation state to ratify the convention on 18 March, 1951. The Convention was finally incorporated into English Law when the Human Rights Act came into force in 1998. These various instruments rest on the appeal to a rights-based morality that assumes that all human beings have rights and it is therefore the responsibility of all human beings to respect the rights of all other human beings.

The use of human rights language is now common and has been used in the struggles for equal opportunities for women and against colonialism, apartheid and oppression in the Soviet Bloc. Globalisation may now be increasing a shared sense of the inevitable interrelationship and interdependence between peoples across the world that makes the language of rights even more attractive. There has been a developing recognition that a rights-based morality, rather than one based on the principle of utility, may be necessary if we are to resolve some of the major problems in the world.

Only by accepting that all human beings have rights are we able to engage appropriately with these problems. The work of the UN is based on the premise of a rights-based morality. In practice this rights-based morality seeks to ensure that the global community of human beings actively works to secure the rights of all human beings. The right to life implies that the world community, represented currently by the UN, has a responsibility to intervene wherever life is in danger. This danger may come from active attempts to destroy the life of others, as in ethnic cleansing and genocide, or in passive cases where people are dying from starvation or disease.

Is it possible to justify a rights-based morality?

Some people would claim that it is self-evident that human beings have these rights and therefore the claim to rights needs no justification. Nevertheless a number of justifications are possible. The most significant of these is provided by John Rawls (1972). He suggests that we should imagine ourselves behind a 'veil of ignorance' where we know nothing about our own position or prospects. In this 'original position' we are invited as individuals to come together to decide on the principles of the society in which we would like to live. Rawls argues that we would agree on two principles. The first would be to allow everyone to have as much liberty as possible consistent with equal liberty for everyone else and the second would allow for liberties, powers, opportunities and wealth to be distributed equally unless an unequal distribution works to the advantage of society in general and particularly to the advantage of the most vulnerable groups in society. Rawls believes we would be aware that we might be born into a vulnerable group in society where, for example, we were disabled or had no source of clean water. Given this, we would wish to develop a society that would take the responsibility for alleviating these difficulties for us, a fair society in which we knew we would be cared for.

Rawls's views are contentious. He has been accused of assuming that other people would share his instincts and take up the same cautious position. It is suggested that some of us may choose to gamble in the hope that we might be born lucky! A much more significant challenge to Rawls comes from Nozick (1975). He argues that Rawls' position ignores the concept of entitlement and suggests that we are entitled to keep what we earn. He accuses Rawls of asking us to imagine that goods are just 'there', not worked for or earned. It is clear that some people are capable of, and do make, a more significant contribution to society than others. We might suggest a brain surgeon deserves more, should be paid more and should be entitled to keep it. However, this argument ignores the circumstances of our birth, our genetic inheritance and our upbringing and access to education.

What Rawls really shows us is that if we wish to claim rights for ourselves we need a new kind of social contract. We need to take seriously our obligations to work towards a fairer society. We need to be willing to sacrifice our own interests for the interests of others. Whether we accept the arguments of Rawls or reject them, we need to recognise that his work has been appropriated in the defence of liberal democracy. Liberal democracies have begun to use it to empower them to take action in a way that allows them to set aside one of the key precepts known as 'The Peace of Westphalia' (1648). According to this key precept nation states were inviolable and each agreed not to interfere with another's internal affairs. So peace is maintained, but at the cost of not intervening to rectify injustice. However, by claiming that all human beings have rights, we are claiming that human rights are universal. If human beings have rights then inevitably someone has a corresponding responsibility. Having a responsibility implies a duty to act. This means that we have the responsibility and duty to protect the rights, at least those of the life and liberty of all other human beings, not just those in our own nation state. Liberal democracies now use this argument to justify the claim that it is morally right to intervene in another country where human rights are being abused.

Cultural rights

There are those who argue that the UDHR and the rights claimed within it are just another expression of Western imperialism. The values embodied in it are the values of the Western powers and we are wrong to project these as universal. The argument here is that the West may not like the values it sees in operation in other countries, but within the context of the culture of that nation state they have a validity of their own by ensuring a society that is socially cohesive. We may be in sympathy with this, but we have to ask ourselves whether it was appropriate for the UN to intervene in Afghanistan when the Taliban denied women access to education or whether currently the UN should intervene to stop genocide in Darfur or starvation in Zimbabwe where the government is regarded as corrupt. The justification given for intervening in these cases is that there are some values that transcend culture. Of these the most generally held remain the right to life and liberty. If any of the customs or practices of other cultures conflict with the right to life or liberty then life and liberty must take priority. This allows those who accept rights-based morality, not merely the right to challenge cultural practices they believe conflict with the right to life or liberty, but the *responsibility* to do so wherever such practices are found.

The Convention of the Rights of the Child

If we accept that all human beings have rights, at least the fundamental rights of life and liberty, we must accept that children as well as adults have the same fundamental rights. The Convention of the Rights of the Child came into force as international law in 1990. This is the UN convention and has been signed by 193 nation states. Only the USA and Somalia are not parties to the Convention. A superficial examination of the Convention could lead you to the belief that the English education system is compliant with it. The clauses on education are largely implemented. A more thorough analysis demonstrates that the clauses fall into three main areas: participation, provision and protection. In general there is acceptance of the need to comply with the clauses on provision and protection but little understanding or commitment to the prior requirements of participation. Article 12 of the Convention reads:

> States Parties shall assure to the child who is capable of forming his or her own views the right to express those views freely in all matters affecting the child, the views of the child being given due weight in accordance with the age and maturity of the child.
>
> For this purpose, the child shall in particular be provided the opportunity to be heard in any judicial and administrative proceedings affecting the child, either directly, or through a representative or an appropriate body, in a manner consistent with the procedural rules of national law (UN, 1989)

The Convention makes it clear that a child has the same rights as an adult. The role of the adult is not to exercise the rights of the child *for* the child but to provide appropriate direction to the child in the exercise '*by the child*' of the rights recognised within the Convention.

There is a case to be made for the liberation of children just as there was for the liberation of black people, women and the disabled. Children should be recognised as young people and no longer excluded from decisions affecting their own lives. Before movements demanding the liberation of women or of black people, men claimed that they knew what was in the best interests of women and white people believed that they knew what was in the best interests of black people. As adults we believe that we know what is in the best interests of children. We believe our major responsibility is to protect children and provide for them. The Convention on the Rights of the Child makes it clear that our priority should be to ensure that the rights of participation are fully respected.

The Education Reform Act (HMSO, 1988) does not address the role of the child in its own education. The Children Act (HMSO, 1989), in marked contrast, does require the child's voice to be heard. When a court is discharging its duties in respect of a particular child the court is required to have particular regard for the 'ascertainable wishes and feelings' of the child concerned. If an infant's views are expected to be taken seriously in the case of divorce or adoption, why not in its education? Harris (1982) argues that the distinction between adults and children based on the supposed incapacity of children couldn't be sustained. Were we to use the criteria of competence to decide who should have full political status, then many adults would need to be excluded and many children included in the numbers of those granted such status. Lindley (1986) argues that we deny children the opportunity to exercise an autonomous choice. A genuine respect for young people would generate an educational programme that would lead young people to claim control over their own lives and ultimately to seek the power to vote.

HUMAN RIGHTS AND EDUCATION

It is generally recognised that the main aim of government policy over the last thirty years has been the maintenance and development of economic strength, to ensure that the economy has an ever-greater competitive edge in a global economy (see Chapter 1). Our government has put faith in encouraging high academic achievement in order to ensure that young people will be in a position to gain employment in a thriving economy, but could it be that we are already failing young people by pursuing this path to the exclusion of others? Given the major changes facing our world it seems appropriate to look again at the aim of education. Should the fundamental aim be to ensure that the next generation exercise both their rights and their responsibilities within a global context where all human beings have the same fundamental rights to life and liberty and the same responsibility to exercise these rights and responsibilities? If this is to happen our expectations of young people need to change and the opportunities we offer them may also need to change. The first priority might be to create opportunities for young people to take responsibility for themselves, to become independent and self-supporting. A second priority might be to empower young people to work to create a fairer and more just world in the hope of removing poverty, disease and conflict.

The world is changing. Developments in communication have led to an understanding that we live in a global community in which individuals and nation states are interdependent. In this world the curriculum needs to have a global focus rather than a narrow national one. At least three major challenges are facing the next generation: poverty, global warming and a significant shift in the balance of power across from West to East. The next generation need to be prepared to face these challenges.

Poverty

A rights-based morality requires us to recognise that it is necessary to 'countervail our limited sympathies and their most damaging effects' (Warnock, 1971: 168). If the rights of all human beings on the globe are to be respected the desire to maintain our own standard of living at the expense of other human beings needs to be resisted. It is necessary to understand the role of human beings in causing poverty, disease and conflict, as well as finding the means to eliminate them. It is necessary to understand, not just the achievements of the past and present generation but much more their failures. It may not be an exaggeration to claim that the current generation, in presiding over world poverty, has been as guilty of as great a crime against humanity as those who prolonged the slave trade. It may not be desirable to sacrifice an ever-higher standard of living but if the principle that all human beings have rights is accepted then it follows that there is a responsibility to act in accordance with this principle and seek to secure the rights of others, if necessary, at the expense of our own standard of living.

Global warming

It is now generally accepted that to avoid the most serious effects of global warming it will be necessary for human beings to change many of their attitudes and values (see Chapter 11). As Al Gore (2006) said this may be an 'inconvenient truth' but the evidence of global warming now seems overwhelming. The next generation need to understand these changes and their perceived consequences not only because they may need to learn to survive in a very different environment, but also because they have a responsibility to ensure that fellow human beings on the globe are also able to maintain a reasonable standard of living.

The balance of power across the world

In recent times the economy of the West has been in the ascendancy. The Western nations have been able to protect their own high standard of living. The growth, in particular, of the economies of China and India is poised to threaten the future of the Western economies. So far the response of our government has been to try to improve the educational level of children in the hope that the skills attained will ensure an ever-improving economy and so protect the current standard of living. This may be important but is there also a case for considering a different approach that recognises the challenges of poverty and global warming and encourages the next generation to become self-supporting?

The recognition that young people should be allowed to exercise their rights and to be expected to carry out their responsibilities together with acceptance of these three major challenges should alert us to the need for a review of our current education system. It seems inappropriate to rely on economic growth alone to secure a reasonable standard of living for everyone across the world.

CONCLUSION – BEYOND THE CURRICULUM

If we are to respect the rights of young people to make their own decisions, they need to be allowed to take responsibility for themselves and to become self-supporting. Young people in some cultures across the world already carry responsibility for maintaining themselves, and often for parents and siblings. It is necessary to recognise that young people can take responsibility at a much younger age than is currently permitted in Western society and that they are denied this fundamental right, often at their long-term cost. They are imprisoned in the values, beliefs and practices of our culture with little recognition of the changed world in which they are likely to live. If we are to allow young people to exercise their rights and responsibilities and to become self-supporting they need to be offered new opportunities alongside formal education.

All young people should have the right to earn money to feed and clothe themselves and to provide themselves with shelter. There are twenty-four hours in the day sufficient to ensure that young people could participate in employment as well as in formal education and take part in physical activity, and it might be wise to expect them to do so. One way of providing these opportunities might be through a series of informal apprenticeships. Adults over sixty who lived through the aftermath of the Second World War and now live on a pension could offer very young people help in learning how to feed themselves well but at very low cost. People with allotments could share their skills in growing food. Builders could offer the opportunity for young people to work alongside the building trades to learn the skills needed to provide shelter. Payment could follow once skills were mastered. In this way young people could be encouraged to become self-supporting by the time they reach puberty and long before the end of formal schooling. This would have the added advantage of making it possible for young people to have children while they are young and healthy.

The welfare state has put the protection of young people before their right to participation. If they are to survive in what may prove to be an increasingly hostile world they need to be encouraged to exercise their fundamental right to freedom.

SUMMARY POINTS

- There are two overarching views of morality. One is based on utilitarianism, which argues that morality is about satisfying the greatest good of the greatest number of people. The other is based on the claim that all human beings have rights, and morality is about respecting those rights.
- If we accept a rights-based morality we must accept that all young people have the same rights as adults and also have the same responsibilities.
- Young people should be expected to earn their own living alongside formal education and to become self-supporting by the time they reach puberty.

QUESTIONS FOR DISCUSSION

1   Should human beings be deprived of their rights if they do not carry out their responsibilities?
2   Should young people be expected to earn their own living as well as attending formal schooling?
3   Do we want to encourage all young people to become self-supporting by the time they reach puberty? If so, what strategies need to be put in place?
4   How would the school curriculum need to change to allow young people to develop an understanding of the responsibility the West has for human rights problems and their own responsibility for assisting in resolving them?

FURTHER READING

Falk, A. (2000) *Human Rights Horizons*, London: Routledge. Falk gives an in-depth study of the pursuit of justice through the development of human rights in a globalised world.

Gore, A. (2006) *An Inconvenient Truth*, DVD, Paramount Home Entertainment. Harrison-Barbet, A. (1990) *Mastering Philosophy*, New York: Palgrave. Sections 6 and 7 (pp. 185–275) provide a useful introduction to moral and political philosophy.

Richardson, R. (1990) *Daring to be a Teacher*, Stoke-on-Trent: Trentham Books. Chapter 4 (pp. 29–44) 'Learning towards justice' argues that the purpose of education is to transform society to make it less unequal and less unjust.

Symonides, J. (2000) *Human Rights: Concepts and Standards*, Aldershot: UNESCO. This is a comprehensive treatment of both the concept of rights and the whole range of rights that are now embodied in human rights instruments.

REFERENCES

Gore, A. (2006) *An Inconvenient Truth*, DVD, Paramount Home Entertainment.

Harris, J. (1982) The political status of children, in K. Graham (ed.) *Contemporary Political Philosophy*, Cambridge: Cambridge University Press.

HMSO (1988) Education Reform Act, London: HMSO.

HMSO (1989) The Children Act, London: HMSO.

Hudson, W.D. (1980) *A Century of Moral Philosophy*, London: Lutterworth.

Kant, I. (1785) *Grundlegung zur Metaphysik der Sitten*, trans. H.J. Paton (1948) *Groundwork of the Metaphysic of Morals*, London: Hutchinson.

Lindley, R. (1986) *Autonomy*, London: Macmillan.

Locke, J. (1690) *Two Treatises of Government*, ed. P. Laslett, Cambridge: Cambridge University Press, 1967.

Mill, J.S. (1861) *Utilitarianism*, ed. M. Warnock, London: Collins/Fontana, 1962.

Nozick, R. (1975) *Anarchy, State and Utopia*, Oxford: Blackwell.

Paine, T. (1791) *The Rights of Man*, Harmondsworth: Penguin, 1969.

Rawls, J.A. (1972) *A Theory of Justice*, Oxford: Oxford University Press.

UN (1989) Convention of the Rights of the Child, London: HMSO.

Vlastos, G. (1984) Justice and equality, in J. Waldron (ed.) *Theories of Rights*, Oxford: Oxford University Press.

Warnock, G.J. (1971) *The Object of Morality*, London: Methuen.

11 Education for Sustainability

David Hicks

INTRODUCTION

Why do teachers need to know about issues to do with environment and development? How can we help young people understand the current crisis of sustainability? What resources are available to assist in teaching about such matters? This chapter sets out to answer questions such as these and, in particular, explores:

- The rationale for an education that explores issues of sustainability.
- Educational initiatives that have contributed to education for sustainability.
- Debates about the meaning and nature of sustainability

Put at its most simple any human activity is sustainable if it can continue fairly indefinitely without causing harm to people or planet. Alternatively, any human activity that results in ongoing harm to people or planet is the opposite – unsustainable.

RATIONALE

In 1992 and 2002 two of the most important events of the last fifty years took place – in Brazil and South Africa – the Earth Summits, attended by leaders from most countries of the world and activists from numerous international non-governmental organisations (NGOs). Why did so many people come together and what did they discuss? They came because since the early 1970s it has been recognised that human activity is increasingly threatening the environment or biosphere – that narrow zone of earth, air, water – on which all life (plants, creatures, humans) depends. They also came because since the early 1970s it has increasingly been recognised that issues of development, i.e. global wealth and poverty, are threatening people's life chances in both rich and poor countries of the world. The welfare of planet and people, issues of environment and development, are thus seen as inextricably related. The term 'sustainable development' is used both to describe these joint concerns and also to highlight what needs to be achieved.

Environmental issues

Many crucial environmental issues have been in the news over the last few years including: the impact of climate change; the safety or otherwise of genetically modified (GM) crops; sources of energy – nuclear or renewable; food safety and the nature of farming; transport problems in our cities. In different ways each of these affects daily life in our own communities. Whilst issues of environment as such are not the focus of this chapter, the way in which education responds to them is. This reflects growing governmental and public awareness of a range of sustainability related issues that we need to face and creatively resolve (see, for example, *The Ecologist* and *Green Futures*).

People respond to such issues in a variety of ways. Many individuals and local authorities are aware of the need to use resources wisely so they recycle paper, glass and plastics and try not to waste water or electricity. In relation to transport many people try to use bus, train and bike as well as car, they may be interested in countryside/urban conservation and in diet and healthy eating. Going a step further we find people who profess a particular interest in environmental matters; they may belong to Friends of the Earth or Greenpeace and perhaps belong to a local wildlife or woodland trust. They are prepared to write to members of parliament (MPs) and newspapers to make their views known and to argue the environmental case.

The most committed and concerned will be expert on specific issues, interested in supporting particular campaigns. They will see connections between issues and espouse a deeper green lifestyle: using renewable energy, sharing a car, living more sustainably. They may be prepared to attend protests and, if necessary, to take direct action in support of chosen causes. What people see as the problem, the causes of the problem and solutions to the problem will vary, of course, depending on their ideological perspective (Pepper, 1996).

Development issues

Many crucial development issues have been in the news over the last few years including: the impact of World Bank and International Monetary Fund (IMF) restructuring policies on the economies of less developed countries (LDCs); plans to cancel LDC debt; the impact of AIDS in Africa; refugees and migrants; patenting of seeds by agribusiness transnational corporations (TNCs); concerns about the impact of globalisation. Many of these issues impact on our own communities too. Development issues as such are not the focus of this chapter but the way in which education responds to them is. This reflects increased public awareness of issues relating to global wealth and poverty and the need for their successful resolution (see, for example, the *New Internationalist*).

It would be true to say that people tend to be more aware of environmental issues than development issues. However, there are still different levels of response and concern. Many people take part in occasional giving to NGOs when particular disasters occur and are reported in the news. This may be to do with famine, lack of water or homelessness, for example. Going a step further there are others who take a particular interest in development issues. They may belong to NGOs such as Oxfam, Christian Aid or Amnesty International. They will be prepared to write to MPs and newspapers to make their views known about appropriate development.

The most committed will be knowledgeable on particular issues, interested in supporting particular campaigns, whether to do with debt, human rights, child labour or supporting a particular community. They will see connections between issues and espouse a less material lifestyle – becoming an ethical consumer and investor, living more sustainably. They may attend demonstrations, e.g. anti-globalisation and take direct action in support of chosen causes. What people see as the problem, the causes of the problem and solutions to the problem will again vary depending on their ideological perspective.

Up until the late 1980s, environmental issues and development issues had largely been seen as separate matters. There were environmentalists and development experts, each with their own interests, government departments and NGOs. Increasingly, however, it was recognised that the welfare of people and the planet were two sides of the same coin. This was officially endorsed at the 1992 Earth Summit when the term sustainable development was used as shorthand to embrace both these interrelated concerns.

Education for sustainability

Education for sustainability (EfS), sometimes also known as education for sustainable development, is a post-Rio phenomenon of the 1990s that highlights these two major concerns (environment and development) in order to prepare young people more effectively for life in the twenty-first century. The importance of education for sustainability in the curriculum is set out by the DfES (2007) in the National Framework for Sustainable Schools.

> Sustainable development is a way of thinking about how we organise our lives and work – including our education system – so that we don't destroy our most precious resource, the planet. From over-fishing to global warming, our way of life is placing increasing burden on the planet, which cannot be sustained. Things which were once taken for granted such as a secure supply of energy or a stable climate do not look so permanent now. We need to help people in all parts of the world to find solutions that improve their quality of life without storing up problems for the future, or impacting unfairly on other people's lives. Sustainable development means much more than recycling bottles or giving money to charity. It is about thinking and working in a profoundly different way.

In order to understand how this important shift in education came about we need to know something about the allied educational fields that were precursors to and influences on education for sustainability (Goldstein and Selby, 2000). These are environmental education, development education and global education, each of which had their origins in the 1960s and 1970s.

CONTRIBUTING FIELDS

Environmental education

Environmental education (EE) has a long history stretching back to the 1960s (Palmer, 1998). It embraces both the natural and built environment although greater emphasis has often tended to be put on the former. The natural environment is seen as a proper focus of educational concern for several important reasons, including the following.

Source of all life

All life depends on the biosphere, that thin film of matter around the planet that supports life, i.e. the soils, water, atmosphere and plants that, together with solar insolation, make Earth a habitable place. Students therefore need to know about the nature of the biosphere and the ways in which it works.

Awe and wonder

The rising and setting of the sun, the turning of year, the ability of the land to bring forth water and food in abundance, our companion creatures, have all long been sources of awe and wonder. Students need to appreciate the natural world because it is a source of beauty, awe, wonder and healing, all prerequisites to human well-being.

Human impact

Humans have always had an impact on the natural environment but in the last two hundred years this has begun to threaten the well-being of the biosphere itself. Worldwide we find: desertification, endangered species, dumping of toxic waste, global warming. Students should be aware of these impacts and understand how to minimise their contribution to this process.

Over the last thirty years the emphasis in environmental education has shifted, from conservation of the countryside in the 1960/1970s (plants, trees, hedgerows, wildlife), to national and global problems in the 1970/1980s (pollution, resource depletion, global warming) and issues of sustainability in the 1990s. International developments in environmental education over this period were very much influenced by NGO activity. In particular UNESCO and the UN Environmental Programme (UNEP) promoted environmental education at milestone international conferences in the 1970s–1980s and gradually agreed definitions of its nature and scope (Palmer, 1998).

In the 1990s the importance of environmental education was officially signalled by documents such as *Teaching Environmental Matters Through the National Curriculum* (SCAA, 1996). In particular this shows how all subjects in the national curriculum can help contribute to an environmental perspective. The greatest body of experience in environmental education lies with NGOs such as the World Wide Fund for Nature (2007) and the National Association for Environmental Education (2007). Each offers invaluable advice and support for teachers and has its own publications and website. Environmental education has made a major contribution to the emergence of the new field of education for sustainability.

Development education

During the late 1960s some of the main development NGOs, i.e. those focusing on issues of global poverty, began to wonder whether they should take on an educational role as well as the fund-raising that was their main aim. Partly this was because they felt that if the public were more informed about issues of global poverty then they would be more likely to give generously to important aid projects. The term development education (DE) was thus coined to refer to the need for education, both formal and informal, which addressed issues of poverty and injustice. In the early 1970s NGOs such as Oxfam and Christian Aid set up their own education programmes. These were run by experienced teachers who were clear that their role was an educational one and they were not, unlike the parent organisation, about campaigning and fund-raising.

During the 1970s and 1980s a number of Development Education Centres (DECs) were set up around the country to provide resources and support on development issues for teachers. At this time the focus of DE was very much on problems of poverty and injustice together with an awareness that issues of racism and discrimination needed challenging both in the UK and globally. The umbrella organisation for DE activity and initiatives in the UK is the Development Education Association (2007) based in London. Some UK DECs have developed impressive resources for teachers, are involved in continuing professional development and are well integrated into the work and life of their own local communities. Two long-standing and excellent examples are Teachers in Development Education (TIDE) (2007) based in Birmingham and Manchester Development Education Project (2007). Both websites are well worth exploring to illustrate good DE practice.

The DEA (2007) sees development education as:

- exploring the links between people living in the 'developed' countries of the North with those of the 'developing' South, enabling people to understand the links between their own lives and those of people throughout the world;
- increasing understanding of the economic, social, political and environmental forces which shape our lives;
- developing the skills, attitudes and values which enable people to work together to take action to bring about change and take control of their own lives;
- working towards achieving a more just and a more sustainable world in which power and resources are more equitably shared.

During the 1980s it became increasingly clear to many development educators that issues relating to the environment, to peace and conflict, to human rights were also inextricably bound up with issues of development. Development education has thus made a major contribution to the emergence of education for sustainability (see Chapter 9).

More recently it has been realised that rather than just pressing for the inclusion of issues relating to inequality and injustice in the curriculum, what was missing more broadly was a 'global dimension' in education. This is the term that is now commonly used in the UK to refer to the need for a range of global issues to be explored in the local and global community.

Global education

At the same time that DE was emerging in the 1970s other radical educators were arguing that a range of global issues, not just development, needed to be included in the school curriculum (Hicks and Holden, 2007). The term originally used for this in the 1970s–1980s in the UK was 'world studies'. Unlike development education world studies was not an initiative tied to NGOs, but more likely to be based in institutions of higher education. In the 1990s the term world studies was replaced by the more international term global education, which is the subject of Chapter 7 in this book.

Practitioners of development education and global education played an important part in raising awareness of the need for a 'global dimension' in the curriculum, now recognised by the DfES (2005). Such official recognition has led to greater awareness of the need for local–global matters, including issues of sustainability, to be explored in the classroom.

It is worth noting that practitioners and advocates of education for sustainability may still sometimes betray their EE or DE origins by the way in which they discuss the field, i.e. some may place more emphasis on environment and others on development. Education for sustainability should be different, however, in giving equal weight to the welfare of both people (social) and the planet (environmental) and the interrelationships between the two. However, it is likely that the meanings of sustainability will always be contested as a result of people's differing beliefs and values about the nature of society.

DEBATES

In its daily practice education for sustainability needs to show awareness of the contested nature of sustainability, i.e. the fact that different political ideologies and worldviews analyse both the perceived problems and possible solutions to them in varying ways. It is important to remind ourselves at this point too that the notion of sustainability can only be seen in relation to its counterpart of unsustainability. They are two sides of the same coin, but a complex one because, as Davison (2001) points out in his *Technology and the Contested Meanings of Sustainability*, our unsustainable Western lifestyle arises out of the industrial revolution and its subsequent technologies that have lead to what we call 'progress' for the few.

> The triumphant history of industrialization is shadowed by a history of social oppression and ecological degradation. The vast, unprecedented affluence that has concentrated in highly technological societies is shadowed by poverty and pollution, the extent of which is also vast and unprecedented. This is so because much of our technology persistently lacks the ability to sustain ecological flourishing and social well-being (p. 59).

One of the best known, but not necessarily most useful, definitions of sustainable development is from the World Commission on Environment and Development (cited in Fien and Tilbury, 2002, p. 2): 'Sustainable development is development that meets the needs of the present without compromising the ability of future generations to meet their own needs.' Radicals, however, argue that neoliberal models of development narrowly focus on economic growth as a measure of progress and discount other costs. Thus actually: i) some people benefit at the expense of others; ii) people benefit at the expense of the environment; iii) people today benefit at the expense of future generations. This is patently unsustainable.

One definition of sustainability might therefore emphasise: i) human well-being: increased levels of social and economic well-being for all, especially the least advantaged; ii) environmental value: increased emphasis on the need to protect the biosphere on which all life depends; iii) future generations: should inherit at least as much wealth, natural and human, as we ourselves inherited.

Growth versus development

A technocentric worldview may deny that there is a crisis of environment/development or, alternatively, sees the route towards a more sustainable future as based chiefly on technical solutions and government regulation. This worldview is a reformist one in that it believes economic growth should continue as before but in a more sustainable way, i.e. sustainable growth. It does not involve any radical rethinking of Western consumerism (Hicks, 2007).

An ecocentric worldview sees the world economic system itself as in need of radical change and social, economic and environmental goals are seen as being of equal importance. Only this, radicals argue, will lead to a more sustainable world. The need for human well-being must not damage the environment, economic growth must promote equity and conservation must not diminish human well-being. This would require a major democratisation of prevailing patterns of power. Davison (2001) points out that although sustainable development has become part of international policy language, its meaning is still widely contested due to fundamental ideological differences. The language of technocratic sustainability, he argues, obscures the deeper sources of what is unsustaining in Western society.

When you come across the terms sustainable growth and sustainable development therefore do not take them at face value. Read between the lines to decide whether the writer is taking a technocentric or ecocentric stance. Notions of technocratic sustainability, of course, derive directly from the neoliberal political and economic ideology (Apple, 2006). It also represents a very Northern view of sustainability.

North versus South

The 1992 Earth Summit highlighted major North–South tensions as the rich and poor countries of the world often saw the problem and their solutions in quite different terms. Rich Northern governments wanted poorer Southern countries to be responsible stewards of the Earth. Southern governments wanted the North to help eradicate poverty. To the poorer countries of the South 'caring for the environment' can seem a luxury that most people cannot afford.

The South saw imperialism, neocolonialism and the strategies of the IMF and World Bank as largely responsible for unsustainable development. They resented Northern demands that they should not exploit their own natural resources for their own benefit accusing the North of environmental neocolonialism. They also saw the corporate neocolonialism of the TNCs as a major factor in supporting unsustainable global practices (Cohen and Kennedy, 2007).

A multidimensional model

A more complex and much richer view of sustainability is seen in the four-dimensional model put forward by UNESCO (2001) in *Teaching and Learning for a Sustainable Future*. It raises questions about what truly sustains us, why it does and how it does this. It illustrates and draws out the different dimensions of sustainability and the values that underpin them. It points out that a holistic or multidimensional notion of sustainability must encompass the ecological, economic, social and political dimensions of life. The *ecological* dimension requires care and protection of the biosphere as our essential life support system. The *economic* dimension requires a society in which jobs and income are protected but not to the detriment of the environment. The *social* dimension requires a society in which peace and equity are valued and present. The *political* dimension requires a democratic society in which both power and decision making are participatory in nature. Models such as this highlight the interconnectedness of all human experience and the ways in which the welfare of people and the welfare of the planet are inextricably intertwined. Working towards such a sustainable society requires personal, social and political change locally, nationally and globally. It would indeed be a radical venture.

These differences and tensions are also going to be present when issues of sustainability are explored in the classroom. Is the form of education for sustainability, as practised in school, one which is non-critical of the existing social/economic order, and which gives a non-problematised and non-political view of sustainability? Or is it a more critical form that suggests that fundamental socio–political changes in lifestyle are needed in order to create a more sustainable society? Sterling (2001) goes further and argues that education for sustainability requires a complete new educational paradigm that would be more far-reaching in its social, environmental, economic and educational implications.

SUPPORT AND GUIDANCE

In order to find out more about how issues of sustainability can be explored at different key stages and in relation to particular subject areas one should consult the DfES website on sustainable schools (2007). Curriculum developments in Wales are also interesting because education for sustainability and global citizenship have been brought together to create a single cross-curricular dimension. Education for sustainable development and global citizenship (ACCAC, 2002) is thus about:

- the links between society, economy and environment and between our own lives and those of people throughout the world;
- the needs and rights of both present and future generations;
- the relationships between power, resources and human rights;
- the local and global implications of everything we do and the actions that individuals and organisations can take in response to local and global issues.

The DfES (2007) strategy on Sustainable Schools identifies eight 'doorways' into education for sustainability. These are: i) food and drink; ii) energy and water; iii) travel and traffic; iv) purchasing and waste; v) buildings and grounds; vi) inclusion and participation; vii) local well-being; viii) global citizenship. Excellent ways in which such themes can creatively be explored in the classroom are found in Webster's (2004) *Rethink, Refuse, Reduce ... Education for Sustainability in a Changing World* and Stone and Barlow's (2005) *Ecological Literacy: Educating our Children for a Sustainable World*.

In order to work towards a sustainable future we need to be able to envision some of the features of such a society. The exploration of preferred futures, which is central to any notion of education for sustainability or indeed good education, is the subject of Chapter 12 in this book.

CONCLUSION

This chapter has set out the rationale for an education that explores issues of sustainability by looking at some of the critical global issues that face us in the twenty-first century. It has highlighted the educational initiatives that preceded and have contributed to the emergence of education for sustainability – environmental education, development education and global education. The contested nature of sustainability and of sustainable development has also been highlighted by identifying some of the ongoing ideological debates, and issues such as these also need to be reflected in classroom practice.

SUMMARY POINTS

- Any human activity causing ongoing harm to people or environment is unsustainable.
- Issues of environment (planet) and development (people) are key educational concerns.
- They both lie at the heart of educating for a more sustainable future.
- A number of long-standing educational fields contribute to education for sustainability.
- Discussions in schools should explore significant debates about the nature of sustainability.

QUESTIONS FOR DISCUSSION

1   This chapter argues that issues of sustainability, local and global, should be at the heart of the curriculum today. Do you agree?
2   How can different school subjects contribute to education for sustainability?
3   Which of the resources listed do you find most valuable and why?

FURTHER READING

Clark, D. (2006) *The Rough Guide to Ethical Living*, London: Rough Guides Ltd. An excellent primer on issues relating to sustainability from low-carbon living to ethical shopping.

Fien, J. (ed.) (2001) *Teaching and Learning for a Sustainable Future*, Paris: UNESCO (CD ROM). Also available http://www.unesco.org/education/tlsf/. A comprehensive online resource that allows the user to explore many aspects of the need for a more sustainable society.

Hicks, D. (2007) Education for sustainability: how should we teach about climate change? in H. Claire and C. Holden (eds) *The Challenge of Teaching Controversial Issues*, Stoke-on-Trent: Trentham Books. Looks at the issue of climate change and questions that arise in relation to how this may be taught about in the classroom.

Orr, D. (2004) *Earth in Mind: On Education, Environment and the Human Prospect*, 10th anniversary edition, Washington DC: Island Press. A classic work on issues relating to sustainability and the contribution of education to resolving or worsening the human and planetary condition.

Webster, K. (2004) *Rethink, Refuse, Reduce ... Education for Sustainability in a Changing World*, Preston Montford: Field Studies Council. A thought-provoking, challenging and practical book for those engaging in education for sustainability.

REFERENCES

ACCAC (2002) *Education for Sustainable Development and Global Citizenship*, Qualifications, Curriculum and Assessment Authority for Wales, Birmingham: ACCAC Publications.

Apple, M. (2006) *Educating the 'Right' Way: Markets, Standards, God, and Inequality* (2nd edition), London: RoutledgeFalmer.

Cohen, R. and Kennedy, P. (2007) *Global Sociology*, Basingstoke: Palgrave.

Davison, A. (2001) *Technology and the Contested Meanings of Sustainability*, Albany: State University of New York Press.

Development Education Association, *What is Development Education?* Online. Available http://www.dea.org.uk (accessed 13 September 2007).

DfES (2005) *Developing the Global Dimension in the School Curriculum*, London: DfES.

DfES (2007) National framework for sustainable schools. Online. Available http://www.teachernet.gov.uk/sustainableschools/ (accessed 13 September, 2007).

Ecologist. Online. Available http://www.theecologist.org.uk (accessed 13 September 2007).

Fien, J. and Tilbury, D. (2002) The global challenge of sustainability, in D. Tilbury (ed.) *Education and Sustainability: Responding to the global challenge*, Gland, Switzerland: IUCN (World Conservation Union).

Goldstein, T. and Selby, D. (eds) (2000) *Weaving Connections: Educating for Peace, Social and Environmental Justice*, Toronto: Sumach Press.

Green Futures. Online. Available http://www.greenfutures.org.uk (accessed 13 September 2007).

Hicks, D. (2007) Education for sustainability: how should we teach about climate change? in H. Claire and C. Holden (eds) *The Challenge of Teaching Controversial Issues*, Stoke-on-Trent: Trentham Books.

Hicks, D. and Holden, C. (eds) (2007) *Teaching the Global Dimension: Key Principles and Effective Practice*, London: Routledge.

Manchester Development Education Project. Online. Available http://www.dep.org.uk (accessed 13 September 2007).

National Association for Environmental Education. Online. Available http://www.naeeuk.plus.com/ (accessed 6 September 2007).

New Internationalist. Online. Available http://www.newint.org (accessed 13 September 2007).

Palmer, J. (1998) *Environmental Education in the 21st Century*, London: Routledge.

Pepper, D. (1996) Defining environmentalism, in *Modern Environmentalism: An Introduction*, London: Routledge.

SCAA (1996) *Teaching Environmental Matters Through the National Curriculum*, London: SCAA.

Sterling, S. (2001) *Sustainable Education: Re-visioning Learning and Change*, Dartington: Green Books.

Stone, M. and Barlow, Z. (2005) *Ecological Literacy: Educating our Children for a Sustainable World*, San Francisco: Sierra Club Books.

Teachers in Development Education. Online. Available http://www.tidec.org/ (accessed 13 September 2007).

UNESCO (2001) *Teaching and Learning for a Sustainable Future*, CD-ROM, Paris: UNESCO.

Webster, K. (2004) *Rethink, Refuse, Reduce … Education for Sustainability in a Changing World*, Preston Montford: Field Studies Council.

World Wide Fund for Nature. Online. Available http://www.wwflearning.co.uk/ (accessed 13 September 2007).

12 A Futures Perspective in Education

David Hicks

INTRODUCTION

Why do teachers need to address future events and trends with their students? How can we help young people think more critically and creatively about the future? What resources are available to assist in teaching about such matters? This chapter sets out to answer questions such as these and, in particular, explores:

- The rationale for students acquiring a futures perspective in their life and work.
- The international field of futures studies and the conceptual framework this offers for educators.
- How futures related ideas and issues, from the personal to the global, can make a significant contribution to good classroom practice.

RATIONALE

It is as vital for young people to understand the temporal relationships between past, present and future as it is the spatial interrelationships between local, national and global (see Chapter 7). Yet, if all education is in some sense a preparation for the future, when, where and how are students given the opportunity to explore possible futures for themselves and society more widely? Whilst historians deal with time past and all teachers deal with the present, explicit exploration of the future is still generally missing from the curriculum (Hicks, 2006).

So why should it be important to help young people think critically and creatively about the future? Here are eight important reasons.

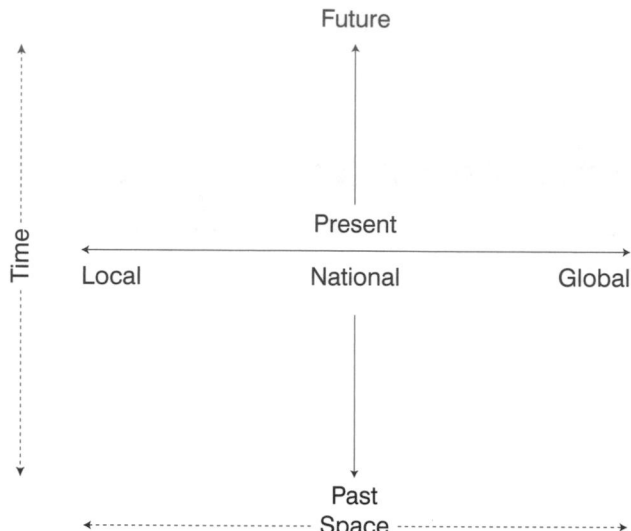

Figure 12.1   The spatial and temporal dimensions

Student motivation

Student expectation about the future can affect behaviour in the present, e.g. that something is, or is not, worth working for. Clear images of desired personal goals can help stimulate motivation and achievement.

Anticipating change

Anticipatory skills and flexibility of mind are important in times of rapid change. Such skills enable students to deal more effectively with uncertainty and to initiate, rather than merely respond to, change.

Critical thinking

In weighing up information, considering trends and imagining alternatives, students need to exercise reflective and critical thinking. This is often triggered by realising the contradictions between how the world is now and how one would like it to be.

Clarifying values

All images of the future are underpinned by differing value assumptions about human nature and society. In a democratic society students need to be able to begin to identify such value judgements before they can themselves make appropriate choices between alternatives.

Decision making

Becoming more aware of trends and events that are likely to influence one's future and investigating the possible consequences of one's actions on others in the future, lead to more thoughtful decision making in the present.

Creative imagination

One faculty that can contribute to, and which is particularly enhanced by, designing possible futures is the creative imagination. Both this *and* critical thinking are needed to envision a range of preferable futures from the personal to the global.

A better world

It is important in a democratic society that students develop their sense of vision particularly in relation to more just and sustainable futures. Such forward-looking thinking is an essential ingredient in both preserving and improving society.

Responsible citizenship

Critical participation in democratic life leads to the development of political skills and thus more active and responsible citizenship. Future generations are then more likely to benefit, rather than lose, from decisions made today.

These eight reasons are a reminder that, whilst the future is yet to come, it plays a vital part in all our lives. Although the future has not happened, we nevertheless think about it, plan for it and may also be concerned about it. In the same way that the today we inherit is yesterday's future, so we can play a part in shaping our future and the future of society – or leave it to others to do, in which case we inhabit someone else's vision of the future. How might one therefore begin to think more critically and creatively about the future?

FUTURES STUDIES

Although interest in the future is as old as humanity itself, serious investigation into different possible futures did not emerge until after the Second World War in the form of strategic planning, technological forecasting, economic analysis and the first major think tanks. Whilst much of this endeavour focused on economic and military forecasting, there were other, largely European, initiatives that were more concerned with how such thinking could be used to help create better social futures.

Futures studies as a field of academic enquiry emerged in the 1960s and Inayatullah (1993) notes that it 'largely straddles two dominant modes of knowledge – the technical concerned with predicting the future and the humanist concerned with developing a good society' (p. 236). It is the latter strand that is of particular interest to educators. Key resources in the field are texts such as the *Knowledge Base of Futures Studies* (Slaughter, 2005), *Foundations of Futures Studies* (Bell, 1997) and *Advancing Futures* (Dator, 2002).

Bell (1997) argues that the purpose of futures studies is to 'discover or invent, examine, evaluate and propose possible, probable and preferable futures'. He continues, 'futurists seek to know: what can or could be (the possible), what is likely to be (the probable), and what ought to be (the preferable)' (p. 73). Dator (2005) elaborates:

> The future cannot be studied because the future does not exist. Futures studies does not …
> pretend to study the future. It studies ideas about the future … [which] often serve as the
> basis for actions in the present … Different groups often have very different images of the
> future. Men's images may differ from women's. Western images may differ from non-Western,
> and so on.
>
> One of the main tasks of futures studies is to identify and examine the major alternative
> futures which exist at any given time and place. The future cannot be predicted, but preferred
> futures can and should be envisioned, invented, implemented, continuously evaluated, revised,
> and re-envisioned. Thus, another major task of futures studies is to facilitate individuals and
> groups in formulating, implementing, and re-envisioning their preferred futures.

The field of futures studies is a rich and vital resource for teachers and educators more widely. The field provides various conceptual frameworks for thinking about and analysing futures as well as a variety of key concepts that can be adapted for use at all levels in the classroom.

FUTURES IN EDUCATION

Educators who are concerned about this neglected aspect of the curriculum talk about the need for a 'futures dimension' within the curriculum and the need for pupils to develop a 'futures perspective', i.e. the ability to think more critically and creatively about the future. The purpose of such a dimension in the curriculum is to help teachers and pupils to:

- develop a more future-orientated perspective on their lives and events in the wider world;
- identify and envision alternative futures that are more just and sustainable;
- exercise critical thinking skills and the creative imagination more effectively;
- participate in more thoughtful and informed decision making in the present;
- engage in active and responsible citizenship, both in the local, national and global community, and on behalf of present and future generations.

Toffler (1974) was one of the first writers to argue that the curriculum needed to be more future-orientated but progress has been slow in developing this dimension of the curriculum (Hicks, 2006). Nevertheless, valuable surveys of contemporary work in schools can be found, such as that by Gidley *et al.* (2004).

Young people and the future

So what is known about how young people themselves view the future? Understanding how children and young people develop such ideas is crucial because it is from this formative period that adult perceptions of the future emerge. This then affects what people feel is, and is not, worth working for in their own lives, their community or the wider world. Here are some of the things we know.

Early years

Whilst it might be thought that younger children have little concept of the future, early years specialist Page (2000), in her work with 4–5-year-olds, found this not to be so. At this age time is viewed in terms of the child's own activities: in four sleeps rather than four days time. They do not understand that time exists independently of themselves, but there is a growing sense of progression beginning with notions of 'before' and 'after', moving on to 'yesterday' and 'tomorrow.' The 'future' means being older or things changing. There is a growing awareness of issues such as the environment, war, music, places and events in the news. Thinking about the future at this age involves imaginative fantasy, which gives a great sense of control and freedom over the future. Whilst this may seem unrealistic from an adult point of view, it is a vital developmental stage. Young children develop positive feelings about their place in the future and their role in its creation.

Primary level

Whilst different levels of ability are found in conceptualising the future at 7–8, this is when a more 'adult' understanding of time begins to appear. Research by Hicks and Holden (1995) and Holden (2007) shows the emergence of an ability to think ahead and the realisation that the future may be something to work towards as well as something to be concerned about. Reality and fantasy may still sit side by side and children sometimes fear that their own area may be subject to violence and conflict seen in other places on TV. There is a growing awareness of social and environmental issues and children are generally optimistic that the future will be better both for themselves and others.

Secondary level

As they grow older young people's concerns for the future tend to reflect current national and global issues and events although these may change over time (Hutchinson, 1996; Holden, 2007). In personal terms secondary students are often concerned about getting a good job, having a good life and doing well at school. In relation to the future of their local community, issues such as crime and violence, employment, and environmental threats are important concerns. In terms of the global future there is often concern about the environment, conflict and inequality. Pessimism appears to increase with age and many secondary students feel that they have not learnt enough about these issues at school.

Youth futures

A recent survey by UCAS and Forum for the Future (2007) invited university applicants in the UK to say what they felt about the future. It asked what they felt life would be like in 2031, in twenty-five years time, when respondents would be in their forties and at the height of their careers. Some of the main findings were:

- Respondents expect the world they'll be living in to be technologically advanced, but environmentally impoverished.
- Three-quarters believe lifestyles will need to change radically for civilisation to survive into the twenty-second century.

- Compared to their parents at the same age, 42% see themselves as more worried about the future.
- Most (69%) believe that individuals are responsible for the change required for civilisation to continue.
- Women are less optimistic about the future than men, feel more change is necessary and are more prepared to contribute to that change.

(UCAS/Forum for the Future, 2007)

What would one need to know and what skills would one need to have therefore in order to think more critically and creatively about the future? Here are nine key concepts which should underpin all subject areas of the curriculum and which highlight the key elements of futures thinking and a futures-orientated school.

Key concepts

State of the world

In the early twenty-first century the state of the world continues to give cause for concern. Issues to do with sustainability, wealth and poverty, peace and conflict, and human rights, all have a major impact both locally and globally. Students need to know about the causes of such problems, how they will affect their lives now and in the future, and the action needed to help resolve them.

Managing change

In periods of rapid social and technological change the past cannot provide an accurate guide to the future. Anticipation and adaptability, foresight and flexibility, innovation and intuition, become essential tools for survival. Students need to develop such skills in order to become more adaptable and proactive towards change.

Views of the future

People's views of the future may vary greatly depending, for example, on age, gender, class and culture, as well as their attitudes to change, the environment and technology. Students need to be aware of how views of the future differ and the ways in which these affect people's priorities in the present.

Alternative futures

At any point in time a range of different futures is possible. It is useful to distinguish between probable futures, i.e. those that seem *likely* to come about, and preferable futures, i.e. those one feels *should* come about. Students need to explore a range of probable and preferable futures, from the personal and local to the global.

Hopes and fears

Hopes and fears for the future often influence decision making in the present. Fears can lead to the avoidance of problems rather than their resolution. Clarifying hopes for the future can enhance motivation in the present and thus positive action for change. Students need to explore their own hopes and fears for the future and learn to work creatively with them.

Past/present/future

Interdependence exists across both space and time. Past, present and future are inextricably connected. We are directly linked back in time by the oldest members of the community and forward nearly a century by those born today. Students need to explore these links and to gain a sense of both continuity and change as well as of responsibility for the future.

Visions for the future

The first decade of a new century provides a valuable opportunity for reviewing the state of society. What needs to be left behind and what taken forward? In particular, what visions of a better future are needed to motivate active and responsible citizenship in the present? Students therefore need to develop their skills of envisioning, and use of the creative imagination.

Future generations

Economists, philosophers and international lawyers increasingly recognise the rights of future generations. It has been suggested that no generation should inherit less human and natural wealth than the one that preceded it. Students need to discuss the rights of future generations and what the responsibility to uphold these may involve.

Sustainable futures

Current consumerist lifestyles on this planet are increasingly seen as unsustainable, often causing more damage than benefit. A sustainable society would prioritise concern for the environment, the poorest members of the community and the needs of future generations. Students need to understand how this applies to their everyday lives and possible future employment.

GOOD PRACTICE

Hutchinson (1996) has shown that school textbooks often fail to give any consideration to the future and that comics and computer games tend to offer violent and uncritical technological views of the future. It is not surprising, therefore, that young people often have stereotypical views of the future themselves. Most Hollywood movies that are about the future are apocalyptic and violent. What, therefore, does good practice, which helps young people interrogate the images offered them by society, look like? Here are some examples of activities that can be adapted for use with different age groups and different subject areas.

Trends shaping the future

A significant trend of any sort may well have an influence on the future. This might be to do with traffic increase, population growth or global warming. Any trend may increase over a period of time; it may decline or remain stable. Trends do not predict the future but they do indicate important social, economic, political and environmental shifts that are going on. One of the most useful resources for teachers on global trends is the annual Worldwatch Institute publication *Vital Signs: The Trends Which are Shaping our Future* (2007). This comprises a series of double-page spreads each of which crisply summarises an important trend together with succinct figures and graphs.

Some current trends include:

- The global economy continues to grow.
- The world fish harvest is stable but threatened.
- The impact of climate change is increasing.
- The use of wind and solar energy is increasing.
- Vehicle production continues to expand.
- HIV/AIDS is threatening development.
- The number of violent conflicts in the world is dropping.
- Obesity has reached epidemic proportions.

A number of interesting questions arise. Which of these trends will have a local impact in your community? Will that trend bring benefits or disbenefits locally? What will they be? Will some people benefit or suffer more than others? What action is being taken to support or diminish this trend locally, nationally and globally? Who or what provides the driving power behind this trend?

Probable futures

One of the most useful distinctions that futurists make is between probable and preferable futures. Probable futures are those that one thinks are most *likely* to come about. This can relate to your own personal future, e.g. I will be studying at university for the next three years; the local future, e.g. it's likely that traffic congestion will continue to get worse in my town; the global future, e.g. climate change means more floods are likely in the UK. It is important and useful to think about probable futures because these are the futures we are most likely to have to deal with. Civil servants, local government departments, town planners, business and industry are all concerned with probable futures, asking questions such as: How many hospital beds will we need in the near future? How can we meet the public demand for more organic foods? Do coastal sea defences need improving at this place? We are constantly planning for probable futures. This does not mean that people necessarily agree on what the future will probably be like. It partly depends on what is happening in relation to particular local, national and global trends and how their possible impacts on the future (short, middle and long term) are interpreted.

Preferable futures

Preferable futures are an entirely different temporal category from probable futures. Preferable futures are those that one would most *wish* to come about. They arise out of our deepest hopes, aspirations and dreams, for ourselves, for others and the planet. They may also relate to political and spiritual beliefs about how one would like the world to be. This can relate to your own personal future, e.g. I would like to become a really good teacher; the local future, e.g. we really need to reduce the amount of traffic in the town centre in order to make this a better place for shoppers; the global future, e.g. what needs to be done in order to help create a more, rather than less, sustainable future. Politicians, non-governmental organisations, faith groups, town planners, business and industry are also concerned with preferable futures. They have a vision of what, for them, the future ought to be like and they work towards achieving this. People therefore do not necessarily agree on what a preferable future for society would look like, in the short, middle and long term, although they may well be clear about the preferred future for their own personal life.

In some research at a number of institutions (Hicks, 2006) undergraduates were asked to write about what the main features of their preferable future for society would be. None of them had been asked this question before. Table 12.1 shows the features they came up with in order of importance.

It is likely that the last four features would rank higher now as these issues have been very much in the news in the years since this research was carried out. What would your key features be?

Table 12.1 Students' preferred futures 2020

	%
Green – clean air and water, trees, wildlife, flowers	79
Convivial – cooperative, relaxed, happy, caring, laughter	74
Transport – no cars, no pollution, public transport, bikes	55
Peaceful – absence of violent conflict, security, global harmony	53
Equity – no poverty, fair shares for all, no hunger	38
Justice – equal rights of people and planet, no discrimination	36
Community – local, small, friendly, simpler, sense of community	36
Education – for all, ongoing for life, holistic, community	30
Energy – lower consumption, renewable and clean resources	26
Work – for all, satisfying, shared, shorter hours	23
Healthy – better health care, alternative, longer life	19
Food – organic farming, locally grown, balanced diet	15

$N = 90$

Timelines

An excellent way of exploring probable and preferable futures is through the use of timelines as shown in Figure 12.2.

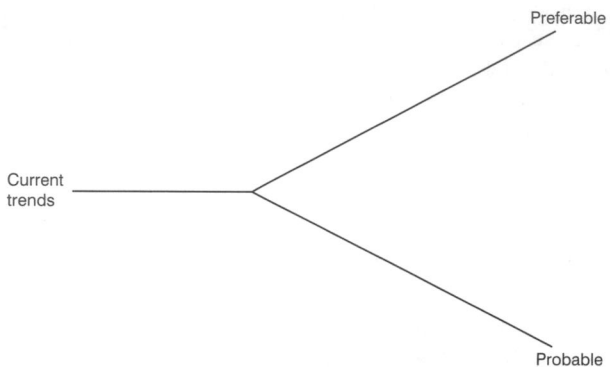

Figure 12.2   Using timelines

The simplest form of timeline is just a straight line with today's date at the left-hand side and some future date at the right-hand side. One then annotates the line with key words, dates, cartoons, icons to indicate the changes that seem appropriate, recorded in sequential order. You may, for example, have used timelines in history to record past events that are already known.

This timeline is more complex in that it is designed to record both probable and preferable futures, as well as recent and current trends that may shape those futures. Where the lines intersect is the present. What is mapped on the timeline and what its overall time frame is depends on the context in which it is used. For younger children a horizon of a year would be sufficient; for older pupils it could be a decade or longer. It also depends on the subject matter.

Firstly, one invites students to note down briefly important current trends that seem relevant to the topic in question. If this was 'climate change in the UK' it might include recent floods, extreme weather, IPCC (Intergovernmental Panel on Climate Change) reports, melting glaciers. Secondly, and the order is important, students should complete the probable timeline. Given these recent events and current trends what is most likely to happen over the next, say, twenty years? Key words, icons, cartoons are used to illustrate it. Lastly, the preferable line is completed. Given the probable future what would students prefer to see happening? Timelines should then be displayed so everyone can see them. Do the probable futures have any common features? If so, what are they? Do the preferred futures have any common features? If so, what are they? With many topics there will be a gap between what students expect and what they hope for. This should then lead on to an exploration of who else shares elements of such a preferable future and is working to help bring this about.

It is important to note that such an activity also highlights for the teacher what young people know (and don't know) about climate change or any other topic that has been chosen.

Vision and action

One of the purposes of this chapter has been to set out different ways in which one can begin to think more critically and creatively about the future. It is important to note, however, that people's images of the future will vary depending on their age, gender and culture as they all deeply affect our views of the world. What may appear 'normal' in Europe and North America may look quite different elsewhere and this applies as much to the future as the present (Sardar, 1999; Hammond, 1999). However, some futures are clearly preferable to others: most people would prefer a less rather than a more violent future. Similarly many people would prefer a more equitable and just future rather than an inequitable and unjust one. For many educators today the crucial question is: What does a more sustainable future look like? (See Chapter 11.) Past generations have always had their visions of a better future and many of the things we take for granted in the twenty-first century we only have because our ancestors struggled to create a better world for their children and grandchildren. We inherit both their successes and their failures.

Chapters 7 and 11 highlight the major issues facing world society today and these will continue to challenge us in different ways for much of the century. Thinking about the future should not, therefore, occur in a vacuum. It should, as Dator (2005) argues, help individuals and groups formulate and implement their preferred futures. This could relate to your own personal and professional life, organisations in the community, the school you may teach in, the work of a voluntary group, an activist organisation or an international network (Hicks, 2002). In particular we need to be able to envision clearly what a more sustainable future would look like. However, Meadows et al. (2005) point out that.

> We should say immediately, for the sake of sceptics … we do not believe vision makes anything happen. Vision without action is useless. But without action vision is directionless and feeble. Vision is absolutely necessary to guide and motivate. More than that, vision, when widely shared and firmly kept in sight, does bring into being new systems (p. 272).

Taking responsibility for oneself and others in the local and global community is a vital life skill that requires critical and creative thinking about both present and future. Geographers have been amongst the first to embrace the need for a futures dimension in the curriculum (Roberts, 2003; Morgan, 2006), which is equally important in Personal, Social and Health Education (PSHE), in citizenship, religious education and other subjects too. Being able to take a more critical futures-orientated perspective on life allows us to learn from our mistakes, individually and as a species, so that future generations will benefit, rather than suffer, from our endeavours here in the present.

CONCLUSION

This chapter has set out the rationale for a more futures-orientated curriculum that will help students to think critically and creatively about the sort of society that they would like to live in. It highlights the importance and value of the international field of futures studies as a source of key concepts and insights that can fruitfully be adapted for classroom use. Examples have also been given of practical ideas that can be adapted for use with different age groups in the classroom.

SUMMARY POINTS

- All education requires more critical and creative thinking about the future.
- Up until recently this has been a neglected dimension of the curriculum.
- The international field of futures studies provides a vital source for ideas.
- A number of key concepts are identified to aid in curriculum planning.
- Understanding probable and preferable futures is a vital educational task.

QUESTIONS FOR DISCUSSION

1   What argument would you use to persuade colleagues of the need for a futures perspective in the curriculum?

2   What would be the key features of your preferred future: a) for a school; and b) for your community?

3   Which of the resources listed below do you find most useful and why?

FURTHER READING

Gidley, J. and Inayatullah, S. (eds) (2002) *Youth Futures: Comparative Research and Transformative Visions*, Westport, CT: Praeger. An authoritative source that looks at what young people feel about their future in different parts of the world.

Hicks, D. (2001) *Citizenship for the Future: A Practical Classroom Guide*, Godalming: World Wide Fund for Nature UK. Designed for Key Stages 2 and 3 this book is full of lively activities to help children think more critically and creatively about the future.

Hicks, D. (2006) *Lessons for the Future: The Missing Dimension in Education*, Victoria BC: Trafford Publications. A thought-provoking book about the need for a clearer futures perspective in education, drawing on innovative work with both teachers and students.

Hicks, D. and Holden, C. (2007) Remembering the future: what do children think? *Environmental Education Research*, 13(4): 501–12. A useful overview and review of the research on children's views of the future.

Pilot GCSE 'Geography 21'. Online. Available http://www.geography.org.uk/projects/pilotgcse. An excellent example of how one subject area, geography, has embraced the need for a futures perspective in the curriculum.

REFERENCES

Bell, W. (1997) *Foundations of Futures Studies*, 2 vols, New Brunswick, NJ: Transaction Publishers.

Dator, J. (ed.) (2002) *Advancing Futures: Futures Studies in Higher Education*, Westport, CT: Praeger.

Dator, J. (2005) Foreword, in R. Slaughter (ed.) *Knowledge Base of Futures Studies, the Future*, CD-ROM, Brisbane: Foresight International.

Gidley, J., Bateman, D. and Smith, C. (2004) *Futures Education: Principles, Practice and Potential*, AFI Monograph 5, Melbourne: Swindon University of Technology.

Hammond, A. (1999) *Which World? Scenarios for the 21st Century*, London: Earthscan.

Hicks, D. (2002) Envisioning a better world, in M. Smith (ed.) *Aspects of Teaching Secondary Geography*, London: RoutledgeFalmer.

Hicks, D. (2006) *Lessons for the Future: The Missing Dimension in Education*, Victoria BC: Trafford Publications.

Hicks, D. and Holden, C. (1995) *Visions of the Future: Why we Need to Teach for Tomorrow*, Stoke-on-Trent: Trentham Books.

Holden, C. (2007) Young people's concerns, in D. Hicks and C. Holden (eds) *Teaching the Global Dimension*, London: Routledge.

Hutchinson, F. (1996) *Educating Beyond Violent Futures*, London: Routledge.

Inayatullah, S. (1993) From 'who am I?' to 'when am I?' Framing the shape and time of the future, *Futures*, 25: 235–53.

Meadows, D., Randers, J. and Meadows, D. (2005) *Limits to Growth: The 30-year Update*, London: Earthscan.

Morgan, A. (2006) Teaching geography for a sustainable future, in D. Balderstone (ed.) *Secondary Geography Handbook*, Sheffield: Geographical Association.

Page, J. (2000) *Reframing the Early Childhood Curriculum: Educational Imperatives for the Future*, London: RoutledgeFalmer.

Roberts, M. (2003) *Learning Through Enquiry: Making Sense of Geography in the Key Stage 3 Classroom*, Sheffield: Geographical Association.

Sardar, Z. (1999) *Rescuing All Our Futures: The Future of Futures Studies*, Westport: CT, Praeger.

Slaughter, R. (ed.) (2005) *Knowledge Base of Futures Studies*, Professional Edition CD-ROM, Brisbane: Foresight Institute.

Toffler, A. (1974) *Learning for Tomorrow: The Role of the Future in Education*, New York, Vintage Books.

UCAS/Forum for the Future (2007) *The Future Leaders Survey 2006/07*. Online. Available http://www.forumforthefuture.org.uk/future_test_head_page499.aspx (accessed 13 September 2007).

Worldwatch Institute (2006) *Vital Signs 2006–2007: The Trends that are Shaping our Future*. Washington, DC: Worldwatch Institute.

Part III

Learning, Knowledge and the Curriculum

13 Education and the Curriculum: Is Knowledge a Dangerous Thing?

Alan Howe and Dan Davies

INTRODUCTION

In this chapter we consider a concept that is central to education – the curriculum. After considering what is meant by the term 'curriculum', we will ask why a curriculum is deemed to be necessary and how it might come into existence. We discuss the role of the state, teachers and pupils in deciding on the content of the National Curriculum in England, whilst arguing that such a curriculum can be a dangerous thing. This argument can be illustrated by considering how a subject such as science has become part of the 'core' of that curriculum. The case study will give us an opportunity to ask questions such as:

- How is a curriculum written?
- Why does a curriculum change?
- How does assessment determine the nature of a curriculum?
- Is the notion of a curriculum useful?

We conclude by considering ways in which we can critically evaluate curricula.

WHAT IS MEANT BY 'CURRICULUM'?

In the following paragraphs we consider some of the ways in which people have conceptualised the curriculum and how the differing views carry with them assumptions about teaching and learning.

Curriculum as a body of knowledge

One way of thinking about the curriculum is to see it as a 'body of knowledge'. As we shall see when we later discuss scientific knowledge, the question of whether 'true' knowledge exists has been discussed for a long time and a branch of philosophy – 'epistemology' – seeks to answer questions about what 'counts' as knowledge. One apparently straightforward view is to see knowledge as propositional – it tells us *that* 2 + 2 = 4 or *that* fish can swim. A curriculum based on such a propositional view might contain a selection from all the factual information that humans claim to know. Imagine for a moment a website that contained every scrap of human knowledge and that you had been set the task of exploring that website with some children. Where would you start? How long would you need? What would you leave out? What would be the most important pages to highlight and revisit? For example, would 'how to save a drowning boy' take priority over 'how to use speech marks' or 'farming in the UK'? Conceiving a curriculum in this way inevitably requires difficult decisions to be made. It suggests that some types of knowledge will be more important than others, some ideas more fundamental, some information unnecessary. It calls into question the nature of the knowledge selected: does it have the status of 'universal truth' or 'working hypothesis'? Seeing a curriculum as a body of knowledge also suggests that its content can be transmitted from where it is stored (e.g. in the head of a teacher) to the learner. But what happens if there are 'faults' in that transmission process? Does it matter if each learner carries his or her own version of that knowledge in their heads, rather than the 'official' version the teacher sought to impart? This definition of curriculum is problematic.

Curriculum as a way to achieve a product

Alternatively, curriculum can be thought of as a set of experiences that will achieve a desired outcome. That outcome might be expressed in terms of aims, objectives or targets. If the target is for the learner to become literate and numerate then the curriculum will be directed towards that end. If the aim is for a learner to gain a set of qualifications, the curriculum will be focused on pupils passing the examinations. The fundamental problem with this approach is that the curriculum becomes linear (headed in a preordained direction), instrumental (concerned with achieving the aim without considering the value of the journey) and leads to a loss of freedom for the pupil and teacher.

Curriculum as a process

Criticisms of the two ways of conceiving a curriculum outlined above have led to the development of a third alternative. Seeing the curriculum as a *process* promotes the notion that clear curriculum *principles* will be informed by ideas about human development and its potentials (Blenkin and Kelly, 1981). This view regards education as valuable in itself rather than as a means to an end, such that learners' needs shape the curriculum rather than *vice versa*. The strength of this approach, according to its proponents, is that it is fundamentally 'moral', in that principles will be based on the needs of learners to attain intrinsically worthwhile outcomes such as cognitive functioning and intellectual development, and 'democratic' in that any changes or developments to the curriculum will need to be clearly linked to the attainment of these principles (Kelly, 2004).

Another advantage of the 'process' approach is that the whole of the educational experience can and should be included in the concept of curriculum – not just the 'official knowledge'. Many educators have noted that much of what learners experience in schools is not published in any official subject or exam syllabus. The social relationships (e.g. between teacher and pupil) and organisational features (e.g. setting by ability) in schools communicate to learners very strong messages about their place in society. Shute (1993), taking an extreme view, refers to the 'tyranny' of the unwritten curriculum where children learn that 'passive acceptance is preferable to active criticism' and that 'education consists of memorising the provided Right Answers' (p. 7). Bernstein (1997, cited in Kelly, 2004, p. 89) offers a radical alternative that identifies three rights of learners: the right to individual enhancement, the right to be included and the right to participate. These rights, he argues, should be fundamental curriculum principles. This is a view of curriculum to which the authors subscribe, whilst acknowledging that it has faced sustained criticism over the last thirty years by proponents of the other two models on the grounds that it neither helps to define a standardised content for all learners (model 1) nor equips them with the skills needed for employment (model 2). Governments, whilst paying lip service to learners' needs and development, tend to shy away from this model since its outcomes are difficult to measure, making national 'standards' impossible to define and the notion of 'value for money' irrelevant.

This brief discussion of 'definitions' can only hint at the complex debates, arguments and counter arguments that whirl around the concept of curriculum.

WHY IS A CURRICULUM DEEMED TO BE NECESSARY?

If we define curriculum as the entire content of children's experience in schools then we cannot escape having one. If, however, we look at it as a selection from human knowledge, the nature of the selection made and how closely it should be prescribed is dependent on views of the purposes of education, which successive governments have shifted significantly in the last thirty years. The supremacy of *subjects* as fundamental units of the school curriculum was firmly established during the first half of the twentieth century, largely as a result of the dominance of a traditional view of knowledge perpetuated by senior academics and politicians who themselves had experienced a knowledge-based curriculum and a school examinations system that reflected subject boundaries. However, for much of the twentieth century, teachers in schools in the UK managed without a nationally prescribed curriculum of any sort (see Chapter 1).

This is not to say that local and national education officials endorsed an ad hoc approach to curriculum selection, but rather that there was a widespread recognition that the school community was in the best position to make judgements about their pupils' education. Between 1927 and 1944 the *Handbook of Suggestions for the Consideration of Teachers and Others Concerned with the Work of Public Elementary Schools* noted that, 'it is not possible to lay down any rule as to the exact number of subjects which should be taken in an individual school' (Board of Education, 1927, p. 38). Changes in subject terminology – from arithmetic to mathematics, from nature study to science, from scripture to religious education – do, however, suggest that the school curriculum was attempting to become a more complete reflection of the important cultural activities of a modern Britain.

Lawton (1992) suggests that another reason for the lack of a national curriculum was the fear of the politics of the totalitarian regimes that dominated Europe during the mid-twentieth century. Nazi and communist governments had introduced tight control of their education policies, making them into propaganda machines to support the state. Politicians in the UK were anxious not to be seen to be anti-democratic and were reluctant to impose national control of the school curriculum. Indeed, the only subject that was compulsory during this period was religious instruction and there was no serious desire on the part of government to introduce greater prescription.

During the 1960s those involved in education began to question the nature of the curriculum, particularly that in primary schools, in two respects. Firstly it was proposed by champions of 'progressive' education that the curriculum should reflect the way that children acquire knowledge through exploration and discovery without reference to what were seen as artificially constructed subject boundaries. The influential Plowden Report (1967) claimed that:

> [in] the appraisal we have made of the curriculum, and of the methods which have proved to be the most fruitful ... 'finding out' has proved to be better for children than 'being told' ... The third of the three Rs is no longer mere mechanical arithmetic, French has made its way into the primary school, nature study is becoming science ... The gloomy forebodings of the decline of knowledge which would follow progressive methods have been discredited. (para. 1233)

In 1967 young people too were commenting critically on the curriculum that they had received. Schoolchildren were invited to submit their ideas in a newspaper competition with resulting entries published in a book: *The School that I'd Like* (Blishen, 1969). Blishen noted that young people disliked subject boundaries and wanted to discover how to be responsible for themselves and their own ideas. He cites 'K., a boy, 17' who hoped that '(i)n the future schools will try to present material so the student will become deeply involved... To this end there would be no such things as set "lessons" and subject boundaries between subjects would be freely crossed' (p. 90).

The Plowden Report did concede that subject-based teaching would be appropriate for older children. It called for a review of curriculum content, for example recommending an expansion of the science curriculum to ensure a smoother transition between primary and secondary school learning. However, it railed against the idea of introducing recognised scientific disciplines into primary schools:

> The conventional ways of categorising these phenomena as biology, branches of physics such as optics, electricity and magnetism, chemistry, engineering and so on are neither natural nor, except very crudely, understandable classifications to young children of primary school age. If, for the terms used above, rabbits, railway engines, telescopes, TV sets and aeroplanes are substituted, these are at once seen to be things about which children show a spontaneous curiosity and ask endless questions. The subject matter of primary school science thus almost settles itself.
>
> (Plowden, 1967, para. 668)

Plowden's discussion of the science curriculum was concluded by addressing concerns from teachers of science in secondary schools who feared that children would come to them possessing 'all kinds of fragmentary unclassified information' (para. 673).

During the 1970s, Britain began an economic decline that led to low productivity, higher inflation and social unrest. The 'problems' were perceived as indicative of a declining society with significant blame directed towards poor teaching and schooling that had become unfit for purpose, partly as a result of the direction primary schools had taken on recommendations from the Plowden Report. The then Labour Prime Minister James Callaghan (1976) argued for society's right to have more influence in what was taught in schools – through establishing a core curriculum of basic knowledge; his so-called 'Ruskin speech' of 1976 kick-started modern debate on education. A central concern of the government was the perceived 'sorry state' of science education, its performance deemed unacceptable in three respects: the unwillingness of young people to seek employment in technological industries, the high proportion of girls abandoning science and the large quantity of empty places on university science and technology courses. The proposed solution to these problems was curriculum reform to ensure a clear focus on the needs of industry and employability of young people. The rate of subsequent curriculum change seems in retrospect remarkably slow when compared to the hurried implementation of new initiatives in the recent past. Nine years after the debate began, science became the second subject to be compulsory in the school curriculum after the publication of the *Science 5–16* policy document, which began with the phrase: 'science should have a place in the education of all pupils of compulsory school age' (DES, 1985, p. 1). In 1988 the Education Reform Act built on this move towards compulsion by establishing a 'core national curriculum' of three subjects – English, mathematics and science.

This tale, of the elevation of primary school science from occasional 'nature study' to a statutory and core curriculum subject, shows in one way the necessity of a curriculum: if, in the view of government, teachers and schools cannot be relied upon to provide an education that is sufficient to meet national priorities, then legislation must enforce a curriculum as a means to that end. This principle has, of course, been applied to the curriculum in England with increasing enthusiasm by governments over the last twenty years.

The current National Curriculum for England (DfEE/QCA, 1999) claims four purposes:

- to establish an entitlement of access for all pupils;
- to establish standards, which in turn inform judgements about performance of pupils, teachers and school;
- to promote continuity and coherence in pupils' learning;
- to promote public understanding of the work of school.

While points one and three relate to the learning experience, the second and fourth point relate closely to the concept of 'accountability'. Education now costs the taxpayer considerably more than the £6bn in 1976 prices quoted by Callaghan and it is now generally uncontested that the public have a right to know whether expenditure represents value for money.

CURRICULUM AND POWER

If a centrally prescribed curriculum is necessary to control what is taught in schools, the next matter to consider is who the authors of that curriculum should be. In a democratic society we would expect it to be unacceptable for unelected representatives to make key decisions about the education of our children. However, that is exactly what happened. In setting up the National Curriculum for England and Wales in 1987, the then Secretary of State for Education, Kenneth Baker appointed 'working parties' of 'experts' to advise and draft the curriculum but maintained, and exercised, the authority to accept, reject and change any proposal.

The idea that the curriculum might be constructed upon anything other than subjects was not seriously considered; working parties were appointed along traditional subject lines, reflecting the school curriculum of the previous centuries. The membership of these groups, whilst not claiming to be in any way representative of society in general, was drawn from some of the 'stakeholders' of the education system – subject experts, industrialists, those from commerce, schools and teacher training institutions. The working party for the art curriculum, for example, included an art critic, a head teacher, a county advisor, a lecturer in primary education, a member of the arts council, an artist and an art columnist. It could be argued that this membership epitomised the assertion that far from being rational entities, school subjects are 'in fact the creation of interest groups whose prime concern has been maintaining and extending their own status' (Kelly, 2004, p. 32). This can also be illustrated in the creation – after an initial joint 'science and technology' working group had failed to reach agreement – of a new and distinct subject named 'design and technology', unique in the developed world at the time. So the actual process of curriculum construction had a momentum towards subject separation (Coulby, 1990), with powerful groups in the ascendancy.

There were many education 'experts' who were not happy with the resulting National Curriculum. It has since gone through many changes to address some of the shortcomings of the day. Some argue that it has not improved at all and still requires radical changes. The process, however, has at least been played out in the public domain; it has been possible to observe a democratic process at work as elected representatives seek to control and direct the education of our young people, negotiating a path between interested parties of subject associations, parents, business and commerce. The fundamental concern for educators is that the state will not necessarily maintain a relatively 'benign' dominance over the school curriculum. It is not difficult to imagine an alternative future where an imposed hierarchy of subjects does not represent any kind of consensus. A curriculum that expresses explicit values at odds with those of minority or disempowered groups, that furthers national interests above those of global concerns, that promotes certain lifestyles and sexual orientation and discredits others, is possible. Some argue that this is what we already have.

EVALUATING A CURRICULUM

In moving on to consider how we might evaluate a curriculum, we continue our focus on the emergence of science as a core subject, because its 'epistemology' (or theory of knowledge) has changed fundamentally over the years, and is still the subject of debate. In some ways, this debate mirrors that about the content of curricula summarised above. For example, the notion of scientific knowledge as having the status of some independent truth, transcendent and incontestable, has dominated rationalist and modernist views of science from the ancient Greeks to the eighteenth-century Enlightenment. More recently, less certain, 'postmodern' perspectives, represented by writers such as Thomas Kuhn, Ernst von Glasersfeld and Paul Feyerabend, have emphasised the 'procedural' elements of scientific knowledge – how it is constructed within the social culture of the scientific community. We can use these different views as lenses through which to look at what is currently in the science curriculum.

In a 'modernist', knowledge-based model of science education, we might expect scientific theories to be presented as 'laws' governing nature, and science education to be seen as the process by which these laws are transmitted to the next generation. The representation of science in the current national curriculum for England (DfEE/QCA, 1999) includes several such statements, particularly in the conceptual components of the Programme of Study. For example, at Key Stage 2 (ages 7–11) pupils are expected to be taught: 'that objects are pulled downwards because of the gravitational attraction between them and the Earth' (Sc4:2b).

This is a restatement of part of Newton's general law of gravitation, which, whilst not generally disputed, could be expressed in other ways. For example, it could be: 'because the Earth causes a curvature of space–time' (Einstein's General Theory of Relativity) or 'because the Earth sends out gravity waves' (a highly controversial scientific statement as no evidence for the existence of gravity waves has yet been found). Whilst we would not suggest that pupils should be confronted with these university-level alternative explanations, it is the presentation of Newton's theory as the definitive statement of scientific truth that is potentially misleading. Many of us can perhaps remember a science teacher who told us that everything we'd previously learned was 'wrong'; this common but disconcerting experience is largely the result of simplified versions of scientific principles being presented as 'facts' to us when we were younger.

Fortunately, such statements are relatively rare in the science Programme of Study. Most of the conceptual statements are phrased in ways that indicate the area of knowledge to be taught but without prescribing specific theories or 'facts'. Examples include Key Stage 2, during which pupils are to be taught: '… about the different plants and animals found in different habitats' (Sc2:5b).

Such a statement, whilst assuming the biological classification into animal and plant kingdoms and the ecological concept of a 'habitat', does not constitute a claim to scientific truth, leaving this to the teacher. The majority of conceptual phrases are similarly inclusive, leading us to the conclusion that the epistemology that matters here may be the teacher's rather than that of the curriculum. If this is the case, then recent developments in science pedagogy may be significant in changing the representation of knowledge within the science curriculum as actually taught in schools. An image of scientific knowledge as 'socially constructed' places an emphasis upon pupils' 'conceptual change' from everyday ideas to more scientific ones (Harlen and Osborne, 1985). This occurs through a process of discussion, exploration and investigation of phenomena, using their existing ideas or 'alternative frameworks' (Driver, 1983) as starting points and teaching them to question explanations critically. This approach has in turn influenced the science curriculum, particularly in its portrayal of scientific 'procedural knowledge'. For example, the National Curriculum for England (DfEE/QCA, 1999) contains a statement summarising the importance of science in children's education, including the following:

> Scientific method is about developing and evaluating explanations through experimental evidence and modelling. This is a spur to critical and creative thought … They learn to question and discuss science-based issues that may affect their own lives, the direction of society and the future of the world. (p. 15)

This emphasis on questioning scientific explanations and focusing upon issues about which scientists may not agree is evidence of a postmodern epistemology creeping into the science curriculum. It finds particular expression in the section of Sc1 ('Scientific Enquiry') entitled 'Ideas and Evidence', the area dealing with the nature of the scientific enterprise itself. However, the postmodern influence on the 'Ideas and Evidence' component is not obvious at primary level, where at Key Stage 1 pupils should be taught: '… that it is important to collect evidence by making observations and measurements when trying to answer a question' (Sc1:1a), whilst at Key Stage 2 they are to learn: '… that it is important to test ideas using evidence from observation and measurement' (Sc1:1b).

These two statements taken together constitute a fairly standard formulation of 'the scientific method'. However, at Key Stage 4 (ages 14–16) the emphasis shifts towards a more questioning approach to the work of scientists, with pupils to be taught: '… how scientific controversies can arise from different ways of interpreting empirical evidence [for example, Darwin's theory of evolution]' (Sc1:1b) and '… ways in which scientific work may be affected by the contexts in which it takes place [for example, social, historical, moral, spiritual], and how these contexts may affect whether or not ideas are accepted' (Sc1:1c).

This representation of scientific procedure is much closer to the idea of science as a social network within society as suggested by Thomas Kuhn (1970) than it is to the logical, objective ideal of the scientist promoted by modernism.

The influence of postmodernism on scientific curricula has intensified recently with the publication of new GCSE syllabuses for science including *21st Century Science* (University of York/Nuffield), which has an emphasis upon science in society, controversial issues and scientific literacy for citizens. In the new GCSE criteria (QCA, 2005), 'Ideas and Evidence' has been replaced by 'How Science Works', a phrase implying that a critical insight into how scientists generate knowledge may be more important than the knowledge itself. For example, the criteria stress the importance of: '… recalling, analysing, interpreting, applying and *questioning* scientific information or ideas' (iii a, our italics) and '…evaluating methods of data collection, and considering their validity and reliability as evidence' (ii d).

Predictably, the shifting epistemology of science away from positivist statements of fact towards one in which scientific knowledge is portrayed as socially constructed by a community of scientists has attracted the criticism of 'dumbing down' by some teachers (Jeandron, 2007). Whilst appealing to students (Donelly *et al.*, 2007) – clearly significant in a context of falling applications for science subjects at university – a socially constructed version of science in the curriculum risks avoiding 'hard' concepts in the pursuit of relevance and controversy. Much as we would support the notion of science for citizenship, the danger of science education becoming merely a sub-branch of media education has to be taken seriously.

CONCLUSION

The science curriculum currently in place in England can be seen as representing a shifting balance between two different strands of thought about the status of knowledge and its role in the education of children. The balance appears to have moved in recent years towards a more postmodern view of 'how science works', although the very construction of the curriculum in terms of knowledge to be imparted suggests a traditional model. Another way of evaluating the National Curriculum would be to measure its effects in terms of its four aims as stated above. By laying down by statute what all pupils should be taught, it has arguably established an 'entitlement' (aim 1), although the teaching methods employed and the ways in which teachers interpret and represent the science written in the document will clearly affect that entitlement. Through its prescription of level descriptors of attainment for scientific enquiry and the conceptual components it certainly appears to have established standards (aim 2), although again the precise nature of assessment (whether externally set tests or ongoing teacher assessment for example) will influence how such 'standards' are represented. By specifying content and overlapping levels of attainment from Key Stages 1 to 4 the curriculum appears to have provided for continuity and coherence in pupils' learning (aim 3), though there is continuing evidence (e.g. Galton *et al.*, 1999) of discontinuity between primary and secondary learning in science. Finally, it could be argued that by adopting a relatively traditional model of the science curriculum, which would not be unfamiliar to adults educated several decades ago, the National Curriculum for science promotes public understanding – or at least recognition – of what is happening in classrooms (aim 4). Against its own aims, this curriculum appears to be relatively successful, although we might wish to question those aims in the first place.

SUMMARY POINTS

- There are various conceptions and definitions of 'curriculum', which reflect different epistemological assumptions.
- Politics, power and economics influenced the development of the statutory curriculum in England
- The National Curriculum is dominated by subjects and particular domains of knowledge have assumed core status.
- A curriculum can be evaluated in terms of the views of knowledge that it represents and against its own stated aims.

QUESTIONS FOR DISCUSSION

1   How would you characterise the differences between the kinds of primary curriculum advocated by the Plowden Report in 1967 and the current national curriculum for England?
2   Why might a curriculum be viewed as being 'dangerous'?
3   How has your own education led you to see the nature and status of scientific knowledge in the curriculum?

FURTHER READING

Kelly, A.V. (2004) *The Curriculum: Theory and Practice*, London: Sage Publications. This provides a powerful analysis of different views of curriculum and provides arguments for a process model of curriculum based on notions of human development.

Moyles, J. and Hargreaves, L. (1998). *The Primary Curriculum: Learning from International Perspectives*, London: Routledge. This offers a comparative perspective on the national curriculum in English primary schools by contrasting it with models adopted by other countries.

REFERENCES

Blenkin, G.M. and Kelly, A.V. (1981) *Primary Curriculum*, London: Sage Publications

Blishen, E. (1969) *The School That I'd Like*, London: Penguin.

Board of Education (1927) *Handbook of Suggestions for the Consideration of Teachers and Others Concerned with the Work of Public Elementary Schools*, London: Board of Education.

Callaghan, J. (1976) Towards a national debate, speech at a foundation stone-laying ceremony at Ruskin College, Oxford, 18 October 1976.

Coulby, D (1990) The construction and implementation of the Primary Core Curriculum, in D. Coulby and S. Ward (eds) *The Primary Core National Curriculum: Policy into Practice*, London: Cassell.

DES (1985) *Science 5–16*, London: HMSO.

DfEE/QCA (1999) *The National Curriculum: Handbook for Primary Teachers in England*, London: DfEE/QCA.

Donelly, J., Osborne, J., Ratcliffe, M., Scott, P. and Bennet, J. (2007) *Twenty First Century Science Pilot Evaluation Report*. Online. Available http://www.21stcenturyscience.org/data/files/c21-evaln-rpt-feb07-10101.pdf (accessed 15 November 2007).

Driver, R. (1983) *The Pupil as Scientist?* Milton Keynes: Open University Press.

Galton, M., Gray, J. and Rudduck, J. (1999) *The Impact of School Transitions and Transfers on Pupil Progress and Attainment*, research report RR131, Nottingham: DfEE.

Harlen, W. and Osborne, R. (1985) A model for learning and teaching applied to primary science, *Journal of Curriculum Studies*, 2(17): 133–46.

Jeandron, M. (2007) GCSE science comes under attack, *Physics World*, September 2007: 7.

Kelly, A.V. (2004) *The Curriculum: Theory and Practice*, London: Sage Publications.

Kuhn, T.S. (1970) *The Structure of Scientific Revolutions*, Chicago: University of Chicago Press.

Lawton, D. (1992) *Education and Politics in the 1990s*, London: Falmer Press.

Plowden, B. (1967) *Children and their Primary Schools: A Report of the Central Advisory Council for Education*, London: HMSO.

QCA (2005) *GCSE Criteria for Science*, London: QCA.

Shute, C. (1993) *Compulsory Schooling Disease: How Children Absorb Fascist Values*, Nottingham: Educational Heretics Press.

University of York/Nuffield Curriculum Centre *21st Century Science*. Online. Available http://www.21stcenturyscience.org/. (accessed 15 November 2007).

14   The Ecology of Learning

Mim Hutchings

INTRODUCTION

This chapter examines ways of understanding people's experiences of learning. It is designed as a tool for you to reflect on your own learning and to understand how personal experience and choice interact with the place we are learning in and with the wider world. It is based on two assumptions: first that understanding your own learning is likely to trigger more informed choices about strategies for improvement. Second, all learning stems from our histories as learners and how we are connected to others in our learning. Some frameworks for observing, analysing and supporting the learning experiences of others are introduced.

REFLECTING ON LEARNING

The importance of reflection has long tradition in education. There is a specific kind of reflection: critical reflection on experience, which is a key concept underpinning transformative learning processes. Mezirow (cited in Merriam *et al.*, 2006) suggests that 'premise reflection' involves exploring the deeply rooted assumptions, beliefs and values socially constructed through our lives and lies at the core of transformative learning. The change could be a radical new view of ourselves and the world we inhabit, or a deeper understanding of existing beliefs and values in how we view the world. Other kinds of reflection contribute to the process. First 'content reflection': thinking about an experience, such as understanding the ideas in this chapter. Second 'process reflection': thinking about the strategies for managing the experience or problem solving around ideas that are new or difficult to understand. Transformational learning is about change: 'dramatic, fundamental change in the way we see ourselves and the world in which we live' (Merriam *et al.*, 2006:130).

Learning is an intensely personal activity influenced by experiences, views and approaches to life. Yet at the same time it seldom happens in isolation and is influenced by whom we learn with and the places where we learn. Illeris (2003) suggests that the first step in constructing a view of learning is to appreciate that learning requires the integration of two processes:

> ... an external interaction process between the learner and his or her social, cultural or material environment, and an internal psychological process of acquisition and elaboration (p. 398).

Most theories of learning depict these processes separately giving a partial view of the whole field. For example, psychological perspectives on thinking tend to focus on the procedures within the mind, the internal processes of cognition such as recognising, understanding, storing information and monitoring performance. For educationalists this translates into an emphasis on productive thinking skills such as planning, reasoning and remembering within problem solving as a way to support learners in becoming more aware of and able to improve their learning. Similar limitations can be observed within social learning theories, which have a tendency to concentrate on external processes of social interaction, influences and power relationships. For example, from the perspective of situated learning (Lave and Wenger, 1991), learning happens through participation within a community and cannot be separated from the place, social experiences, learning activities and available tools. Perkins (1993) talks about 'the person plus': how individuals and communities of learners make use of 'tools' or the immediate physical and social resources (such as people, technology or pictures) to learn. This includes the idea that intelligence does not reside only within the individual but also within the resources used to accomplish learning. Within the classroom this might be viewed as thinking of all the people in the classroom (pupils, teachers, support assistants) working as a community, plus the physical support systems of pens, white boards, books and multimedia stories.

Illeris (2003) points out that this tendency towards separating cognitive, emotional and environmental aspects does not mean that these theories are worthless; it is simply that they do not cover the 'whole field of learning' (p. 398). He also suggests that transformative learning is an example of a point in time when all three dimensions (cognitive, emotional and social) undergo dramatic restructuring as new challenges make change necessary in order to progress. What is required to aid us in personal critical reflection, studying, watching and supporting learning are frameworks that afford an overview of the landscape of learning. With this landscape it is possible to see how themes from a variety of theories and concepts about learning run in parallel, each contributing differing but significant understandings of what is going on as we look at, or participate in, learning in specific places. Transition, such as moving countries, starting school or university, are times in our lives when we are most likely to feel changes or transformation most strongly.

ARRIVING IN A NEW PLACE – A CASE STUDY OF LEARNING

Laila has spent the first six years of her life in Norway. She grew up speaking Arabic with her father and Norwegian with her mother and in kindergarten. Now she is spending her first day in a primary school in England. She is nervous about the changes in her life but confident about coping, as she has always been encouraged to join in everything at kindergarten and had good friends in Norway. All the children in her new class know the morning routine and start reading with a partner. Laila's teacher has put her with a partner, who smiles and begins to read her book to her. Laila is puzzled. In her kindergarten in Norway no one had a reading book. She listens carefully to her partner who is reading aloud slowly, struggling to work out the words on the page. As Laila looks around the class everyone has a reading book. She was quiet that day, immersing herself in this new environment, watching, listening but getting quite cross. She had never felt that she couldn't do at least the same as everyone else. That evening she went home, determined to teach herself to read. She collected together all her books, asked her parents to help and by the next week was immersed in the reading partners game, determined to be a participant in her new environment.

Laila has what might be called 'a feel for the game' in the field of education. So, despite meeting new practices in the classroom, she has the cultural capital to understand, interpret and act in this new social world. She uses the practical social competencies learned in Norwegian education to make a choice about how and what she will do in this situation. Laila's choice is to accept the new values and immerse herself in what is required, to take ownership of her learning by learning to read. In order to do this she has to overcome her emotions of initial impatience, frustration and anxiety, to organise her cognitive resources, reflect on what she has to do and, with the support of strong learning relationships within the home, takes the first step in belonging in this new learning environment. This description emphasises the external and internal factors in Laila's transformation as a learner that might have remained hidden by concentrating on a single dimension. In this example Illeris's (2003) three dimensions of learning – cognitive, emotional (internal) and environment (external) –interact.

ECOLOGICAL SYSTEMS

Bronfenbrenner's (2005) ecological approach suggests that all aspects of learning are interconnected and cannot be understood in isolation. The individual learner lives within a complex series of interactive systems. An alternative way of understanding Laila's experiences would be to consider the different systems that she inhabits: first, her experiences of home and education in Norway and England; second, political and policy factors such as differences in the age that children begin formal schooling.

At the core is an individual, living within a 'microsystem' consisting of all the environments a learner inhabits, together with the face-to-face interactions within those environments. Examples include the home, the family and relationships with parents, grandparents, siblings and language/s used. Children inhabit more than one microsystem of places, relationships and languages such as home, education setting, play/social environments, both within school and the neighbourhood.

The microsystems are connected to the 'mesosystems' through interaction between two or more systems, which influence the learner directly. Examples include: how and whether an education setting values and builds positive home/school relationships; how language/s used at home are valued and used within education settings. Another example is parents' perceptions of the safety of their local area and whether there are safe play/social environments where children can meet their friends. The relationships between the systems can be either singly or multi-linked. When systems work collaboratively, rather than in tension, then the child's experiences and learning are more likely to be positive.

'Exosystem' systems refer to the environments and relationships that the child does not experience first hand, but which have an indirect influence on them. Examples are: opportunities for employment in the locality or parents' working hours and levels of stress within a workplace influencing a child's home life; whether the education setting actively pursues multilingual policies. Another example is whether the organisation of safe play/social environments for young people is a local community and political priority. Although the exosystem is experienced second hand, its influence on the individual can be strong.

The broadest context is the macrosystem in which all the other systems are embedded. Every person is a part of a wider political, economic, social and cultural setting, which influences the world of individual learners. Economic decisions about relocating a manufacturing industry to another part of the world can change employment opportunities in a locality and have an impact on the embedded systems. Changing government policies affect individuals' experiences of education. Examples are the different foundation stage curriculum in England, Wales and Scotland; and how community languages and knowledge are marginalised or absent from mainstream English schools.

An ecological system suggests ways of understanding the interactions between a range of influences on learning. The ecology of learning within a setting becomes not just about how the learner changes, but also about the climate for learning: what kinds of learning relationships educators value; how resourceful settings and individual educators are in drawing on languages, literacies and knowledge within their local environment. Although at first an ecological systems approach appears complicated, the concept of nested systems opens up opportunities for analysing connections across (lateral) systems and through time (temporal). As a child develops so associated systems change; as political, economic and social worlds change so does the experience of the individual.

So far two different frameworks for understanding the experiences of learners have been reviewed. Illeris's (2003) three dimensions suggest ways of understanding learners and learning within specific places such as classrooms. It offers potential for understanding why individuals learn something different from the same lesson, or the way a learner feels about a lesson, subject or teacher can affect learning. Bronfenbrenner's ecological system suggests that learning is embedded in a web of influences where changes within one of the systems can have a profound effect on learners and learning. This framework offers understanding of questions such as how transition from home into school or from kindergarten in one country to school in another, or from school to university, changes learners. The final frameworks turn to successful learning in education and how they could be used as tools for personal reflection. The emphasis in these recent frameworks is on identifying core dimensions of effective learning. Although the focus is on the individual learner, the cultural context of learning in classrooms is seen as a crucial part of an 'ecology of learning'.

Both of the frameworks discussed here stem from systematic reviews of research about learning and are often accompanied by catch phrases designed to interest teachers such as 'developing the mind to learn', 'learning power' (Claxton, 2002) or 'learning energy' (Deakin Crick, 2006). Nevertheless they are helpful tools for making explicit what is known about effective learning. They also represent a long tradition of recognising processes of learning as well as knowledge to enhance our ability to improve learning. Claxton's (2002) *Building Learning Power*, written for teachers, focuses on developing the mind to learn by working on four aspects of students' learning: resilience, resourcefulness, reflectiveness and reciprocity.

> The first task is to help them become more resilient: able to lock on to learning and to resist distractions either from outside or within. The second is helping them become more resourceful: able to draw on a wide range of learning methods and strategies as appropriate. The third is building the ability to be reflective: to think profitably about learning and themselves as learners. And the fourth task is to make them capable of being reciprocal: making use of relationships in the most productive, enjoyable and responsible way (p. 17).

The second approach finds recurring themes that are significant to personal development and learning. 'Evaluating Lifelong Learning Inventory' (ELLI) is an instrument that can identify elements of an individual's capacity for lifelong learning. Through a series of research projects, mainly with school-age pupils, a database of around 6,000 pupils was accumulated of 'seven dimensions of learning power and reliable scales to assess these' (Deakin Crick *et al.*, 2004: 247). Currently the ELLI profile is used by a growing number of schools nationally and internationally to support pupils' and teachers' reflection on learning (Deakin Crick, 2006). More recently the profile has been introduced within higher education as part of students' professional development profiles and as a tool to support reflection on learning in university and work placements.

In a recent project in an Education Studies module 'Learning through Life' students worked through a process of reflecting on their growing knowledge of research about learning and influences on their learning. During the module students went through a three-step process of:

1   using the ELLI online self-report questionnaire;
2   undertaking a personal project investigating influences on their learning;
3   reflecting on what they had learnt and how they had changed through the process.

The purpose of the three-step approach was to support students through discussion, reflection and action in order to facilitate personal change.

The first step, using the profile, provided students with a visual profile of their learning and information about the seven dimensions associated with effective learning. The ELLI online self-report questionnaire measures what individuals say about their learning at a particular point in time. Individual learners' responses to the questionnaire may change over time and within different contexts. The research from the ELLI project suggests that for most learners there are likely to be enduring characteristics such as critical curiosity. The learner reflects on all seven dimensions at once in relation to each other. The following summary of the seven dimensions draws on Deakin Crick (2006) and Deakin Crick *et al.* (2004). As you read each of the dimensions identify which parts of each dimension seem most like you.

Dimensions of learning

Changing and learning

Some learners know that learning itself is learnable. They see learning as a lifelong process and gain pleasure and self-esteem from expanding their ability to learn. Changing and learning includes a sense of getting better at learning over time and of growing and changing and adapting as a learner in the whole of life. There is a sense of history, hope and aspiration. The opposite end of the spectrum is fixity: the belief that the ability to learn is fixed. These learners tend to experience difficulties negatively, as revealing their limitations. They are less likely to see challenging situations as opportunities to become a better learner. Their feeling of self-efficacy is weak.

Critical curiosity

Some learners show a desire to find things out: to get below the surface of things and try to find out what is going on. They are more likely to adopt 'deep' rather than 'surface' learning strategies. They are less likely to accept what they are told uncritically, enjoy asking questions and are more willing to reveal their questions and uncertainties in public. They like to come to their own conclusions about things and are inclined to see knowledge, at least in part, as a product of human inquiry. They take ownership of their own learning and enjoy a challenge. At the opposite end of the spectrum learners are more passive, accepting what they are told uncritically. They appear less thoughtful and less likely to engage spontaneously in active speculation and exploratory discussion.

Meaning making

Some learners are on the lookout for links between what they are learning and what they already know. They get pleasure from seeing how things 'fit together'. They like it when they can make sense of new things in terms of their own experience and when they can see how learning relates to their own concerns. Their questions reflect an orientation towards coherence. They are interested in the big picture and how the new learning fits within it. At the opposite end of the spectrum is fragmentation: learners who tend to approach learning situations piecemeal and to respond to them on their own individual merits. They may be more interested in knowing the criteria for successful performance than in looking for joined-up meanings and connections.

Creativity

Some learners are able to look at things in different ways and to imagine new possibilities. They enjoy lateral thinking, playing with ideas and taking different perspectives, even when they don't quite know where their trains of thought are leading. They are more receptive to hunches that bubble up into their minds and make use of imagination, visual imagery in their learning. They understand that learning often needs playfulness as well as purposeful, systematic thinking. At the opposite end of the spectrum are rule-bound learners who prefer clear-cut information and tried-and-tested ways of approaching things. They feel safer when they know how they are meant to proceed. They function well in problem-solving situations with unambiguous answers.

Learning relationships – interdependence

Some learners are good at managing the balance between being sociable and being private in their learning. They are not completely independent, nor are they dependent. They like to learn with and from others and to share their difficulties. They recognise important people in their lives who help them learn, though they may vary in who those people are. They know the value of learning by watching and emulating other people, including their peers. They make use of others as resources, as partners and as sources of emotional support. They also know that effective learning may also require times of studying, enquiring and even 'dreaming' on their own. At the opposite end of the spectrum are learners who may be isolated or dependent. They are more likely to be stuck either in their over-dependency on others for reassurance or guidance, or in their lack of engagement with other people.

Strategic awareness

Learners with strategic awareness tend to be more aware of, and talk about, their learning. They like trying out different approaches to learning to see what happens. They are more reflective and better at self-evaluation. They can judge how much time or what resources a learning task will require. They know how to repair their own emotional mood when they get frustrated or disappointed. They like being given responsibility for planning and organising their own learning. At the opposite end of the spectrum are learners who are less self-aware, who are less likely to be able to explain the reasons for the ways they choose to go about things. They don't tend to reflect on their own processes and experiences in such a way as to 'name them' and learn from them. They might plunge into a task with little planning or forethought.

Resilience

Resilient learners like a challenge and are willing to 'give it a go', even when the outcome and the way to proceed are uncertain. They accept that learning is sometimes hard for everyone and are not frightened of finding things difficult. They are persistent and can readily overcome feelings of frustration and impatience. They stick with learning even though they may, for a while, feel confused or even anxious. They don't mind making mistakes and can learn from them. At the opposite end of the spectrum are learners who are dependent and fragile who more easily go to pieces when they get stuck or make mistakes. They prefer not to take too many risks and often seek and prefer less challenging situations. They are dependent upon other people and external structures for their learning and for their sense of self-esteem. They are passive receivers of knowledge, rather than active agents of their own learning, constructing meaning from their experience.

Findings from students

On completing the online profile students filled in a reflective questionnaire on how they felt about using the profile: how easy was it to understand and complete? Did they feel it accurately represented their view of themselves as learners? The majority of students rated the experience of doing the profile as positive and as an accurate representation of themselves as learners. In addition students were asked to reflect on their strengths, weaknesses and priorities for improvement. Student responses suggested that the profile and information was clear, easy to understand and offered most of them an accurate picture of their learning. Typical responses were:

> 'I feel it correctly highlighted the areas of learning where I am not as efficient as I should be.'

> 'It is a good reflection of the learner I am. Although in the past I have been stronger in different learner dimensions.'

However, even when students disagreed with aspects of their profile it prompted thoughtful analysis of why this might be the case and starting points for developing a critique of the construction and use of questionnaires about learning generally.

> 'I have no idea of what type of learner I am, but of course I am not certain, especially as there are so many varying models and instruments to help you identify this. I have always thought of myself as a varied learner with the ability to adapt my learning to differing situations and my profile didn't reflect this. The profile results suggest that I have a weakness in the learning relationships dimension but it would be too obvious to suggest that it is something I need to improve. I feel that the questions asked were the problem. I am the first person in my family to go to university and just because my learning is not strongly influenced by my family and friends, it does not mean that I am weak when working with other people.'

All students could identify specific strengths and weaknesses and identify areas for improvement. However, at this stage the emphasis was what could be improved (content reflection) rather than how (process reflection).

'My profile suggests that my strengths are learning relationships, creativity and meaning making. I like to make links with what I am learning and what I know already as it helps my understanding. I also find that I learn better through exploring ideas in different ways. My main weakness is strategic learning; this may be because I am not very confident about my own learning and its differences from others.'

The second step asked students to complete a personal project on their learning that included their ELLI profile. The model used to prompt student's reflections was inspired by Brookfield's (cited in Merriam *et al.*, 2006) five phases of critical thinking and the seven dimensions. The projects began with the trigger of selecting a variety of images of places or objects of significance in their learning and moved to a self-examination of ideas and questions associated with these images.

In the third phase – exploration – students were asked to 'dig deep' with one image: to question and examine its connections to themselves as learners and to their developing knowledge about learning.

'I believe that my rebellious nature, my strong-mindedness, my individuality and my want to help others is as a direct result of the picture … I've never really thought about it or made a connection until doing this project.'

The fourth phase was developing alternative perspectives through theorising about their experiences. One student selected a series of images of situations that challenged her thinking on morality and asked 'What are my morals and how did I acquire them?' leading into an exploration of theories of moral development.

The fifth phase was also the final step: integrating these new ways of thinking into a critical reflection on their learning journey through the project and the module.

'My main reflection, from analysing myself in relation to these theories, is that my strength as a learner lies in having proved to myself that resilience brings results. I conclude, from my research into moral development and its theories in relation to culture, that questions surround the universality of the higher stages of Kohlberg's theory.'

'My final conclusion, and the main point that I would like to communicate, is the importance and power in learning about oneself as a learner. Apart from being able to identify weaknesses to improve, the realisation of learning strengths will aid in applying them sooner to learning situations.'

From this group of undergraduate students emerges a picture of learners taking control and recognising how their learning has changed in response to developing knowledge about learning, skills of reflection and personal perspective on theories of learning. Whether this was transformational learning remains a question and reveals difficulties surrounding this approach. Learning is an intensely personal activity, even though it inhabits public spaces. Transformation is an uncertain process that is only partially predictable and never complete. Nevertheless, having a source that is accessible and makes explicit some of the dimensions underlying effective learning together with a process that invites learners to engage in critical reflective practice is worth pursuing.

CONCLUSION

This chapter has introduced some frameworks for theorising about learning. The criterion for selection has been their potential for explaining how individuals' educational careers are linked to wider contexts. They all suggest the importance of understanding how learning is connected to histories of experience and across structures that frame our opportunities for learning. Much of what happens in educational settings operates in a murky world of hidden practices and is based on collectively assumed values. At the same time the places and the policies of education are increasingly influenced by external forces locally, nationally and globally. These frameworks suggest that theory should engage with dilemmas, tensions, contradictions and the partiality of current Western research on learning. A fully comprehensive theory of learning is probably not achievable. However, it is possible and practical to work with multiple perspectives to inform our thinking. To have schools and universities suitable for the education of diverse learners and capable of including vulnerable learners, we need tools to trigger reflection on what it means to be a learner in this place and at this time.

SUMMARY POINTS

- Reflecting on learning is an important step in understanding yourself as a learner, engaging with theories and processes of learning.
- The frameworks introduced are potential 'tools' for personal reflection, studying, watching and supporting learning. As such they offer some starting points for theorising about learning in education settings.
- A central theme has been the importance of making connections: to the histories of learners and across a range of influences on learners.
- Multiple perspectives offer opportunities to view different theories and concepts of learning as part of or contributing to a wider picture.
- Theoretical frameworks are 'tools' for analysing and questioning assumptions and practice in education.

QUESTIONS FOR DISCUSSION AND REFLECTION

1   How do these frameworks help you identify the influences on strengths and weaknesses of your learning?
2   How would you describe your strengths and weaknesses as a learner and how would you improve?
3   Where and when would it be appropriate to use these frameworks to observe, analyse and reflect on learning?
4   What connections can you make to other theories of learning?

FURTHER READING

Claxton, G. (1999) *Wise Up: Living the Learning Life*, London: Bloomsbury/Network. Explores a range of themes about learning through life in an accessible way.

Deakin Crick, R. (2006) *Learning Power in Practice*, London: Paul Chapman Publishing. Provides a more detailed overview of learning power and the seven dimensions of learning. It also includes chapters written by teachers on implementing the ideas and concepts of learning power.

Kail, R. and Cavanaugh, J. (2004) *Human Development: A Life Span View*, Belmont, CA: Wadsworth/Thomson Learning. A United States college text that introduces psychological perspectives on the study of human development, including most 'traditional' learning theories.

Moseley, D., Baumfield, V., Elliot, J., Gregson, M., Higgens, S., Miller, J. and Newton, D. (2005). *Frameworks for Thinking*, Cambridge: Cambridge University Press. Provides descriptions and evaluations of major frameworks about the thinking processes associated with learning: a detailed, accessible and up-to-date overview.

REFERENCES

Bronfenbrenner, U. (ed.) (2005) *Making Human Beings Human: Bioecological Perspectives on Human Development*, London: Sage.

Claxton, G. (2002) *Building Learning Power*, Bristol: Bristol TLO.

Deakin Crick, R. (2006) *Learning Power in Practice*, London: Paul Chapman Publishing.

Deakin Crick, R., Broadfoot, P. and Claxton, G. (2004) Developing an effective lifelong learning inventory: the ELLI project, *Assessment in Education*, 11(3): 247–72.

Illeris, K. (2003) Towards a contemporary and comprehensive theory of learning, *International Journal of Lifelong Learning*, 22(4): 396–406.

Lave, J. and Wenger, E. (1991) *Situated Learning: Legitimate Peripheral Participation*, Cambridge: Cambridge University Press.

Merriam, S.B., Cafferalla, R. and Baumgartner, L. (2006) *Learning in Adulthood: A Comprehensive Guide* (3rd edition), San Francisco: Jossey-Bass.

Perkins, D.N. (1993) Person-plus: a distributed view of thinking and learning, in G. Salomon (ed.) *Distributed Cognitions: Psychological and Educational Considerations*, Cambridge: Cambridge University Press.

15 Young Children Learning

Viki Bennett and Nicki O'Brien

INTRODUCTION

Learning for young children is a naturally creative and rewarding experience. This chapter explores the repertoire of strategies that young children employ in their learning. Drawing on the findings of key theorists, the first section explains young children's learning under each of these headings:

- investigation;
- movement;
- schema;
- repetition;
- communication.

Children learn best when they feel secure and motivated, particularly when they play. The final section shows the orchestrating nature of play in learning across the different strategies. Each is illustrated by an observation of children – a 'scenario'. Examples of good practice in early years education are also included.

INVESTIGATION

Young children have a natural desire to investigate the world around them. Research by Pascal and Bertram (2006) demonstrates that 'from birth, children have a strong exploratory drive to experiment, explore, interact with and make sense of their world' (p. 59). Investigation involves first-hand discovery and children use all of their senses to increase their knowledge and understanding. They examine and look closely, handle and take things apart, put things in their mouths to taste and test, and seek out the potential for making and responding to sound.

Scenario 1 – in a puddle

India (3 years 7 months) is jumping in the puddles. She investigates the movement of the water by varying the style of her jump. She feels the water on her legs, her hands and sometimes on her face. She can hear the splash every time she lands and can see the water travelling outwards and upwards. This active investigation enables her to find out more about water and the impact that her own body can make on it.

Jean Piaget (1896–1980) was the first major developmental psychologist who explained that children learn and develop as they investigate new and familiar aspects of their environment. He defined stages of cognitive development and the ages at which these occur. Piaget's theories have occupied the dominant discourse in understanding children's learning and development, although subsequent thinking has disputed this principle of assigning milestones to a specific chronological age.

India is investigating some familiar and unfamiliar aspects of water. As she encounters a new phenomenon – stamping hard enough to force water up to her face – she seeks to understand the experience. Piaget suggests that when this happens a 'disequilibrium' occurs, which the child can resolve through cognitive adaptation. Adaptation takes two forms:

1   Assimilation – the child incorporates the new phenomenon into her current understanding of the world. India already knew that water travelled in lots of directions. Her discovery that water can reach her face by the force of stamping feet would lead her to 'assimilate' this into her existing knowledge of water.
2   Accommodation – the child makes changes to her previous understanding of the world. For example, Jessie had established that all words that began with 'ch' sounded the same at the beginning, e.g. 'church, chicken, children'. When her brother Christopher was born, however, she had to adjust her knowledge and recognise that the consonant cluster could also made a different sound.

Jerome Bruner (1915–) has developed Piaget's ideas and proposes 'learning as discovery': children's independent exploration helps them to understand and remember crucial concepts. Similarly, Laevers (1999) suggests that only 'by acknowledging [children's] interests, giving them room for experimentation, letting them decide upon the way an activity is performed will children be satisfied with their learning' (p. 5). In order to investigate, young children need opportunities to explore a wide range of materials at their own pace. They are entitled to have their ideas valued and extended by supportive and interested adults.

MOVEMENT

Children love to move and be physical. Even before birth they learn by being active and interactive. During the foetal period this becomes apparent to the mother who feels the developing baby moving in response to her voice, her body movements and other environmental stimuli. David and Powell (2007) suggest that children's 'ability to investigate increases as they become physically more able' (p. 15). Piaget recognised that the foundation of young children's learning is dependent upon their early sensory and motor experiences. He argued that children, particularly from birth to two years, find out about the world through their 'motor activity'. He called this critical time the 'sensorimotor stage'. More recent research confirms the power of movement as a tool for learning. Maude (2003) declares it to be 'the main medium of exploration for the young child' (p. 211).

Movement is made up of both gross and fine motor actions and involves children exploring and manipulating their environment. It allows them to take control, feel confident, build a sense of self, take risks and recognise cause and effect.

Scenario 2 – height and speed

> Harry (4 years 2 months) is sitting on a see-saw with his friend Alice. He propels himself from the floor using his legs and enjoys the effect of the upward movement on his body, particularly the jolt as Alice reaches the ground. He notices that the speed and height of his travel is controlled by the force of his leg push and experiments with this. He recognises that Alice's movement and his own are connected. Harry is having fun and is happy with the physical risk that this activity involves. He can decide to increase the height and speed each time and is therefore becoming more confident as he does so.

Howard Gardner (1993) is well known for his theory of multiple intelligences. According to Gardner, intelligence is not a single entity, or 'general intelligence'. Instead individuals have different strengths in various cognitive areas such as language, mathematics or music and 'bodily-kinaesthetic'. He suggests that children are able both to experience and to demonstrate their understanding of the world through a physical movement. Harry is moving his body with skill and control and is making sense of a range of physical processes. He is using his bodily-kinaesthetic intelligence to hypothesise, try out, draw conclusions and demonstrate new understanding.

The impact of physical movement to cognitive function has been widely acknowledged:

> … learning to move cannot be divorced from the fact that physically oriented experiences, as well as cultural and social experiences, encourage the ways and extent to which the brain develops.

> (Davies, 2003, p.30)

Research described by Doherty and Bailey (2003) demonstrates that movement experiences are of fundamental importance in each child's development and education: children 'would rather take part in physical activities than any other endeavour' (p. 2). Young children need to have frequent opportunities to move and have access to space, stimulating materials and equipment. They also need to be with adults who respect and promote bodily-kinaesthetic learning.

SCHEMAS

Children can be seen to engage in certain actions and behaviours that may seem to adults to be random and lacking in purpose: lining up and connecting small toys, wrapping objects, carrying items from place to place and hiding themselves under coverings. Piaget (1962) observed these patterns of behaviour and called them 'schemas'. He describes them as 'coordinated systems of movements and perceptions, which constitute any elementary behaviour capable of being repeated and applied to new situations' (p. 274). He suggests that children explore the world by trying out schemas on everything they meet in the environment. At first explorations will be action-based and generalised: all objects can be bitten. But as they are repeated, learning becomes more thought-based: apples are good to bite, but stones are not. In this way schemas are instrumental in facilitating new learning at certain crucial stages. His hypothesis has been developed by later theorists, most notably Athey, who in 1990 noted that children's schemas clearly influence their learning. Indeed it has been suggested that schemas continue from childhood into adulthood and can influence lifelong interests and learning (Bruce, 2005a: 84). Athey defines a schema as 'a pattern of repeatable behaviour into which experiences are assimilated and that are gradually coordinated' (p. 37). She observed that more than one schema or cluster may present at a given time and, building on Piaget's original work, named and grouped these according to the characteristics of the behaviour. Examples include dynamic vertical schemas, circular direction and rotation, going over or under and enveloping and containing.

Scenario 3 – dropping the boat

Alfie (9 months) is sitting in his high chair. He drops his toy boat to the floor and looks down at it. His mother picks it up and gives it back to him saying 'here you are'. Alfie drops the boat again and the sequence is repeated a number of times. Both Alfie and his mother smile and giggle throughout.

Scenario 4 – musical circles

Surinda is 3 years 9 months. Recently her parents have noticed her regularly painting circular patterns. She repeats this circular movement when using her crayons and stirring her ice-cream. When dancing to her favourite music she loves to swirl round and round with her arms outstretched.

Alfie displays an early schematic behavioural pattern often seen in babies. He is captivated by the way an object moves up and down. Athey has identified and named this behaviour as a 'dynamic vertical schema' (p. 116). Surinda is fascinated by exploring the round-and-round movement, which Athey describes as a 'rotation schema'. Surinda is seeking opportunities to explore circular movements in different contexts. Bruce (2005b) suggests that the importance of schemas is that they provide a mechanism for analysing 'where the learner is' and help to predict other situations that will be of interest to the child. To kindle Surinda's learning, experiences such as a trip to a fair or theme park, dancing with streamers and ribbons, playing with hoops and wheels will enhance her language, her social and physical development and her knowledge and understanding of the world.

REPETITION

Young children relish the opportunity for repetition and through it steer their learning and gain satisfaction. Neuro-scientific research in the 1990s revealed the power of repetition on the human brain, which is important to studying how young children learn. The findings suggest that the brain is a network of physical pathways made up of neurons, axons and dendrites. The pathways are strengthened by repetition of a certain behaviour or action. Put simply, the tracks that come to be used most often are developed because of the increased level of energy and muscle activity. Conversely, tracks that are not used or used less will atrophy and eventually disappear. The overwhelming majority of these connections are formed in the first few years: 'Everything a baby sees, hears, tastes, touches and smells influences the way the brain gets hooked up' (Gopnik et al., 2001: 181). Babies are active participants in their own brain development and the repetitive experiences that they select at this time are crucial in constructing and consolidating meaning.

Scenario 5 – repeated patterns

> Molly (5 years 2 months) is listening to her favourite story. She turns the pages and recognises her favourite character. Throughout the story she anticipates and predicts events by pointing at the pictures and making statements. She notices when two pages are turned at once and that the pattern of the story is different from previous readings. She joins in with the repetitive phrases and on completion asks her father for the story to be read again.

Molly has become familiar with book conventions and is able to choose stories that particularly interest and excite her. She knows how to open and handle the book, is familiar with the story structure, recognises individual specific events and understands the relationship between the spoken and written word. This repeated experience, in a safe and secure environment, has helped her to develop confidence, preference and satisfaction, and will enable her to transfer these skills into new situations.

Scenario 6 – goal kicks

> Luke (2 years 9 months) is playing with a collection of balls. He is practising his favourite activity of aiming the balls at the goal. He holds each one with both hands out in front of him and as he drops the ball he attempts to kick it into the goal. Sometimes his kick and aim are successful and he shows how pleased he is by exclaiming 'yes!' He repeats these actions with all his balls and gathers them back to play the game again continuing for a further 30 minutes. He chooses to play this game regularly for the next six weeks during which his ability to aim and kick improves.

Luke is practising and consolidating, motivated to repeat this game by the rewarding experience of a goal. Laevers (1999) concludes that children learn best when they are deeply involved and satisfied by an activity. He recognises persistence and precision as key signals of involvement and suggests that the amount of energy and concentration invested contributes to successful learning. Luke will draw on this experience and find that the elements of repetition – trial and error, persistence, concentration and energy – are valid strategies to apply to any learning situation. Claxton (1999) is concerned with cultivating effective habits and attitudes for lifelong learning in order to develop 'learning power'. He identifies four key aspects of learning: resilience, resourcefulness, reflectiveness and reciprocity. Luke's resilience and self-belief can therefore be acknowledged as essential to this learning experience.

In order to facilitate repetition, children need time and space to return to their chosen activities. Children's learning will only *deepen* and *flourish* if adults recognise that when a concept or skill has been mastered, the levels of complexity and challenge need to be increased. This is in line with Bruner's (1977) view of learning as a spiral: children should have opportunities to revisit the same concept over time but at more sophisticated levels. For example, wheeled vehicles are often provided in early years settings. As they ride on a range of surfaces children learn about the differences in speed and effort required to make the vehicle move over them. These early experiences should be revisited and built upon later in a more complex study of friction using materials and vocabulary that are developmentally appropriate. Bruner (1977) states that 'any subject can be taught to any child at any age in some form that is honest' (p. ix). This theory continues to serve as a prompt for practitioners to plan according to children's current understandings.

COMMUNICATION

Communication is at the heart of young children's learning. From birth, they are highly skilful and effective at conveying and receiving messages from those around them. They achieve this by using an increasing range of verbal and non-verbal language strategies. These include speaking and listening; body language such as facial expression, eye contact and gesture; representation such as the written word, mathematical and musical notation, role play, dance and picture.

Lev Vygotsky (1896–1934) shows that children learn best when they are able to use language to clarify their thoughts. Children engage in 'inner speech' – a spoken commentary on what they are doing or have done. Vygotsky suggests that as children grow older the 'inner speech' becomes less apparent or internalised because they are able to recall and clarify their learning through thought. Bruner (1977) also identified this process and describes language as a 'tool of thought'. His research confirms that inner speech enables children to consolidate and apply knowledge.

In addition Vygotsky (1978) recognised the importance of children interacting with adults and more experienced others who question, describe, model, demonstrate and listen. With appropriate language and support, a child can move beyond the edge of his or her capability and understanding into a new level of understanding – the Zone of Proximal Development. Building on this notion Bruner (1986) recommends 'scaffolding' as a teaching strategy – the supportive process of advising, encouraging and facilitating.

Scenario 7 – chicken and eggs

> Annabelle (5 years 7 months) is helping her childminder to feed the chickens. As they approach the hen house Annabelle speculates about the number of eggs that will have been laid today stating 'I think there will be six'. 'What makes you think that?' asks the childminder. Annabelle replies, 'There were six yesterday so there will be six today'. 'Oh yes you're right. Good thinking! I wonder why there have been six every day?'

In this exchange the childminder is encouraging Annabelle to verbalise her language for thinking. She is helping her to identify patterns and to draw conclusions. She is affirming Annabelle's reasoning by showing a genuine interest in what she thinks. As the conversation continues the childminder may choose to introduce new and specific language appropriate to the activity, such as 'half-dozen, dozen, broody, cluck, peck, scratch'.

Recent research confirms that children's learning is most effective when adults offer opportunities for sustained dialogue and exploration. The EPPE project (Sylva *et al.*, 2004) investigated the effects of preschool education and care on the development of children aged 3–7 years. It emphasises the quality of adult–child verbal interactions and recommends episodes of 'sustained shared thinking' with children:

> 'Sustained shared thinking' occurs when two or more individuals 'work together' in an intellectual way to solve a problem, clarify a concept, evaluate an activity, extend a narrative etc. Both parties must contribute to the thinking and it must develop and extend the understanding. It was more likely to occur when children were interacting 1:1 with an adult or with a single peer partner and during focussed group work … Adult 'modelling' skills or appropriate behaviour was often combined with sustained periods of shared thinking; open-ended questioning and modelling were also associated with better cognitive achievement. (p. 13)

The philosophy and pedagogy of the Reggio Emilia Pre-schools in Northern Italy are internationally acclaimed. Reciprocal relationships are recognised as fundamental to children's learning. Value is placed on the interaction and mutual trust between teachers, children and parents: 'the interactive partners of the educational process' (Rinaldi, 1998: 118). This is facilitated through a pedagogy of listening, encapsulated in the following example:

Scenario 8 – shadow bird

A group of children notice a shadow in the shape of a bird on the wall of the role-play area. Initially they are not aware that this is created by a mobile hanging in the window. They are fascinated by the movement of the shadow and use their hands and available resources (tape, boxes) to try and 'stop the bird' and 'keep it from leaving'. The practitioner uses her skills in questioning and encouragement to elicit the children's thoughts and knowledge as they return to the shadow bird throughout the day. The activity also captures the imagination of a group of older children who use their previous understanding of the effects of the sun to suggest reasons why the 'shadow bird' keeps moving beyond the confines of the children's cage creations. As the children talk, hypothesise and discover, the practitioner records the children's 'learning journey' by taking photographs and writing down what the children say. The practitioner is able to analyse this information to make suggestions about what the children know and think. This process of 'documentation' allows the children's learning to be made visible and crucially involves other teachers, parents and the children themselves.

Malaguzzi (1997), the founder of the Reggio Emilia approach to early years education, celebrates children's range of communication strategies as a 'hundred languages' in his poem 'No way. The hundred is there'. This is a fundamental consideration for all those concerned with young children's learning.

PLAY

Although it has been recognised that children may learn in other ways, much has been written about the importance of play in young children's learning. A predominant theme is that through play there is no risk of failure. This is because young children naturally choose to play. While playing they create their own rules and goals and manage materials, people and time. This enables their confidence and self-belief to flourish, which in turn contributes to a state of emotional security. The more secure children feel the higher their level of cognitive operation will be. Vygotsky (1978) states that, particularly in imaginative play, children are 'a head taller than themselves' (p. 102): they operate at higher levels of thought and action than they would in any other context. For Bruce (2005b) play is an 'integrating mechanism' that helps children 'to consolidate, coordinate and get to together what they know, feel and understand in ways which give them a sense of control over what is happening to them' (p. 130). Play is the most effective context in which young children can manage and pursue the learning mechanisms that this chapter examines: investigation, movement, schema, repetition and communication.

Scenario 9 – bathing baby

Moses (4 years 7 months) regularly chooses to play in the role play area themed as a bathroom. He selects a jug from a shelf that he then uses to fill a baby bath with water. He pretends adding bubble bath and then washes a doll. Moses supports his doll carefully in the water with one hand and gently washes it with the other. 'All clean!' he says as he lifts the doll out of the water. He wraps the doll in a towel and then puts it to bed, covering it with a blanket. Throughout his play Moses provides a verbal commentary.

In his bath-time play Moses is learning about the needs of others. He shows genuine care and concern for the doll and handles it as if it were a real baby (movement). He is familiar with the bath-time routine (repetition) and through role play represents his understanding with confidence and security (communication). His inner speech is helping him to connect ideas and explain what is happening (communication). Moses manages the resources with increasing dexterity (movement). The play provides an appropriate context in which he can explore and develop his schematic interest in enveloping. He enjoys controlling the timing of the events and demonstrates a sense of pride in his achievements.

Scenario 10 – log ladder

> Tamsin (4 years 1 month), Donny (4 years 11 months) and Susie (5 years 10 months) are playing in the park with their grandfather and have collected some small logs. The children decide to lay the logs on the ground in a line. 'It looks like a ladder!' shouts Susie, 'I'm going to climb it!' She jumps over each log in turn and the other children do the same. They repeat the action again and again and, as Susie jumps, she starts to count out loud. Tamsin asks her grandfather to count her jumps, which he is happy to do. After five minutes, Donny withdraws from the ladder game and starts collecting leaves.

The children have created their own game using the skills of negotiation and problem solving, adapting and refining the ladder layout as they play (repetition). They have established their own set of rules and eventually agreed how the play should proceed (communication). The game is based on physical movement and the children show their physical prowess by jumping over the logs successfully (movement). The enthusiasm for the game motivates Susie to add a new dimension to the play by introducing the language of number. She represents her knowledge by counting as she jumps and inspires the other children to count higher than they have felt confident to do before (communication).

Scenario 11 – peek-a-boo

> Anja (6 months) is in the baby seat of a supermarket trolley. Whilst her mother is packing the shopping, Anja attracts the attention of the adult standing in the queue behind. She does this by babbling, smiling and using eye contact. The adult responds warmly smiling back and saying hello. This exchange continues and the adult then begins a game of peek-a-boo, hiding her face behind a cereal box. Anja shows she is enjoying this by bouncing up and down and laughing out loud.

Anja is learning that she can initiate and develop interactions with others by using both verbal and non-verbal modes of communication. This reciprocal exchange is not only emotionally rewarding (fun) but also serves to teach Anja elements of social convention. Anja learns to respond appropriately within the pattern of the game (repetition) and develops her understanding of timing, turn-taking and expression (communication). Anja is encouraged to increase her powers of observation and is able to anticipate where the adult is hiding (investigation). The humour of the game serves to consolidate and extend the learning opportunities.

Scenario 12 – building bridges

> Aaron (6 years 1 month) and his class have been studying local bridges. Aaron has chosen to use the wooden bricks to build a suspension bridge for his red toy car to travel over. He

places two chairs at roughly a metre distance apart and selects bricks of the same size to create a supporting stack adjacent to one of the chairs. He then selects flatter bricks and lays them on the chair seat overlapping them onto the supporting stack, creating the beginnings of a road. He notices that the road is not level and carefully adds another brick to his stack to reconcile this. He builds a further two supporting stacks and carefully balances more flat bricks over them to continue the road. Throughout the play he handles the bricks with precision and steps back to view the stability of structure.

Aaron's construction represents his knowledge of bridges (communication). He knows that the bridge needs to be level and that it has to be stable enough to allow his red car to cross from one side of the gap to the other. Aaron is familiar with brick play and has an ongoing vertical schema (repetition, schema). He is confident to make choices about the types of bricks he needs and through a process of trial and error tests the bricks and adjusts them in order that they fit his required purpose (investigation). Aaron displays high levels of concentration and precision as demonstrated in his ability to use his hands to make refined and deliberate adjustments (movement). Throughout the play Aaron shows resilience and determination. He is not distracted by the other children around him. He overcomes possible failures and is rewarded by the successful journey his red toy car makes.

CONCLUSION

Only through play are children able to utilise the full range of learning strategies. During play children are empowered, take control, take risks, overcome failure, consolidate skills and understanding, think creatively and imaginatively and above all learn positive attitudes about themselves as learners.

SUMMARY POINTS

- Children are capable and competent learners.
- They learn at different rates and in different ways.
- They need the support of caring, sensitive and knowledgeable adults.
- The early years are critical in children's learning and development.
- Learning depends on children's emotional security.
- Meaningful contexts are important.
- Children learn and represent their learning through a repertoire of communication strategies.

QUESTIONS FOR DISCUSSION

1   What is the difference between assimilation and accommodation?
2   What movement experiences might a young child engage in at home or in an early years setting?
3   What are the benefits of observing schematic behaviour?
4   What value do you place on reciprocal relationships in your own learning?
5   Do you agree with the theory that there is no risk of failure for young children when they play?

FURTHER READING

Edgington, M. (2004) *The Foundation Stage Teacher in Action: Teaching 3, 4 and 5 Year Olds*, London: Paul Chapman Publishing. Offers an in-depth consideration of recent guidance, theory and research about young children's learning and effective early years pedagogy.

Moyles, J. (ed.) (2007) *Early Years Foundations: Meeting the Challenge*, Maidenhead: Oxford University Press. By exploring the nature of how children learn through the perspective of the principles of the *Early Years Foundations*, the writers offer early years professionals support to direct their thinking and provision.

Taylor, J. and Woods, M. (eds.) (2005) *Early Childhood Studies: An Holistic Approach* (2nd edition), London: Hodder Arnold. Considers children's holistic development and learning with a focus on current UK policy.

Wood, D. (1998) *How Children Think and Learn* (2nd edition), Oxford: Blackwell Publishing. Wood explores the theories and research about how children think and learn from a psychological perspective. He offers guidance for the practical implications of this theory and research.

REFERENCES

Bruce, T. (2005a) *Early Childhood Education* (3rd edition), London: Hodder Education.

Bruce, T. (2005b) Play matters, in L. Abbott and A. Langston (eds) *Birth to Three Matters: Supporting the Framework of Effective Practice*, Maidenhead: Open University Press.

Bruner, J. (1977) *The Process of Education* (2nd edition), Cambridge, MA: Harvard University Press.

Bruner, J. (1986) *Actual Minds Possible Worlds*, Cambridge, MA: Harvard University Press.

Claxton, G. (1999) *Building Learning Power*, Bristol: Teaching and Learning.

David, T. and Powell, S. (2007) Beginning at the beginning, in J. Moyles (ed.) *Beginning Teaching, Beginning Learning* (3rd edition), Maidenhead: Open University Press.

Davies, M. (2003) *Movement and Dance in Early Childhood* (2nd edition) London: Paul Chapman Publishing.

Doherty, J. and Bailey, R. (2003) *Supporting Physical Development and Physical Education in the Early Years*, Buckingham: Open University Press.

Gardner, H. (1993) *Frames of Mind: The Theory of Multiple Intelligences*, London: Fontana.

Gopnik, A., Meltzoff, A. N. and Kuhl, P. (2001) *How Babies Think: The Science of Childhood*, London: Phoenix.

Laevers, F. (1999) The project 'Experiential Education': concepts and experiences at the level of context, process and outcome, paper presented at *7th Early Childhood Convention*, Nelson, New Zealand (27–30 September 1999). Online. Available http://www.ecd.govt.nz/publications/convention/Laevers.pdf (accessed 21 November 2007).

Malaguzzi, T. (1977) No way. The hundred is there, in T. Filippini and V. Vecchi (eds) *The Hundred Languages of Children: Narrative of the Possible*, Reggio Emilia: Reggio Children.

Maude, P. (2003) How do I do this better? From movement development into physical literacy, in D. Whitebread (ed.) *Teaching and Learning in the Early Years* (2nd edition), London: RoutledgeFalmer.

Pascal, C. and Bertram, T. (2006) Introducing child development, in T. Bruce (ed.) *Early Childhood: A Guide for Students*, London: Sage.

Piaget, J. (1962) *Play, Dreams and Imitation in Childhood*, London: Routledge and Kegan Paul.

Rinaldi, C. (1998) Projected curriculum constructed through documentation – progettazione, in C. Edwards, L. Gandini and G. Forman (eds) *The Hundred Languages of Children: The Reggio Emilia approach – Advanced Reflections* (2nd edition), London: Ablex Publishing Corporation.

Sylva, K., Meluish, E., Sammons, P., Siraj-Blatchford, I. and Taggart, B. (2004) *The Effective Provision of Pre-School Education (EPPE) Project, Technical Paper 12, Final Report*, London: DfES/Institute of Education, University of London.

Vygotsky, L. (1978) *Mind in Society*, Cambridge, MA: Harvard University Press.

16 ICT, Computer Games and Learning

Graham Downes and Susan Haywood

INTRODUCTION

Focusing on computer games as texts, this chapter explores their potential for learning. It identifies some games' typologies and the commonalities and differences between them. It argues that the types of interaction that are recognised as specific to this domain have the potential to promote learning, but that this opportunity is not always realised. If the learning potential of 'pure' computer games is to be harnessed within our system of education, for girls as well as boys, fundamental changes in pedagogy are required.

WHAT'S IN A GAME?

The term 'computer game' is used here to cover a diverse collection of resources that involve a variety of different user interactions. The differences between computer games affect the way they are played and their learning potential.

Hertz (1997) identifies two main categories emerging from contrasting environments. The first, arcade-style games, emerged from the fast action, rapid wrist action world of pinball machines. The second originated from a role playing culture in games such as Dungeons and Dragons. These were slower, less visual and required considerable background reading. A number of subcategories have developed: action, adventure, fighting, puzzle, role playing, simulations, sports and strategy. Although the parameters of these categories have become blurred as genres have evolved, they 'hold firm in the middle [because] there are certain strategies that are inherently satisfying' (p. 25) when playing computer games.

GAMES AS TEXTS

In the relatively short time in which computer games have been subject to academic study, debates have come to be focused around two approaches to gaming: narratology and ludology. Narratology views games as narratives, identifying them with features of stories such as chronology, pace, characterisation, and focusing on the similarities between games and other story-telling media. Ludology is the 'ludic' or play-related aspects of the games. Ludologists stress the differences between games and other media in which narrative plays a part, focusing on the game-specific aspects of the genre such as the relationship between rules, strategy and outcomes. Narratology and ludology is a continuum; both disciplines make an important and distinctive contribution to game theory.

Aarseth (1997) describes computer games as 'texts'. Later Frasca (1999) developed a theoretical model of computer games as a new 'semiotic domain', the study of how meaning is constructed and understood in specific contexts. For example, in a printed text a question mark denotes interrogation; in the context of a game, the same mark denotes 'help' or 'information'. A key on the floor in a computer game infers that at a later point a door will need to be unlocked. The key, in this example, is a connotative sign, where meaning is conveyed by commonly held assumptions within the domain.

An important distinction between computer games as texts and other narrative genres is that games are more ludic than narratologic, because of the degree of control exercised by the reader/player. Dillon (2005) summarises the distinctions:

> … [ludolgy focuses on] the kind of simulation the game provides and the mechanics of the gameplay – the rules, strategies, typologies and models … On the other hand, narratologists consider video and computer games as part of an extended tradition of how humans use tools to express themselves and tell their stories.

In education this has led to problems in attempting to draw firm conclusions from existing work. As Kirriemuir and McFarlane (2004) state 'from the range of perspectives taken by researchers, there are few hard and fast findings in the literature' (p. 2). Opinions vary about the potential of computer gaming for learning. This debate, characterised by Demos (Green and Hannon, 2007), ranges from 'moral panic' to 'digital faith' and risks obscuring legitimate consideration of the value of children's digital culture.

Media representations of gaming focus on the assumed and unwelcome influence of violent computer games on young people's behaviour, attitudes and health and have attempted to link computer games with childhood depression. In contrast, academics such as Johnson (2005) and Prensky (2002) have sought to highlight the potential benefits of games, arguing that those who condemn this new order are themselves outsiders from the digital future that is being created. Some academic literature has focused on games as a learning tool. With the exception of a few enthusiasts, there is little evidence of any sustained use of games in classroom teaching and considerable reluctance amongst teachers to utilise popular computer games (Kirriemuir and McFarlane, 2004). This research also highlights a fundamental difference between these and 'educational' computer games, used more extensively within the classroom, although the report does not specify how such games differ.

Games as narrative or ludic texts: a new literacy?

Gee (2003) states emphatically, 'When people learn to play video games they are learning a new *literacy*' (p. 13). Unsworth (2006) similarly acknowledges that computer games, forms of hypertextual non-linear literature where the reader determines the pathway through the text, are a new genre of multimedia electronic literary narratives. The introduction of the term 'visual literacy' in the 1960s brought different modes of conveying meaning. This has resulted in a fundamental shift in the balance between words and images as modes of expression, as well as exploration of the interaction between them (Kress and van Leeuwen, 1996).

The term 'literacy', originally applied to relatively informal learning contexts such as adult or family literacy, has come to be applied more generally as a competence or critical facility, and associated with the social and cultural context in which it exists. Lankshear and Knobel (2006) explain that 'whereas "reading" has always been conceived in psychological terms, literacy has always been a much more sociological concept. Literacy is a matter of social, institutional and cultural practices, not just something that goes on in one person's head' (p. 5). Literacies, in this sense, are always associated with discourses, using texts that are integral to the everyday practices associated with specific social situations.

Computer gaming provides a disputed context for the academic and professional discussion of the relationship between popular culture and literacy learning. This is significant, both in respect of games as a literary genre, and the ways in which experience of computer games influences the attitudes and competences with which young people approach learning in general and in particular literary genres. Video games differ from conventional book narratives in that events may not be linked in chronological order, but in the order determined by the player's decisions. In addition, the player is a participant and so narratives are 'embodied' stories, embodied in the player's choices in a way that is not possible in books and films.

In his framework for describing electronic game narratives, Unsworth (2006) distinguishes between 'game focused stories' and 'story focused games'. In game focused stories, such as video games, the game forms all or part of the story. Such games are often strong on 'back story', the events which pre-date those of the game, and weak on narrative during the game itself. Story-focused games, in contrast, are based on previously published books such as the Harry Potter series or *Lord of the Rings*. In some cases games are included in e-stories for young children, as in the case of *The Jolly Postman* or *The Rainbow Fish*.

Theoretical perspectives on literacy have moved from representing the reader as a passive decoder of text, to recognition of literacy as a meaning-making practice embedded in a social and cultural context. From birth onwards children engage in a range of culturally specific literacy activities that lead not only to cognitive development but also to participation in culturally defined structures, knowledge and forms of communication (Kress, 2003). School definitions of literacy have been slow to change and the pedagogical literature shows that some literacy practices are supported, valued and reinforced by formal schooling whilst others are not. This has led leading to the marginalisation of some practices and the empowerment or disempowerment of particular groups.

Marsh and Millard (2006) describe three dominant mindsets relating to the relationship between computer games and school literacy practices:

- new technologies enhance learning; their effects on learners should be documented and evaluated in order to support reading and writing;
- new technologies are 'flashy and entertaining', intrinsically harmful to children's language and development;
- children involve themselves in a range of social and technological practices and these should be used to inform literacy pedagogy.

Across all age phases, researchers report a dissonance between the literacy practices of the home and the school. In early years education a case has been made for recognising the importance of popular culture and literacy practices of the home for developing young children's literacy (Marsh, 2005). Green and Hannon (2007) warn that teachers cannot afford to neglect the skills and understanding developed by young people in non-school settings:

The change needed in schools is two-fold. First they need to find ways to recognize and value the learning that goes on outside the classroom. Second they need to support this learning by providing a space to reflect on it, galvanize and develop it so students can recognize and transfer those skills in new situations and contexts. (p. 25)

This imperative, sometimes referred to as the 'Third Space' requires educationalists to find ways to capitalise on the authentic learning that can take place in informal environments, a requirement that is likely to challenge school culture in fundamental ways. Unsworth (2006) argues that schools should integrate computer games into their literacy teaching to provide a range of literary narratives for young people whose literary landscape is ever changing. He bases this argument on:

- the richness of the narrative scenarios within which many games are set;
- the opportunity provided to relate game narratives to literary narratives and so develop students' critical appreciation of the narrative space and the range of ways in which a story can be interpreted;
- research suggesting that avid game-players are also avid readers but do not privilege book, electronic or game formats;
- work with literary texts should include discussions of all narrative formats, including games.

Games that emerge from a role playing environment are likely to have objectives that are numerous and complex, with a varied timescale. Arcade-style games such as PacMan have relatively few objectives and occur within a fast time frame. They demand rapid reactions from the player, who is required to modify her objectives as the game progresses. Iversen (2003) identifies three genres of computer game: action, strategy and adventure. This is a more flexible, overlapping model. A game might contain features of all three types but shows strong characteristics of one more than the other two.

WHAT CAN WE LEARN FROM COMPUTER GAMES?

Multiplicitous activity

Johnson (2005) claims that the emerging intelligences of the digital generation are largely unnoticed. The process of 'telescoping', defined as the 'mental labour of managing simultaneous objectives' is crucial. Johnson argues that telescoping is becoming an increasingly elaborate part of the computer gaming environment, identifying more than twenty telescoped objectives a gamer would be required to retain while playing a typical game. One aspect of ludological games is the motivational nature of rules and challenge. Juul (2003) defines games as:

> (1) a rule-based formal system with (2) a variable and quantifiable outcome, where (3) different outcomes are assigned different values, (4) the player exerts effort in order to influence the outcome, (5) the player feels attached to the outcome, and (6) the consequences of the activity are optional and negotiable.

Iversen's (2003) framework for the study of user interaction stresses the contract of more or less clearly stated rules that players create whenever they enter a playful environment. In the case of computer games, the contract is between the player and the game itself and there is always something at stake. The player may not necessarily win, and the challenge can be motivating. Iversen identifies five main types of challenge:

- finding your way around the game;
- interacting with characters and objects
- staying alive, gaining points or power;
- setting yourself challenges;
- solving puzzles.

A player may respond to some or all of these challenges at different points in the game, but the key point for learning is the negotiable and flexible nature of these challenges. Although the player does not have complete control over the objectives, she is presented with combinations of choices. On occasion, the player may decide to construct her own objectives that subvert the designed objectives of the game; for example a player in a football game may choose to see how many own goals can be scored.

Multiple objectives and multiple challenges have parallels with multi-mediation, which is transforming the nature of literacy. The term refers to the act of working on a number of tasks simultaneously, an opportunity that a computer environment uniquely affords due to the immediacy with which resources can be accessed. Some have questioned the usefulness of such skills, pointing out that people often seem distracted from the main task they are attempting. Such skills are necessary, however, when working on tasks defined solely within the computer environment. For example, the number of windows can quickly burgeon when undertaking a complex computer-based task. Windows may involve very different tasks, all critical to the development process and may need to be referenced at every stage. Any computer-user will recognise that they regularly need to multitask in this way. There is some evidence linking the processes of telescoping and multi-mediating. Children who do not engage with computer games may not develop the skills necessary to use electronic media effectively. The evidence is, however, limited and more research is required.

Problem solving

Seymour Papert (1993), a seminal theorist on computers and learning, identified the opportunity to problem solve within a computer-mediated environment. He used the term 'debugging' to explain the procedure of identifying and solving computer-based problems. This allows the user to imitate, articulate and analyse the process of 'mechanical thinking', that is, employing a 'step-by-step, literal' approach to a problem. Computer games are computer programs based on algorithms that require a mechanistic approach if one is to progress. Papert distinguished between this logical, computer-based problem solving and that taught in the mathematics curriculum. Computer-based problems arise directly from the game, relate to it and can be saved and revisited. This approach is the basis of problem-centred teaching and learning.

Gee (2003) proposes that humans are compulsive pattern-makers, finding patterns even where these are not obvious. Consider the urge for people to make pictures from clouds in the sky or flames in a fire. The relationship between the patterns we create to form meaning are continually being revised based on our life experiences. Gee refers to this reflective practice as the 'probing cycle', a four-step process:

- probing: 'looking around,' focusing on a specific course of action;
- hypothesising: reflecting upon outcomes of probing and developing a hypothesis (an underlining pattern which links all the information);
- reprobing: utilising this hypothesis to predict positive outcomes when probing;
- rethinking: considering feedback from reprobing and considering impact on the hypothesis. (p. 90)

Although the cycle is a critical part of all our meaning making, it is the only analytical model that works within the context of learning to play a computer game. Learning endless lists of game-related facts without consideration of the underlying rules would render the game impossible to play, akin to attempting to master a game by only reading the instructions.

Prensky's (2002) hierarchical model of learning within a computer game environment offers a description of the processes undertaken by the gamer as well as offering a value judgment about its relative sophistication. This model consists of five levels of learning:

- How: referring to the basic manipulation of on screen images, their patterns and spatial meaning.
- What: an understanding of the rules within a computer game environment.
- Why: the emergence of a strategy based on the knowledge of rules.
- Where: the understanding of the world of the game and the values it represents.
- When/Whether: at this final level, the player learns to make decisions which accord with the values of the game. (p. 2)

What can we learn from problem-solving activities?

That computer games develop problem-solving skills of some kind is undisputed. The types of problem solving and the transferability of these skills are more contentious. The Kirriemuir and McFarlane (2004) review concluded that teachers and pupils felt that using computer games developed their general problem-solving skills. Research carried out by Futurelab, however, suggests that playing computer games does not help players to identify problems and develop hypotheses in situations outside the game itself (Kirriemuir and McFarlane, 2004). Prensky (2002), in contrast, argues that the type of game is crucial and, when appropriate, the transferability of skills becomes obvious:

... the more a game's content 'simulates' anything in the real world, the more one learns about how to do things in that world ... Can you learn to find your way around a real-life oil platform, trade financial instruments, manage a theme park, or aim a gun and be stealthy? You bet you can. (p. 3)

Some evidence links gaming with the ability to problem solve within a computer-mediated environment. For example, children who play computer games from an early age are likely to approach computer-related problems without seeking assistance, using 'trial and error' methods rather than referring to linear-based manuals.

Engagement: the experience of flow

Csikszentmihalyi's (1992) notion of 'flow', often applied to computer gaming, developed from observations of very complex tasks such as playing a musical instrument. Csikszentmihalyi noted that 'Participants observed undertaking these complex activities reported a sensation of ecstasy, losing a sense of self and time' (p. 49). This state of being was termed 'flow'. To enter such a mental state requires a delicate balance between complexity of task and individual ability. If a task is too difficult, the user cannot achieve the required level of automated control. If the task is too easy, there is not the necessary level of challenge. Csikszentmihalyi described such activities as 'autotelic', those that are enjoyed without the necessity for beneficial outcomes. His work has informed studies and theoretical frameworks relating to computer games.

In order to achieve flow, accessing the appropriate level within the gaming environment is critical. The success of computer games is largely due to the multiplicity and flexibility of the tasks that can be undertaken at any one time. Where content is imposed or carefully controlled, computer games are unlikely to motivate learners in the classroom. The mismatch between current classroom pedagogy and computer games is never more apparent than in the numerous attempts that have been made to conceal learning outcomes within 'fun' educational games, an approach described as irrelevant by Kirremiur and McFarlane (2004).

TOYS FOR THE BOYS?

If computer games have educational value, then gender difference in gaming is an area of legitimate enquiry and potential concern. Discussion of gender difference focused on children's perceptions of computers as 'boys' toys' and the real or perceived danger of girls' exclusion from this area of learning. Games were seen as an overwhelmingly male domain. The issues were twofold: the under representation of girls in game-playing and the way in which female characters were portrayed – or overlooked in the games. Concerns increased as educationalists asserted the educational value of games and the transferable technological skills developed through computer gaming. Cassell and Jenkins (1998) argue:

> The problem in the differential attraction to computer games stems from the fact that here, as is often the case, the cultural constructions of gender are not separate from those of power. It is not just that girls seem to like today's computer games less than boys do, but that these differential preferences are associated with differential access to technological fields as children grow older. (p. 11)

The dilemma of girls and gaming was characterised as 'chess for girls'. Chess is recognised to be a high status and intellectually demanding game. Many more boys than girls play chess, so how should parents and educators respond? Should girls be given 'girlie' chess sets containing ponies and princesses, or should they be encouraged to compete with the boys in a rigorous and intellectually demanding pursuit? The responses of the industry and girls themselves reflected this duality. In 1994 the first commercially successful computer game marketed for girls 'Barbie Fashion Designer' was launched and, 'pink packaging', to be attractive to girls, became common. At the same time, feminists, academics and some gaming executives argued for the development of computer games with stronger female characters. In 1995, Tomb Raider achieved this aim. Lara Croft, its heroine, was intended to appeal to girls as a tough, self-reliant role model but remained a sexually attractive character for the core male market. As new games were developed further female characters emerged, ranging from gladiatorial monsters and bodybuilders to manga-influenced and more girlish, but no less deadly, street fighters. Hertz (1997) describes a typical character thus:

> A martial arts superbabe is the girl next door who'll also trounce you with a heart-rending smile. … She's a Jeet Kune Do expert built like an Olympic swimmer. She's not delicate or curvy. She's not even particularly thin. This woman has powerful shoulders and strong legs, and she's tall – usually taller than her male opponents. All in all, she's considerably more realistic than Pamela Anderson. (p. 179)

Parallel to the marketing of the Barbie-derived games and of new games with female characters such as Quake and Mortal Combat, was the emergence of organisations of female gamers in the 'Game Grrls' movement. Here, in physical and virtual subculture groups, girls played traditional fighting games, adopting aggressive or sexually explicit group identities such as 'Crack Whores' or 'Clan CMS Psycho Men Slayers'.

The development of online gaming environments has done much to make gaming attractive to female players of all ages. Gee (2003) commenting on the emergence of online multi-user role playing games writes:

> I have no doubt that video games, like most other popular cultural forms, overstress young, buxom and beautiful women in their content … However, as more girls and women play games this will change. And indeed, in role playing games you can design your own character … Games, of course reflect the culture we live in – a culture we can change. As to the issue of girls and women playing games, they are quickly catching up with the boys and the men, though they often play different games. (p. 11)

Sites such as Club Penguin, a version of a social networking site, have lowered the age range of online computer gaming and produced environments in which girl players outnumber boys. Adopting the persona of a penguin in a North Pole virtual community, players interact with others in real time. They buy or win clothes and accessories, decorate their igloos, go to virtual parties and take part in competitions. Such games have moved computer gaming from a peripheral interest for girls to a mainstream activity in which they participate in ever-growing numbers. They introduce pre-teen girls to computer-based discourses such as those enjoyed by their older sisters in social networking sites like MySpace and virtual worlds such as Second Life. In this respect they are examples of effective, if subtle, pink packaging, but do, at least, offer girls the opportunity to develop the transferable technological and cognitive skills that gaming can promote.

CONCLUSION

There are a number of reasons why computer games merit serious consideration by teachers. Games can legitimately be considered as narrative and ludic texts, requiring and developing a new literacy that is part of the digital landscape that children and young people occupy. The games themselves support the development of new ways of thinking and reasoning, attributes required for this new world. The Demos Report (Green and Hannon, 2007) puts it succinctly:

> It's about the knowledge economy, stupid. We cannot afford to make the mistake of trying to prepare children for today's jobs. We know that as the knowledge economy continues to expand, and more traditional sectors decline, the creative and cultural sector will rise to take their place. (p. 21)

This fundamental change will require the reinvention of the workplace and the society and will bring with it new technologies, new ways of communicating, participating, problem solving and thinking. This is a world in which, arguably, understanding and being able to use the context, skills and structure of the computer game will be an important attribute, for young women, as well as young men.

SUMMARY POINTS

- Computer games are texts and part of a new semiotic domain.
- These differ from traditional printed texts in that they include significant ludic elements as well as narrative.

- The types of interaction that are required to play a computer game have the potential to promote learning, but this opportunity is rarely realised.
- If the learning potential of 'pure' computer games is to be harnessed within our system of education, fundamental changes in pedagogy may be required.
- The experience of gaming may be different for girls and boys and this could have implications for their learning.
- This type of learning often takes place within the 'Third Space', non-school settings in which authentic but informal learning occurs.

QUESTIONS FOR DISCUSSION

1   What are the main differences between ludic and narrative elements of computer games and what potential for learning could games provide?
2   What are the main issues preventing schools from using computer games as teaching tools?
3   How does existing pedagogy need to change for schools to effectively utilise computer games in the future?
4   Why is it important to address the issue of differential access to computer games between girls and boys? How might schools do this?

FURTHER READING

Cassell, J. and Jenkins, H. (eds) (1998) *From Barbie to Mortal Kombat: Gender and Computer Games*, London: MIT Press. This is a seminal work on computer games and gender. It is based on an academic symposium on this subject held at Massachusetts Institute of Technology.

Gee, J. (2003) *What Video Games Have to Teach us About Learning and Literacy*, New York: Palgrave Macmillan. Gee takes a semiotic approach to literacy, technology and learning. This book provides an academic perspective on the use of games for learning and challenges traditional approaches to the use of games for teaching.

Green, H. and Hannon, C. (2007) *Their Space: Education for a Digital Generation*, Demos. Online. Available http://www.demos.co.uk/files/Their%20space%20-%20web.pdf (accessed 11 January 2008). This report from the prestigious think tank, Demos, challenges current approaches to the formal education of children and young people. It argues for approaches that better prepare young people for future economic and societal needs.

Kirriemuir, J. and McFarlane, A. (2004) *Literature Review in Games and Learning*, Futurelab (Futurelab series publication 8). Online. Available http://www.futurelab.org.uk/research/reviews/08_01.htm (accessed 5 January 2008). This is a literature review outlining and problematising current thinking and research into the use of computer games in education.

Unsworth, L. (2006) *E-literature for Children: Enhancing Digital Literacy Learning*, Oxon: Routledge. Unsworth discusses children's literature and literacy in the digital age, and also focuses on e-literature and the use of games for literacy teaching.

REFERENCES

Aarseth, E.J. (1997) *Cybertext: Perspectives on Ergodic Literature*, Baltimore: Johns Hopkins University Press.

Cassell, J. and Jenkins, H. (eds) (1998) From *Barbie to Mortal Kombat: Gender and Computer Games*, London: MIT Press.

Csikszentmihalyi, M. (1992) *Flow: The Classic Work on How to Achieve Happiness* (2nd edition), London: Rider.

Dillon, T. (2005) *Computer Game Theory: Narrative Versus Ludology*, Futurelab (viewpoint series). Online. Available http://www.futurelab.org.uk/viewpoint/archive_2005.htm (accessed 10 December 2007).

Frasca, G. (1999) *Ludology Meets Narratology: Similitude and Differences Between (Video) Games and Narrative*, Ludology. org. Online. Available http://www.ludology.org/articles/ludology.htm (accessed 4 December 2007).

Gee, J. (2003) *What Video Games Have to Teach us About Learning and Literacy*, New York: Palgrave Macmillan.

Green, H. and Hannon, C. (2007) *Their Space: Education for a Digital Generation*, Demos. Online. Available http://www.demos.co.uk/files/Their%20space%20-%20web.pdf (accessed 11 January 2008).

Hertz, J.C. (1997) *Joystick Nation: How Videogames Gobbled our Money, Won our Hearts and Rewired our Minds*, London: Abacus.

Iversen, S. (2003) Struggling towards a goal: challenges and the computer game, unpublished PhD Thesis, Aarhus University.

Johnson, S. (2005) *Everything Bad is Good for You: How Popular Culture is Making us Smarter*, London: Allen Lane.

Juul, J, (2003) *Where the Action is*. Online. Available http://www.gamestudies.org/0501/editorial/ (accessed 4 December 2007)

Kirriemuir, J. and McFarlane, A. (2004) *Literature Review in Games and Learning, Futurelab* (Futurelab series publication 8). Online. Available http://www.futurelab.org.uk/research/reviews/08_01.htm (accessed 5 January 2008).

Kress, G. (2003) *Literacy in the New Media Age*, Oxon: Routledge.

Kress, G. and van Leeuwen, T. (1996) *Reading Images*, London: Routledge.

Lankshear, C. and Knobel, M. (2006) *New Literacies: Everyday Practices and Classroom Learning* (2nd edition), Maidenhead: Open University Press.

Marsh, J. (ed.) (2005) *Popular Culture, New Media and Digital Literacy in Early Childhood*, Oxon: RoutledgeFalmer.

Marsh, J. and Millard, E. (eds) (2006) *Popular Literacies, Childhood and Schooling*, Oxon: Routledge.

Papert, S. (1993) *Mindstorms: Children, Computers and Powerful Ideas*, Hemel Hempstead: Harvester Wheatsheaf.

Prensky, M. (2002) *What Kids Learn That's POSITIVE From Playing Video Games*. Online. Available http://www.marcprensky.com/writing/Prensky%20-%20What%20Kids%20Learn%20Thats%20POSITIVE%20From%20Playing%20Video%20Games.pdf (accessed 12 November 2007).

Unsworth, L. (2006) *E-literature for Children: Enhancing Digital Literacy Learning*, Oxon Routledge.

17 Cultural Connections in Learning

June Bianchi

INTRODUCTION

> Human beings constantly create or construct new mental representations, and so the content of the mind is by its nature an open, infinitely expandable category (Gardner, 2006:21)

Cultural connections are a key factor in a model of education that addresses not only children's academic progress, but also their development across emotional, social, cultural and spiritual dimensions. This 'holistic' approach to education informs the 2004 Children Act and the policy document *Every Child Matters: Change for Children in Schools* (DfES, 2004) (see Chapter 2). The educational agenda seeks to fulfil children's wider potential to contribute, achieve and enjoy. Learning beyond narrowly defined academic achievement is a paramount aspiration for lifelong learning across diverse socio-cultural and educational contexts.

The multidisciplinary links and multiple outcomes of Every Child Matters (ECM) can be daunting to educationalists whose recent agenda has been the delivery of quantifiable curriculum targets. The chapter investigates implementation of the policy through an arts-based approach; it uses ECM as a basis for creative education and holistic development for children and young people. It explains the theory and practice implicit in the wider objectives of ECM, exploring rationales, debates and issues within the cultural connections agenda, as well as providing evidence to support practice in meeting the broader learning requirements. Using studies of successful cultural projects based on cross-agency and interdisciplinary partnerships, it provides models of practice to facilitate an inclusive and creative approach to deliver ECM's outcomes, accessible to any level, ability or setting.

THE POLITICAL BACKGROUND

The 2004 Children Act and ECM policy document extend beyond purely educational concerns to encompass targets for holistic development for children and young people across a range of identifiable areas of need, both academic and social. Nevertheless, the policy espouses a commitment to education and other interventions involving networks of support in addressing problems of social deprivation.

An underlying assumption is that 'educational achievement is the most effective route out of poverty' (QCA 2007b), a phrase occurring in the opening page of the ECM website and quoted extensively in follow-up national and local proposals. Interviewed in September 2007, in response to the Research Report produced by the Campaign to End Child Poverty, Schools Minister Andrew Adonis confirmed that helping children from disadvantaged backgrounds through education was one of New Labour's key objectives (BBC, 2007).

Research published in both ECM and by the Campaign to End Child Poverty (2007) indicates that the quality of the family environment and its relative security, in both economic and social terms, has the most significant impact on children's development, well-being and achievement. It is useful, then, to consider the prominence given to the meeting of educational targets within the policy, an area that appears to take precedence in dissemination of the initiative. As Chapter 2 shows, national policy documents are informed by wider political discourses and agendas, which inform the language, structure and the proposed means of implementation of the initiative. Uniting previously discrete agencies through a shared responsibility for children's welfare aims to improve the safety net for vulnerable children. The allocation of a pivotal role for education in meeting children and young people's wider needs also increases the accountability of educational institutions in implementing government policy. This development could be regarded as having strategic implications for measurability of ECM's policies: auditing the schools' implementation of ECM is arguably more feasible than measuring social improvement through the family. It is also less expensive than economically bolstering needy groups in society.

The panoramic scope of ECM documentation with multi-agency involvement presents a challenge to educationalists. The chapter investigates the cultural connections dimension in relation to previous theoretical debates. It explores the potential for implementation in schools in partnership with other contributors such as the Department for Culture, Media and Sport (DCMS), the Arts Council and a range of cultural settings and practitioners.

THE THEORETICAL BACKGROUND

The significance of the arts and leisure component of the policy has been developed in consultation with young people, who identified, 'things to do and places to go' as their priorities (DCSF, 2007a). DCSF targets seek improved access to culture, sport and play for young people, to facilitate participation and develop talents in culture and sport. The emphasis is on two key areas: 'enjoying and achieving' and 'making a positive contribution' (DCSF, 2007b). There is a recognition that such activities have the potential to offer benefits that extend beyond those of the individual. They provide scope for addressing wider agendas such as promoting diversity, fostering creative partnerships between a range of trusts and agencies and enabling young people to participate in creative and inspiring activities within and beyond the school curriculum. The discovery that children are motivated by agendas other than the cerebral is not new within arts education: cultural educators have long campaigned for education to address needs beyond cognitive development. The significance of creative approaches, spearheaded by the arts, in meeting broader cultural needs is also a familiar rhetoric in educational initiatives. Sir Ken Robinson, influential writer and lecturer argued, in his presentation at the TED Conference, that 'creativity now is as important in education as literacy, and we should treat it with the same status' (2006). This view endorses earlier findings from an extensive report, *All our Futures: Creativity, Culture and Education* (Robinson and National Advisory Committee on Creative and Cultural Education, 1999), and correlates the development of creativity with the raising of cultural awareness. It recommends addressing the needs of society and the individual through a partnership model that is redolent of ECM's cultural connections agenda. It demands government support for creative and cultural education and for training to enable teachers to 'facilitate development of young people's creative abilities and cultural understanding' (p.12).

In his 2001 book *Out of Our Mind: Learning to be Creative*, Robinson suggests that creativity, like culture, is not an isolated individualist phenomenon: 'Creativity can be inspired or stifled by cultural conditions. Understanding the culture of creativity is essential to being able to promote it in organisations and in nations' (p. 167).

ECM's message that cultural experience requires a holistic model of education has informed previous educational agendas and policies. The hierarchy of subjects, with privilege given to subject areas conventionally regarded as 'academic', is prevalent throughout the Western world (see Chapter 13.) But it is contested, as Elliot Eisner (2002) suggests: '... literal language and quantification are not the only means through which human understanding is secured and represented' (p. 204).

Recognition of domains of experience other than the cognitive is well established in the educational community. For example, Howard Gardner's (1999) theory of multiple intelligences sees intelligence as multi-perspectival, rather than entirely logical-deductive. It incorporates traditional spectrums of intelligence such as mathematical and linguistic, as well as modes of engagement associated with the arts: visual and spatial, musical and kinaesthetic; with human consciousness: interpersonal, intrapersonal, spiritual and existential; and with the phenomenological world – naturalist. Gardner's premise is widely respected as an influential theory, with some educational institutions acknowledging the impact of learning styles and intelligence orientation on its learners. However, no radical shift from the traditionally dominant subject hierarchical model of the curriculum has yet occurred and the more readily quantifiable modes of intelligence are still dominant.

The privileging of cognitive intelligences within Western culture and education reflects a society where achievement in these spheres garners respect, status and success. Gardner proposes a wider perspective, valuing cultures predicated on skills other than the mathematical-linguistic. For example, a rural tribal society relying on shared enterprise, spatial skills and physical stamina would foster contrasting modes of intelligence to its Western counterpart. Ethnomusicologist Bruno Nettl (2002) contends that some societies can favour the arts as their central mode of cognition and communication: 'In many societies, including particularly some of those of the South Seas, children and young people learn the important elements and values of their own culture through musical experience' (p. 31).

Yet there is still reluctance to offer such 'non-academic' areas of the curriculum the same importance awarded to the traditionally academic spheres. Such preferences reflect the underlying ethos of a society, indicative of its dominant ideologies, values and aspirations. As Mihaly Csikszentmihalyi (2002) observes: 'Every human culture, by definition, contains meaning systems that can serve as the encompassing purpose by which individuals can order their goals' (p. 218).

Such meaning systems are disseminated implicitly and explicitly throughout its entire cultural milieu; as Raymond Williams (1958) comments, 'culture is ordinary'; it takes place in 'the whole of life' as well as in domains we associate with the notion of culture: 'in institutions, and in arts and learning' (p. 11). Value ascribed to different forms of cultural production is variable, with a hierarchy frequently existing between that designated by society as 'high art' and more populist forms of cultural practice. Cultural institutions such as galleries, theatres and concert halls bestow value on artists' production, establishing and reinforcing stratification of value by their patronage and support. Cultural theorists such as Williams have criticised the hierarchical approach to culture, its social divisiveness and perpetuating inequality of access and opportunity through 'his extraordinary decision to call certain things culture and then separate them, as with a park wall, from ordinary people and ordinary work' (Williams, 1958, cited in Higgins, 2001: 13).

As the sociologist Pierre Bourdieu (1984) contends, the ability to operate across the spectrum of levels of cultural production, demonstrating a grasp of nuances of meaning and function, amounts to a valuable commodity, which he calls 'cultural capital'. While ownership of cultural capital may not convey monetary wealth, it does give 'symbolic profit' (p. 230), the acquisition of cultural knowledge and the corresponding level of social confidence and esteem.

Critical debates over the last three or four decades have challenged such cultural hierarchies. Postmodernists, such as Jean-François Lyotard and Jean Baudrillard, propose the notion of parallel or competing narratives that counter traditional paradigmatic structures. Challenges to colonialism, class and patriarchy, from such quarters as feminists, queer theory, post-colonialism and anti-globalisation activists, all conspire to rock the boat of cultural supremacy. Pluralist discourses present a breakdown of the adherence to past judgements on what constituted quality and value. An example is *Jerry Springer – the Opera*, a synthesis of popular television reality show with the conventions of Wagnerian operatic performance.

Within this arena of cultural synthesis and celebration of difference, educationalists endeavour to acknowledge diversity of experiences and perspectives within the pluralist society that encompasses British life. The National Curriculum champions the importance of respecting and understanding cultural diversity. Yet a tension still exists in striving to balance the needs of antithetical cultural traditions. Nevertheless the curriculum seeks to reflect the melange of socio-cultural experiences that constitute British life and to recognise the diversity of expression and experience in a heterogeneous society. ECM's outcomes espouse the target of equality for all young people to meet their full potential. To this end the educational system must develop cultural strategies to stimulate curiosity, appreciation and respect in celebrating our diversity of cultural idioms.

CULTURAL CONNECTIONS: INITIATIVES WITHIN AND BEYOND THE CURRICULUM

While ECM recognises that education must incorporate children's wider needs, the existing National Curriculum Orders acknowledge the importance of learning extending beyond the boundaries of subject knowledge: 'Education that develops cultural understanding and recognises diversity is crucial for the future well-being of our society' (QCA, 2007a).

The curriculum from the foundation phase through to completion of GCSE examinations at Key Stage 4 and post-16 is constantly under review. Restructuring of curriculum orders build on previous practice with continued commitment to addressing wider societal and cultural issues. Such aspects of education are currently addressed within non-statutory aspects of the curriculum known as 'cross-curriculum dimensions' as well as through specific subjects, particularly the arts and humanities.

'Cross-curriculum dimensions provide important unifying areas of learning that help young people make sense of the world and give education relevance and authenticity. They reflect the major ideas and challenges that face individuals and society' (QCA, 2007a). Cross-curriculum dimensions addresses a broad spectrum of issues impacting upon the well-being of young people, encompassing aspects of their experiences as individuals as well as engaging with their role as citizens and contributing to a changing society. Topics include identity, cultural diversity, health, sustainability, critical thinking and citizenship. Some are highly contested with epistemologies regarded as antithetical to the government-validated pedagogy of the National Curriculum (see Chapter 13).

ECM places pressure on educational institutions to realise the existing agenda to support young people's Spiritual, Moral, Social and Cultural needs (SMSC), along with additional responsibility for their physical, emotional and intellectual personal development. Schools are required to demonstrate the extent to which the curriculum contributes to meeting the five outcomes: addressing children and young people's health, safety, achievement and enjoyment, their ability to contribute to society and their economic well-being. These are laudable aims, but are less easily measured than the statistical data of external examinations and Standard Assessment Tests results published in school league tables. The challenge lies with the government to redress the balance in the priorities set for schools' achievement, and to ensure that support is provided for schools to fulfil their social as well as their academic duty to pupils. Economic and socio-cultural factors are rightly regarded as providing no justification for failure to address the ECM outcomes. However, demands to meet increasing needs within socially deprived environments place greater pressures on schools, which are potentially demoralised by their inability to meet academic targets and successfully compete in league tables.

A number of initiatives have demonstrated an awareness of the role of creative and cultural activity in addressing both academic and wider educational needs in disadvantaged areas as well as across the whole educational sector. The Department for Culture, Media and Sport (DCMS) set up Creative Partnerships in 2002, managed by Arts Council of England. It was designed to provide opportunities for young people aged 5–18 years in deprived areas to develop their creativity and experience working in a collaborative mode with a range of partners. The initiative fostered partnerships between multidisciplinary agencies: schools, individual arts practitioners, creative organisations and businesses. An Ofsted report commissioned by Culture Minister David Lammy, published in September 2006, confirmed the success of its approach. Lammy commented on its findings in an Arts Council's press release:

> When we set up Creative Partnerships in 2002 it was because we believed that the creative and cultural sectors have an essential role to play in exciting minds and enriching educational experiences. I'm delighted that the report published today supports this and that Ofsted found such good evidence that the programme was contributing to each of the Every Child Matters Outcomes.
>
> (Arts Council, 2006)

Schools Minister Andrew Adonis, in the same press release, also praised the Creative Partnerships initiative, but placed emphasis on its role in promoting achievement across academic aspects of learning. He reaffirmed the traditional view of cultural and creative activity as of particular value when it contributes to the rest of the curriculum, rather than as a focus in its own right:

> It is important that young people develop creative skills that can help them with their studies. Creative activities can also help to boost young people's self-confidence and motivation. I am pleased to see that the Creative Partnerships programme is encouraging pupils to enjoy learning and helping schools to improve pupils' achievement in literacy, numeracy and ICT.
>
> (Arts Council, 2006)

Creative Partnerships are based in about thirty-six areas of England, and projects so far have involved children in approximately one third of schools across the educational sector. The aim is not only to inspire young people to be innovative, risk-taking, adventurous and cooperative members of society, but also to rejuvenate teachers through productive and regenerative connections between educationalists, arts professionals and institutions. The Creative Partnerships (2007) website shows the range and scope of the many successful projects spanning diverse topics and issues. These range from the humanitarian focus of 'A Safe Place to Live', a citizenship project on diversity by photographer Rich Wiles, to 'Bel the Giant', using a Leicestershire myth as a starting point for imaginative performances and incorporating cross-cultural multidisciplinary arts. Breadth of vision and sensational outcomes confirm the Creative Partnerships mission statement that: 'Creativity is not simply about doing the arts – it is about questioning, making connections, inventing and reinventing, about flexing the imaginative muscles' (Creative Partnerships, 2007).

These processes cross disciplinary boundaries to foster creative collaborations. Creative partnerships can be formed either informally or through more formal coalitions supported by various local, national and private funding bodies. The success of these linked initiatives is indicated by further joint-funded projects such the 2005 development, 'Cultural Hubs', involving arts organisations, galleries, museums and schools within focal areas. The project's aims include the promotion of cultural activities among young people and the fostering of sustainable networks between schools and cultural sector organisations involved. A key factor is that cultural opportunities not only target young participants but also include continued professional development provision for staff within the educational sector. The *Cultural Hubs Baseline Report*, carried out in 2006 to investigate its potential, indicated a high level of positive expectations from future partners: '[83 per cent of schools, 78 per cent of cultural organisations] expect parents, school governors and the wider community to benefit from participation in the Cultural Hubs' (Hayton Associates, 2006: 17).

While the DCMS and Arts Council initiatives operate within specific regional areas, other options are available to practitioners seeking connectivity between creative partners within their own area in order to gain the educational benefits for young people. *Davies et al.'s* (2004) research project 'Young Designers on Location', (YDoL) was funded by the National Endowment for Science, Technology and the Arts (NESTA). It fostered inventiveness and imagination with groups of 11-year-old children through working partnerships with designers in a supportive working environment in the South West and Midlands. They found that the quality of the working location, in Harrington's terms the 'creative ecosystem' (p. 278), influenced children's responses. Case studies in the research report indicated significant benefits to children participating in creative engagement at this level. There is widespread recognition that generating such conditions within the school system can be problematic due to 'constraints of funding, curriculum, timetable and inspection regime' (Davies *et al.*, 2004: 286). Out-of-school projects like YDoL, while not fully viable within the mainstream curriculum, could be a means to combine ECM's 'extended school'. The cultural connections agenda addresses the outcomes by extending times, beyond the strictures of the timetable.

Schools that invest resources and curriculum time in implementing cultural activities report high-quality outcomes and follow-up impact. Such positive feedback has been generated in response to the work of South West England's arts-based action research organisation, 5×5×5=creativity. The organisation's title is based on its inaugural project in 2000 when five schools, each working in partnership with an artist and a cultural centre, generated artistic outcomes that emerged from an exploratory child-centred methodology. Central to its philosophy and practice is an investigative, process-based approach, informed by the Reggio Emilia system of education (see Chapter 15). Viewing the research process within art-making, not as a preliminary element, but rather a central focus within children's artistic development, 5×5×5=creativity projects foster valuable skills. As Mike Young, former Director of Education for Bath and North East Somerset, suggests, 'creativity, flexibility and above all the ability to think for yourself' (5×5×5=creativity, 2006).

These desirable assets, which, Young maintains, are essential for a changing world, are also the skills that ECM seeks to promote through wider and enhanced learning opportunities. Cultural projects have the potential to build the individual's self-esteem while promoting human rights through understanding and appreciating diversity. Such concepts are pivotal within '*Global Dimension*', the Development Education Association's (DEA) proactive internationalist guide, which 'emphasises the positive contribution of diverse cultures and communities, locally and globally' (DEA, 2006: 5).

ECM's commitment to enable every child to reach full potential must be an anti-racist one as prejudice destroys life's possibilities. This is not just a priority for culturally diverse areas, because the need for education to counter limited cultural understandings is more important in a monoculture. The Essex Intercultural Arts Project, based in an area with few minority ethnic residents, sought to address misunderstanding and prejudice through a cross-arts intercultural approach. The term 'intercultural' acknowledges the complex, mutable and hybrid nature of contemporary cultural identity. Working creatively with international artists across a range of disciplines and gaining respect for the dignity of individuals' beliefs and values, young participants were able to readjust their own personal paradigm and challenge previous preconceptions. Evaluations of the project from teachers and an external examiner praised its impact on participants' SMSC development:

> … difference came to be seen by pupils as something to celebrate, and negative and stereotypical ideas as negative and destructive.
>
> (Tallack *et al.*, 2005: 74)

Addressing parallel issues of cultural diversity, the interdisciplinary arts project, 'Scarves Reveal and Conceal', developed through a creative partnership between the present author and visual artist, writer Carol Cooke, a range of educational institutions, and the Study Gallery of Modern Art in Poole. 'Scarves Reveal and Conceal' was a visual arts interactive installation funded by a range of agencies including the Arts Council. It was first exhibited at The Study Gallery of Modern Art in Poole, Dorset (2006–7). The installation explored and celebrated cultural diversity through the role of the scarf as an individual and collective symbol of socio-cultural meaning and identity. It incorporated an extensive programme of interactive activities during both its developmental and exhibited stages, involving a wide cross section of the community. While images of diversity can be celebrated for their societal enrichment, offering a multiplicity of possibilities and choices, anxiety around notions of 'difference' can create suspicion, confusion and even fear. 'Scarves Reveal and Conceal' workshops and installation provided space to question preconceived ideas that can trigger prejudice, and challenge them through playful and experimental creative engagement. Images from both the exhibition and the workshops are available on the author's web pages on Bath Spa University's website. It is a resource that provides a continued focus for exploratory work on image and identity with a wide range of audiences (Bianchi, 2007).

The installation features four central mask casts from whose mouths flow 'rivers of opinion', a fabric maze printed with poetry, stories and narratives. Surrounding this central sculptural area, twelve images of scarf-wearing people from around the globe display the hijab, turban, headscarf, bandana and stole and invite the viewer to interact with the installation. Their faces are clear so the viewer, inserting their own face, sees the world for a short while, through another's perspective. A post-16 student, attending an exhibition workshop in image and identity commented, 'the exhibition made me rethink the way that I saw different cultures – it was thought-provoking and particularly relevant now'.

By operating on both cognitive and affective levels of the mind, the arts are capable of engendering change in a more powerful and direct form than logical-deductive modes, which are frequently employed.

CONCLUSION

ECM's cultural connections can be effectively met through a range of cultural strategies incorporating practice currently within the domain of the arts educational community. Moreover, fulfilment of ECM's broad-based holistic agenda lies within the scope of arts specialist practitioners who have expertise in addressing key issues of diversity, equity and personal development. ECM demands an inclusive approach with potential for building esteem and achievement across a wider subject profile than the narrow scope of the currently privileged, traditional academic subjects.

The challenge lies with the government and with educationalists to recognise the potential of cultural strategies in delivering many key issues within ECM. Current educational paradigms are predicated on notions of Western society as post-industrial and systems-based. Yet evidence suggests that the new global society is an organism in a state of creative flux, struggling to respond to challenges of an economic, environmental and cultural nature. New possibilities bring new tensions, which are recognised within current educational legislation such as *Guidance on the Duty to Promote Community Cohesion* (DfES, 2007c). This outlines schools' duties and their role in promoting social harmony within a rapidly evolving, diverse society. While publication of such documents signals commitment to the wider issues impacting upon education, arguably teachers need strategies beyond the provision of further reading matter in order to address such aspects of the ECM agenda. If ECM is to be more than a formality then a paradigm shift is required: teachers need different skills to meet the needs of young people in their care.

SUMMARY POINTS

- The 2004 Children Act and the policy document *Every Child Matters: Change for Children in Schools* (DfES, 2004) aim to address children's wider potential to contribute, achieve and enjoy, as well as providing for their academic development.
- Influential theorists such as Howard Gardner and Sir Ken Robinson suggest an approach that recognises a multiplicity of perspectives to intelligence and a correspondingly broader educational agenda.
- Cultural and creative partnerships provide a model for development of key areas of knowledge and skills.
- Arts education incorporates cultural strategies that have the potential to address a holistic educational remit and meet ECM's cultural connections agenda.

QUESTIONS FOR DISCUSSION

1   What wider generic skills are identified within the ECM guidelines and across other new legislation mentioned within the chapter?
2   How can these be developed through a holistic approach to the curriculum?
3   What kind of cultural strategies have you observed in use, within a school or other educational institution, as a focus for the development of wider learning? Discuss and compare your findings with a learning partner who has visited another institution.
4   How can cultural institutions enhance delivery of ECM within the local community?
5   To what extent do creative partnerships between educational and cultural institutions, in your locality, extend provision of ECM?

FURTHER READING

Calloway, G. and Kear, M. (2000) *Improving Teaching and Learning in the Arts*, Lewes: Falmer Press. A range of strategies for developing children's learning through arts education.

Craft, A., Jeffrey, B. and Liebling, M. (eds) (2001) *Creativity in Education*, London: Continuum. A guide to issues of practice, pedagogy and policy within creative education, edited by a highly respected editorial team within the field of creativity.

Craft, A., Gardner, H. and Claxton G. (eds) (2008) *Creativity, Wisdom, and Trusteeship: Exploring the Role of Education*, Thousand Oaks, CA: Corwin Press. Edited by three influential writers on holistic educational approaches, addressing pertinent perspectives and debates within contemporary education.

Eisner, E. W. (2002) *The Arts and the Creation of Mind*, New Haven: Yale University Press. Internationally renowned educationalist, Elliot Eisner, investigates the role of the arts in developing children's cognitive facilities.

Goleman, D. (1996) *Emotional Intelligence: Why it Can Matter more Than IQ*, London: Bloomsbury. A cogent argument for a more holistic approach to intelligence, recognising the significance of affective as well as intellectual processes in learning.

REFERENCES

5×5×5=creativity (2006) *100 Voices*, DVD, Bath: 5×5×5=creativity.

Arts Council (2006) *Ofsted Report Praises Creative Partnerships Programme for Improving Pupils' Personal and Social Skills.* Online. Available http://www.artscouncil.org.uk/pressnews/press_detail.php?id=727&browse=archive (accessed 15 November 2007).

BBC (2007) *Poor Teens Lag Two Years Behind.* Online. Available http://news.bbc.co.uk/1/hi/education/6989177.stm (accessed 14 November 2007).

Bianchi, J. (2007) Online. Available http://users.bathspa.ac.uk/biaj1/ (accessed November 2007).

Bourdieu, P. (1984) *Distinction: A Social Critique of the Judgement of Taste*, translated by R. Nice, London: Routledge and Kegan Paul.

Campaign to End Child Poverty (2007) Online. Available http://www.endchildpoverty.org.uk/index.html (accessed November 2007).

Creative Partnerships (2007) Online. Available http://www.creative-partnerships.com/projects/ (accessed 14 November 2007).

Csikszentmihalyi, M. (2002) *Flow: The Classic Work on How to Achieve Happiness*, Rider: London.

Davies, D., Howe, A. and Haywood, S. (2004) Building a creative ecosystem – the Young Designers on Location Project, *Journal of Art & Design Education*, 23(3): 33–44.

DCSF (2007a) *Things to Do, Places to Go.* Online. Available http://www.everychildmatters.gov.uk/youthmatters/thingstodo/ (accessed November 2007).

DCSF (2007b) *Culture, Sport and Play.* Online. Available http://www.everychildmatters.gov.uk/culturesportplay/ (accessed November 2007).

DCSF (2007c) *Guidance on the Duty to Promote Community Cohesion*, London: DCFS Publications.

DCSF (2007d) *Every Child Matters: Outcomes for Children and Young People.* Online. Available http://www.everychildmatters.gov.uk/aims/outcomes/ (accessed 14 November 2007).

DEA (2006) *The Arts: The Global Dimension*, London: DEA.

DfES (2004) *Every Child Matters: Change for Children in Schools*, London: DfES.

Eisner, E. W. (2002) *The Arts and the Creation of Mind*, New Haven, CT and London: Yale University Press.

Gardner, H. (1999) *Intelligence Reframed*, New York: Basic Books.

Gardner, H. (2006) *Changing Minds*, Boston, MA: HBS Press.

Hayton Associates (2006) *Cultural Hubs Baseline Report*, London: Arts Council England.

Nettl, B. (2002) What's to be learned? Comments on teaching music in the world and teaching world music at home, in L. Bresler and C. Marme Thomson (eds) *The Arts in Children's Lives: Context, Culture and Curriculum*, London: Kluwer Academic Publishers.

QCA (2007a) *National Curriculum: Cross Curriculum Dimensions.* Online. Available http://curriculum.qca.org.uk/cross-curriculum-dimensions/index.aspx (accessed 15 November 2007).

QCA (2007b) *Every Child Matters.* Onlin. Available http://www.qca.org.uk/qca_15305.aspx (accessed November 2007).

Robinson, K. (2001) *Out of our Minds: Learning to be Creative*, Oxford: Capstone Publishing Ltd.

Robinson, K. (2006) webcast speech from TED Conference, California. Online. Available http://www.ted.com/index.php/talks/view/id/66 (accessed 14 November 2007).

Robinson, K. and National Advisory Committee on Creative and Cultural Education (1999) *All Our Futures: Creativity, Culture and Education*, Sudbury, DfEE Publications.

Tallack, M., Knock R., Stokes, A. and Davison, L. (2005) *My culture, your Culture, our Culture: The Essex Intercultural Arts Project*, Chelmsford: Essex County Council.

Williams, R. (1958) Culture is ordinary, in J. Higgins (ed.) (2001) *The Raymond Williams Reader*, Oxford: Blackwell.

18 Educational Research

Dan Davies

INTRODUCTION

Through this chapter you should gain:

- an appreciation of the importance of educational research for effective classroom practice;
- an awareness of the role of research in the life of a university department of education;
- an understanding of the continuity between undergraduate student research and that being undertaken by schools, postgraduate students and university tutors.

RESEARCH AND THE TEACHER

We live in a research-saturated culture. It seems that every day the media report on 'research' emanating from some university or other, often appearing to confirm the blindingly obvious or finding a link between a hitherto benign foodstuff and cancer. Market research is used to develop and sell us new products, whilst a writer might claim to be 'researching my new novel'. The word 'research' appears to have a multiplicity of meanings in the political, commercial and academic worlds – some of them trivial, some respected, some even sinister. It is perhaps not surprising that many teachers are cynical about research in general and educational research in particular. Research can be seen as the opposite of action; finding more out about a situation rather than doing anything about it. But perhaps this is an unfair characterisation. Perhaps we need to look again at research in general, and at educational research in particular, to ascertain whether it has any value to the development of teaching and learning.

Perhaps the tarnished image of research and its misuse as a term by advertisers can obscure its essential purpose and meaning. Cohen *et al.* (2007) characterise three ways of finding out about the world: reasoning, experience and research, the latter differing from the informal, ad hoc nature of the first two in that it is 'systematic, controlled, empirical and self-correcting' (p. 5). Research *should* be able to produce reliable, valid and tested knowledge that will be of as much (or even greater) use to practitioners than their own reasoning and experience, which will necessarily be limited and subjective. Perhaps the most powerful argument that can be made for the importance of educational research, however, is for that undertaken by teachers themselves:

> We believe that lasting improvement in education can come about only through the work of individual teachers and school staffs as they seek, through inquiry into their own practice, to provide optimal learning conditions for the particular students in their care.
>
> (Wells, 2001, p. 2)

Comparisons between the medical and teaching professions (e.g. Hargreaves, 1996) might lead us to question why teaching is not more 'research-led' or 'evidence-based'. A surgeon from the nineteenth century transplanted into a twenty-first century operating theatre would be completely lost. He or she would not recognise the technology employed, would be unfamiliar with the vast majority of drugs used and treatments prescribed. In short, medical research has advanced practice in that profession to such an extent that it bears almost no resemblance to the work of physicians a hundred years ago. By contrast, whilst the nineteenth-century teacher might be baffled by interactive whiteboards and computers, he or she would almost certainly recognise most of the curriculum and the majority of the teaching methods. We might argue that teaching is a social science rather than a physical (or biological) one, dealing with human interactions that are less likely to change than the scientific interventions of drugs, so we might not expect such a radical change, but the lack of apparent 'progress' or sense of engagement with educational research by most teachers is still striking. It is important, however, not to over-sell medical research as a model. Pring (2000) warns that:

> ... caution is required even about this rather selective view of medical research, let alone about the connection between such research and professional practice. The Cochrane Centre in Oxford was established precisely because the connection between such research and professional practice was tenuous indeed. (p. 157)

CRITICISMS OF EDUCATIONAL RESEARCH

One of the reasons for the lack of impact of educational research on practice might be a widespread mistrust of its quality or relevance on the part of teachers and other educational commentators. Educational research has received widespread criticism, rising to a crescendo in the late 1990s. The main thrust of this criticism is summarised in the following quote from a speech given by David Hargreaves to the Teacher Training Agency annual conference: '... educational research is poor value in terms of improving the quality of education in schools' (Hargreaves, 1996, p. 1). This criticism implies either that the 'problems' worked on by educational researchers do not match well with the concerns of teachers, or that the results of such research is poorly disseminated so that it cannot inform and improve practice. The notion of 'value for money' relates to public funding for such research, either directly from government departments or from research councils, and suggests that the time has come for the beneficiaries of expenditure (by implication universities) to be called to account. The implied lack of engagement with the 'real world' of classrooms is echoed in the words of the then chief inspector of schools, who described educational research as 'irrelevance and distraction' (Woodhead, 1998). Its location in university departments of education led the then Secretary of State for Education to describe it as 'ivory-towerism' (Blunkett, 2000), taking place in privileged academic communities divorced from the realities of classroom life.

The quality of educational research also came under criticism at this time, being described as 'sloppy' (Tooley and Darby, 1998), i.e. not fulfilling many of the characteristics of research proposed by Cohen *et al.* (see above): systematic, controlled, empirical and self-correcting. In a study of the criticisms levelled at educational research in the late 1990s, Oancea (2005) found a litany of reported shortcomings in research methodology:

> Educational research was deemed non-reliable and inconclusive. Much of this was charged to flaws of empirical research, especially qualitative – lack of triangulation, sampling bias, purposeful distortion, ideological bias etc; but also to flaws of non-empirical research, such as, contentiousness, superficial literature review, logical incoherence, excessive reliance upon secondary sources, adulation of great thinkers. (p. 167)

As well as being an amplification of the charge of 'sloppiness', the list implies that educational research was mistrusted because of suspicions of ideological bias. This charge has come particularly from official and government critics, perhaps because the research concerned had been critical of government initiatives. Educational researchers have been seen as part of the 'liberal establishment' by market-oriented government education ministers, and were clearly included in the 'forces of conservatism' attacked by the British Prime Minister for criticising market-driven 'reforms'. Generally governments only tend to be interested in educational research that supports the policies they wish to introduce; hence the emphasis on the 'research-basis' for the Rose Review of literacy in the National Curriculum (2007). The small sample size and lack of corroboration for the single study used to justify the exclusive prescription of synthetic phonics for five-year-old children have received little attention, despite its clear resemblance to the characteristics of 'sloppiness' highlighted above.

One of the solutions to the perceived ills of educational research has been to propose a 'new orthodoxy' in the approach adopted by future studies, drawn from the methodology of the physical and social sciences and already prevalent in much American educational research (large sample sizes, quantitative methods, controlled experiments). The likelihood of this approach producing more reliable, useful findings for teachers has been contrasted with the 'inconclusive' interpretative approach adopted by much current educational research:

> Two main possible patterns are largely distinguishable: one characterized by the emphasis on *cumulativeness/convergence/rationality/teleology* (the so-called 'new orthodoxy'); the other by *discontinuity/divergence/non-rationality/non-teleology* in various degrees and combinations. (p. 175)

In this definition of the 'new orthodoxy', cumulativeness refers to the idea of each research study building on the findings of previous ones, so that they converge towards an agreed message. Rationality implies a belief that there is a 'truth' out there to be discovered by such research, and that researchers can be objective, disinterested observers. Teleology is the extent to which the research deals with issues central to educational practice – applied research as opposed to that dealing with philosophical or political issues. Many educational researchers are wary of this model and agree with Richard Pring's (2000) argument that, since educational research deals with the complexity of 'social reality', it can never really be scientific. Yet perhaps they should also heed his warning that questioning '… the relevance of notions such as "truth", "knowledge", "objectivity", "reality", "causality" … [has] caused much harm, playing into the hands of those who wish them ill' (p. 159).

Whilst the 'new orthodoxy' has yet to direct the progress of much educational research in the UK, it has had the effect of concentrating the minds of educational researchers on the usefulness of their findings to practitioners. For example, the General Teaching Council (GTC, 2007) has introduced an online *Research of the Month* update for teachers, while The Research Informed Practice Site (TRIPS) of the Department for Children, Schools and Families (DCSF, 2007) publishes online *Schools Research News*. These represent a purposeful attempt to move away from what Wellington (2000) describes as the 'osmosis' model of research informing practice: 'This is the idea that educational research somehow permeates or percolates into the discourse, thinking and practice of teachers over a long period, often unnoticed' (p. 178).

There has also been a new emphasis on gathering the results of research studies together to accumulate a weight of evidence on particular topics (see Chapter 15), as in the Evidence for Policy and Practice Information (EPPI, 2007) Centre research reviews.

This idea that educational research should be both 'use-inspired' and 'basic' implies that it should produce both practical and theoretical knowledge. The people in the best place to ensure that the knowledge generated is practical are teachers themselves. There is a long tradition of teachers as researchers; Dewey (1929) advocated that they should enquire into their own practice as a means of improving it. Perhaps the golden age of teacher research was the 1970s and 1980s, inspired by the action research movement. The rationale for practitioner action research was clearly articulated by Lawrence Stenhouse:

> … effective curriculum development of the highest quality depends upon the capacity of teachers to take a research stance to their own teaching. By a research stance I mean a disposition to examine one's own practice critically and systematically.
>
> (Stenhouse, 1975, p. 156)

However, while teachers' enquiry into their own teaching will clearly generate practical knowledge, to produce 'basic' theoretical insights, such enquiry might need to be undertaken as part of a wider research community, including academics who are more theoretically orientated and who can help practitioners theorise their work. This is why many teachers undertake research into their own practice in collaboration with a university department of education, perhaps as part of a higher degree. Access to knowledge and expertise from a wide range of sources; a stimulating atmosphere of discussion and debate; and opportunities to be part of larger collaborative projects all contribute to what we might call a 'research culture'. This concept is explored further below.

A RESEARCH CULTURE

Schools can themselves become research cultures, with staffroom discussion becoming dominated by discussion of strategies to improve the learning experiences of pupils. However, in practice this is difficult to maintain because of the many domestic and administrative necessities of the school day. Most schools are too 'full on' to enable teachers to stand back and analyse their practice. While university departments of education might be criticised for being detached from the realities of the classroom, they do at least offer the opportunity for reflection and exchange of ideas. If not too exhausted after a day's work, teachers can find this atmosphere stimulating and refreshing. Tutors in the university need this interchange of views with teachers every bit as much as the teachers do. At one level, they require good relationships with schools in order to gain access for their own research, but the idea of academics doing the research for the teachers to implement is both out of date and deeply flawed, as Wellington argues: 'This metaphor, of one group providing a "commodity" to another (who may take it or leave it) is clearly unacceptable as a future model' (2000, p. 174).

Academics need to undertake their research with teachers as co-researchers, ensuring that it is 'use inspired' and involves the perspective of the user. Some research projects such as the 'Listening to Children' project in Kingswood, Bristol (Barratt and Barratt Hacking, 2007) have involved children as researchers within their own schools. This effectively closes the loop between the originators of research and its ultimate beneficiaries, if we suppose that the ultimate aim of educational research is to improve children's lives.

But there is still a missing group here in our research culture. Most university schools of education exist to teach students, perhaps in the academic study of education as a subject, but also usually in training them to become teachers. Even though these students are often required to undertake some small-scale research as part of their qualification, they are often overlooked when it comes to thinking about the department's research culture. Not only is this missing an opportunity to benefit from the findings of some excellent student projects, but it is neglecting an important part of their induction into the professional life of the teacher. Education Studies is, as the name suggests, the study (i.e. research) of education. Therefore, undergraduate students of education need to be included in the research life of the department as much as possible from an early stage. They then become both the audience for research undertaken by tutors and schools, and later can present the outcomes of their own research to these groups. This is equally true for trainee teachers, particularly those undertaking Master's-level PGCE courses, which require engagement with educational issues at an academic level.

Figure 18.1 is an attempt to represent diagrammatically the overlapping research interests and activities of students, teachers and academics in our research culture. The boxes around the edge represent the various activities undertaken within the department of education that sustain this culture. For example, research seminars could be undertaken as part of an undergraduate module, as a staff-only activity to discuss a colleague's project, as a partnership event to which local schools are invited or as an evening sharing of ideas between teachers on a higher degrees programme. But why not combine some of these contexts and audiences? Undergraduate students can present at the same seminar as PhD students, teachers and tutors, so that there is a building sense of continuity in research at all levels. Similarly, conferences could be combined to mix professional and academic purposes. Instead of mounting a series of events – one aimed at partnership schools, another at students, a third at teacher researchers

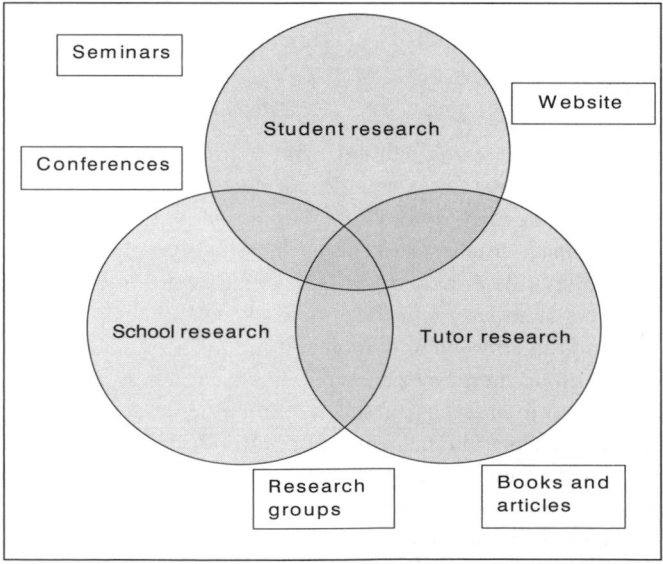

Figure 18.1   Diagrammatic representation of a university department of education research culture

or academics from other universities – a single event can have multiple strands. Often we assume that 'research' is only of interest to one type of audience.

A website is essential to keep members of the research culture up to date with current projects, events and opportunities for collaboration and funding. There might be a regular email newsletter to let everyone know what is going on and to remind or encourage them to get involved. Research groups or centres are another way to break down the isolation often experienced by the educational researcher. Finding other people interested in the same topics or methodologies can save a lot of time in fruitless searches for relevant literature, and can also offer new researchers an apprenticeship by becoming involved in larger collaborative projects led by experienced staff. They should certainly involve tutors, teachers and students with similar research interests working together – perhaps in formal, supervisory relationships but preferably more as equals. Books and articles constitute both the outputs of research activity within the culture (an in-house online journal can also be a useful form of dissemination) and also as resources for sustaining the intellectual life of the department. We all need to keep on learning, so the sharing of published literature in seminars or research groups can help stimulate new ideas or approaches to our work. We can also support each other by writing collaboratively or acting as 'readers' for each other's drafts before submitting them to the *Dragons' Den* of academic publishing. Often the most vital component of a vibrant research culture, however, is that which occurs naturally on an informal basis. Discussions over coffee or in the corridor often spark an idea or move a research project forward just as much as a more formal meeting or seminar.

EXAMPLES OF COLLABORATIVE RESEARCH WITHIN A RESEARCH CULTURE

The chapter concludes with examples of students, schools and tutors researching together. They emphasise the relevance of research to professional practice and show how a practice-based research culture can begin to emerge. Bath Spa University has a large undergraduate education studies programme, which includes a compulsory first-year research module and two other opportunities to undertake school-based research. The School of Education also trains over 500 early years, primary and secondary teachers on Master's-level PGCE courses, each of which includes a research component. The Professional Master's Programme, aimed at practising teachers, includes several practitioner research modules, together with research methodology leading to dissertation. There is a growing interest amongst tutors in joining research groupings and undertaking research in collaboration with their own students and partnership schools.

On the undergraduate Education Studies programme, students have the opportunity to undertake research commissioned by, or in collaboration with, local primary schools. They often work with teachers, to an agenda set by a current interest the school has with an aspect of teaching and learning. Recent examples have included:

- children's choice of play activities in Reception;
- multiple intelligences and children's learning styles;
- children's use of computers in the home;
- ICT and learning with socially disadvantaged pupils.

A research conference at the end of each year enables students to present their findings to peers, tutors and the schools in which they have conducted the research. There is also the opportunity to write for publication in collaboration with staff, or to present at the annual British Education Studies Association (BESA) conference.

For student or trainee teachers on a PGCE course, there is a strong rationale for becoming involved in research on their own practice as part of the professional learning involved in becoming a teacher:

> In adopting a student-teacher as researcher stance, students of teaching might realize new and meaningful ways of becoming more informed about the manner in which their own learning about teaching is shaped and may therefore become better informed about their own professional learning.
>
> (Loughran, 2006, p. 139)

These teachers at the beginning of their careers can also contribute insights into the process of becoming a teacher that can inform the practice of their tutors or mentors:

> Students of teaching are in an ideal position to generate knowledge and insights into learning about teaching and its impact on their own understanding about teaching and learning in ways different to that of more experienced, or distanced others.
>
> (Ibid., p. 140)

Examples of research projects undertaken in collaboration with schools by PGCE trainees on an optional leadership module include:

*   gender-split teaching of primary mathematics;
*   topic work as a catalyst to improving speaking and listening skills;
*   improving boys' writing;
*   developing problem-solving skills in maths;
*   is the Foundation Stage Profile effective?

In these cases the issue for research was identified through analysis of pupil performance data with a senior member of staff. The trainees were able to present their findings in seminars and accredit their work as part of the Professional Master's Programme. Often the dissemination of such research can be the weakest element of an emerging research culture. Tutors, teachers and students alike can feel abashed at the prospect of sharing their work with a wider public, so few potential users benefit from the knowledge generated. Students in particular

> … have limited possibilities or outlets to publish their findings, thus much of their work exists only as university assignment. However, when they are encouraged to describe their learning and their new understandings, the response from others (peers, experienced teachers and teacher educators) can be very positive.
>
> (Loughran, 2006: 144)

The final example is that of a project that combined tutor, teacher and student research. The 'Neston Moonbase' is a four-year action research project undertaken by a Wiltshire primary school, with the aims of enhancing pupils' use of information and communications technology (ICT) in their learning of science, and design and technology, and of increasing their confidence in speaking and listening. The work was supported by a grant from NESTA, and took as its theme the topic of communication in space. Neston became the first UK primary school to link with the International Space Station, conducting a ten-minute live radio interview with astronauts, which gave pupils and staff an insight into the issues of communication and control between Earth-based 'mission control' and remote satellites. The school took this idea a stage further by designing and constructing a 'moonbase' on the school playing field, comprising a geodesic dome connected to a 'rocket' greenhouse and weather station by a living tunnel of willow, simulating the artificial ecosystem that would need to be constructed if such a project were to become reality. The dome contains a computer-controlled robotic arm complete with miniature camera, allowing remote imaging of arm operation, together with another smaller robot. Remote cameras in the dome and school computer suite enable pupils to set parameters and zones around the dome with warning signals. They can also send instructions directly to 'astronauts' working within the dome – either via video link or electronic message display board – and monitor their movements. Monitoring and control software has been installed, with dome-based laptop computers wirelessly linked to the school network, enabling teachers and pupils to conduct a wide variety of science investigations including impact testing, pH testing, temperature logging, sound analysis and light monitoring.

A university tutor was linked to the project throughout its life, offering advice on research methodology, applying for funding and evaluating the project's impact on pupils' learning. An undergraduate Education Studies student undertook observations of pupils designing and working within the moonbase environment and its linked classroom interface as part of her 'research in a school' module. The research questions were as follows:

1   To what extent is the Neston Moonbase project a viable model for other whole-school initiatives in control technology?
2   What evidence is there of pupil learning as a result of the project against the specified learning outcomes?
3   What lessons can be learnt from the process, management and outcomes of this project to inform future work in developing control technology through design and technology and other primary curriculum areas?

The methodology was that of an evaluative case study, employing Jenkins' four-stage evaluation process (1976), examining *context* (questions 1, 3), *input* (question 1), *process* (question 3) and *output* (question 2). The data gathering techniques employed included the following:

*   Classroom observations (six half-day observations were carried out on pupils aged 7–11, between October 2003 and April 2006) – particularly relevant to research question 2.
*   Video and audio recordings, photographs of children working and finished outcomes. These were collected by the researcher during observations and additional material was provided by the senior teacher.
*   Analysis of documentary sources (e.g. reports to NESTA, planning documents) – particularly relevant to research questions 1 and 3.
*   Analysis of email correspondence between members of the project management team and between the team and external personnel – particularly relevant to research question 1 and 3.

Analysis of data relating to pupil learning demonstrated methodical yet creative approaches to problem solving, together with a relatively high degree of autonomy. Pupils' speaking and listening skills have also been enhanced by sending groups of children to the moonbase with specific tasks, and observing them over a live video link. Pupils aged 9–11 years have been able to study group dynamics and how humans respond to different situations. They have learned about team-working skills and how to take on a variety of roles in a group discussion. By taking remote responsibility for the moonbase team, pupils have practised skills of managing and organising others. Pupils have also presented their work to adult audiences in local authority advisory network meetings and through the Bath Spa University and Wiltshire 'Vibrant Schools' project.

CONCLUSION

To some extent, the 'joined-up thinking' that made the Neston Moonbase project a success could equally be applied to the construction of a university department of education research culture. The whole community (staff, students, schools) need to be involved from an early stage, there need to be some 'big ideas' to engage participants' enthusiasm and drive the enterprise forward, and there also needs to be as many links as possible between all of the various agencies involved in improving teaching and learning in schools. Ultimately, that's what we're all here for. Educational researchers of all types need to keep this goal at the front of their minds to ensure that research is a key part of the solution.

SUMMARY POINTS

- Discussion of the role, value and relevance of educational research for teachers and schools, examining some of the criticisms levelled at educational research during the 1990s and some of the responses of government and the research community in making the findings more applicable to classroom practice and readily accessible to users.
- Teachers should themselves be researchers of their own practice, along the lines suggested by the action research movement.
- University departments of education can play a key role in supporting such research and working alongside schools to identify priorities for developing evidence-based practice.
- Students in the university, whether undergraduate, postgraduate trainee teachers or practitioners taking higher degrees, all have an important part to play in this process, together contributing to a research culture.
- A research culture, located within the university–school partnership and supported by seminars, conferences, web-based dialogue and publication, can involve students, staff and schools researching and learning together, as exemplified by the Neston Moonbase project.

QUESTIONS FOR DISCUSSION

1   How would you defend the government funding spent every year on educational research?
2   Do you feel part of a research culture in your university department? If not, what could be done to involve students more in research within the department?
3   What aspects of educational policy or practice do you think merit further research?

FURTHER READING

Bell, J. (2005) *Doing your Research Project: A Guide for First Time Researchers in Education, Health and Social Science* (4th edition), Buckingham: Open University Press. An excellent beginner's guide to the process of designing and undertaking a student research project in education.

Cohen, L., Manion, L. and Morrison, K. (2007) *Research Methods in Education* (6th edition), Oxon: Routledge. This is the standard introductory text, now in its sixth edition. It provides a valuable overview of research paradigms, methodology and data collection methods.

Hitchcock, D. and Hughes, D. (1995) *Research and the Teacher: A Qualitative Introduction to School-based Research* (2nd edition), London: RoutledgeFalmer. This text is invaluable for teachers undertaking small-scale research projects in their own classrooms using ethnographic or action research methodologies. It takes an interpretative approach to the collection and analysis of qualitative data.

REFERENCES

Barratt, R. and Barratt Hacking, E. (2007) A clash of worlds: children talking about their community experience in relation to the school curriculum, in A. Reid, B.B. Jensen, J. Nikel and V. Simovska (eds) *Participation and Learning: Perspectives on Education and the Environment, Health and Sustainability*, Dordrecht: Springer.

Blunkett, D. (2000) Influence or irrelevance: can social science improve government? (speech made by David Blunkett, Secretary of State for Education and Employment, to a meeting convened by the Economic and Social Research Council, 2 February, 2000), *Research Intelligence*, 12–21.

Cohen, L., Manion, L. and Morrison, K. (2007) *Research Methods in Education* (6th edition), Oxon: Routledge.

DCSF (2007) *The Research-informed Practice Site*. Online. Available http://www.standards.dfes.gov.uk/research/ (accessed 12 November 2007).

Dewey, J. (1929) *Experience and Nature*, New York: Dover.

EPPI (2007) *Eppi Centre*. Online. Available http://eppi.ioe.ac.uk/cms/ (accessed 12 November 2007).

GTC (2007) Online. Available http://www.gtce.org.uk/research/romtopics/ (accessed 12 November 2007)

Hargreaves, D.H. (1996) *Teaching as a Research-based Profession: Possibilities and Prospects, Teacher Training Agency Annual Lecture*, London: Teacher Training Agency.

Jenkins, D. (1976) *Open University Course E203, Curriculum Design and Development, Unit 19: Curriculum Evaluation*, Milton Keynes: The Open University.

Loughran, J. (2006) *Developing a Pedagogy of Teacher Education*, Oxon: Routledge.

Oancea, A. (2005) Criticisms of educational research: key topics and levels of analysis, *British Educational Research Journal*, 31(2): 157–84.

Pring, R. (2000) *Philosophy of Educational Research*, London: Continuum.

Rose, J. (2006) *Independent Review of the Teaching of Early Reading – Final Report*, London: DfES. http://www.standards. dfes.gov.uk/phonics/report.pdf (accessed 3 April 2008).

Stenhouse, L. (1975) *An Introduction to Curriculum Research and Development*, London: Heinemann.

Tooley, J. and Darby, D. (eds) (1998) *Educational Research: A Critique. A Survey of Published Educational Research*, London: Ofsted.

Wellington, J. (2000) *Educational Research: Contemporary Issues and Practical Approaches*, London: Continuum.

Wells, G. (2001) *Action, Talk and Text: Learning and Teaching Through Inquiry*, New York: Teacher's College Press.

Woodhead, C. (1998) Foreword, in J. Tooley and D. Darby (eds) *Educational Research: A Critique. A Survey of Published Educational Research*, London: Ofsted.

Index